The Political Writings of Leibniz

The Political Writings of Leibniz

TRANSLATED AND EDITED
WITH AN INTRODUCTION AND NOTES BY
PATRICK RILEY

Assistant Professor of Government
Harvard University

CAMBRIDGE
AT THE UNIVERSITY PRESS
1972

58458

Published by the Syndics of the Cambridge University Press
Bentley House, 200 Euston Road, London NW1 2DB
American Branch: 32 East 57th Street, New York, N.Y.10022

Library of Congress Catalogue Card Number: 78–171681

ISBN: 0 521 08345 1

Printed in Great Britain by
Alden & Mowbray Ltd
at the Alden Press, Oxford

Contents

Abbreviations

Acad. Ed. = G. W. Leibniz, *Sämtliche Schriften und Briefe*, edition of the German (formerly Prussian) Academy of Sciences at Berlin, Darmstadt and Leipzig, 1923–.

Baruzi = Jean Baruzi, *Leibniz et l'Organisation Réligieuse de la Terre*, Felix Alcan, Paris, 1907.

Duncan = G. M. Duncan (trans.), *The Philosophical Works of Leibniz*, 2nd ed., New Haven, 1908.

Dutens = Louis Dutens, *God. Guil. Leibnitii...Opera Omnia*, de Tournes, Geneva, 1768.

F de C = A. Foucher de Careil, *Œuvres de Leibniz*, Didot Frères, Paris, 1859–75.

Ger. = C. I. Gerhardt, *Die Philosophischen Schriften von G. W. Leibniz*, Weidmann, Berlin, 1875–90.

Ger. Math. = C. I. Gerhardt, *Die Mathematische Schriften von G. W. Leibniz*, Berlin and Halle, 1849–55.

Klopp = Onno Klopp, *Die Werke von Leibniz*, Klindworth Verlag, Hanover, 1864–84.

Latta = Robert Latta, *The Monadology and Other Philosophical Writings*, Oxford University Press, 1898.

Loemker = Leroy Loemker, *Leibniz: Philosophical Papers and Letters*, University of Chicago Press, 1956. (As this is the most comprehensive collection of Leibniz' works in English, reference to this edition has been made whenever possible.)

Mollat = G. Mollat, *Rechtsphilosophisches aus Leibnizens Ungedruckten Schriften*, Verlag Robolsky, Leipzig, 1885.

Monadology (cited by propositions, e.g. 'prop. 56').

New Essays on Human Understanding (cited by book, chapter, and part, e.g. '*NE* IV, iii, pt. I').

Principles of Nature and Grace (cited by propositions, e.g. 'prop. 2').

Rommel = C. von Rommel, *Leibniz und Landgraf Ernst von Hessen-Rheinfels*, Frankfurt, 1847.

Ruck = E. Ruck, *Die Leibniz'sche Staatsidee*, Verlag J. C. B. Mohr, Tübingen, 1909.

Russell = Bertrand Russell, *A Critical Exposition of the Philosophy of Leibniz*, George Allen and Unwin, London, 1900.

Textes Inédits = G. Grua (ed.), *Textes Inédits*, Presses Universitaires de France, 1948.

Theodicy (cited by books and propositions, e.g. '*Theodicy* III, pt. 337').

Preface

In a letter to the Jesuit Father Des Bosses, Leibniz had occasion to complain that 'two things usually make publishers hesitate – one is their desire to profit; the other is ignorance. Thus they do not know what they should select. They do not trust scholars enough, because they believe that scholars have a better understanding of what is scholarly than of what will sell.' If Leibniz were alive today, he would be gratified to know that the Cambridge University Press, in consenting to publish an edition of his political writings, showed itself admirably free of all these faults. From the outset the Press trusted my judgment in the selection and translation of the pieces to appear in this volume, but also saw to it that I was provided with a searching critique of some of the more obscure points in the 'editor's introduction'. For this trust, for this willingness to revive interesting and unaccountably neglected political writings of a great contemporary of Hobbes, Spinoza and Locke, I am much in their debt. While it is true that no one can pretend that Leibniz' political writings are equal to those of such contemporaries, or even to his own writings on logic, metaphysics and theology, they are at least intriguing and worthy of some attention.

Anyone who reads the introduction will notice that it draws on a wide range of books, letters, manuscripts etc., and that Leibniz' 'political system' has been assembled out of these materials. I think that there really is a system in these writings – though, since Leibniz never wrote a large-scale, comprehensive treatise on politics, the system which I have explained may look rather artificial. A composite it is, indeed; but not an invention.

In preparing this edition I have incurred many debts. Dr John Gleason, formerly of the Harvard Classics Department, supplied me some years ago with a translation of chapters 9 and 10 of Leibniz' *Caesarinus Fürstenerius*, and I have retained most of his work in the present version. Mr James Zetzel, of the same Department, was kind enough to read over the translations from the Latin, and to suggest important changes. Professor Leroy Loemker, of Emory University, cleared up several difficult points in a letter from which I profited. The present version of the *Meditation on the Common Concept of Justice* was strengthened because I was able to read the actual manuscript, preserved in the Niedersächsische Landes-bibliothek in Hanover, Germany; for the funds which made this trip possible I am grateful to the Harvard Government Department, and for generous assistance at the Landesbibliothek I wish to thank particularly Dr G. Utermöhlen. Finally I want to acknowledge a grant from the Canaday Humanities Fund at Harvard, which made it possible to put the finishing touches on the book, and the patient assistance and advice of Mrs Patricia Skinner of the Cambridge University Press. And, were it not for an inequitable division of labor which keeps my wife at home while I enjoy the freedom to prepare books such as the present one, it would become clear that my right to appear in print is, to say the least, no greater than hers. It is to her that this book is dedicated.

P.R.

Harvard University
Cambridge, Mass.
May 1971

Introduction

Gottfried Wilhelm Leibniz, the son of a Leipzig University professor, was born in 1646, two years before the end of the Thirty Years' War. He was thoroughly educated – partly through his own efforts – in scholastic philosophy and in jurisprudence, including the Roman law (which was later to be important to his theory of justice). At an early age he attempted a correspondence with Hobbes, whom he was already beginning to see as his principal philosophical antagonist; but Hobbes never replied, in part, perhaps, because of Leibniz' left-handed compliments ('certain men are ... wrong in ascribing license and impiety to your hypotheses'). Following a brief period of service to the Elector of Mainz, Leibniz resided in Paris for a few years; here he first observed Louis XIV's expansionist policies, which he was afterwards to combat as a writer and as a diplomatist. In Paris, too, he expanded his interests to take in logic and mathematics, and made a number of important permanent friendships. Unable to secure the diplomatic post he wanted, Leibniz finally attached himself to the house of Brunswick-Lüneburg, rulers of the (soon-to-be) Electorate of Hanover, and became official apologist for and historian of this principality.

At Hanover Leibniz, in addition to his official duties and philosophical efforts, carried on a wide range of political activities and correspondences. He entered into an exchange of letters with Bossuet concerning the reunification of 'Christendom'; this became his lifelong passion, as it had been that of his favorite modern political theorist, Grotius. Though a Protestant, Leibniz became the defender of a reformed and truly universal Papacy; at the same time he vigorously defended the Conciliar movement of the fifteenth century, believing that if it had succeeded, the Reformation would have been unnecessary and the 'universal' authorities (Pope and Holy Roman Emperor) would still be viable. To produce the desired reconciliation, Leibniz recommended toleration and compromise; and this, of course, made all parties suspicious of him. Though he was the last thinker of great stature to defend the Empire as something more than a vestigial oddity, he was also a frequent apologist for the rights of Imperial electors and princes, and tried to strike a balance between the *majestas* of the Empire and the sovereignty of the princes. Sovereignty, for him, meant simply internal control and 'influence' in European affairs, but did not exclude ultimate allegiance to universal authority. His efforts to recast sovereignty led to a broad attack on Hobbes and Pufendorf, and, ultimately, to a more general critique of legal positivism.

In later years, while keeping up his interest in the re-unification of the *Respublica Christiana* and in the refutation of Hobbes, Leibniz devoted considerable time to justifying the Hanoverian succession to the British throne, arguing that a Stuart restoration would make France the absolute arbiter of Europe. On behalf of the Empire, he wrote tracts attacking French seizure of Imperial territories; against Louis XIV's devastations, he urged that charity and benevolence were the proper course for a true prince, and was instrumental in trying to set up academies of arts and sciences, as well as economic and educational councils, in Germany and – at the behest of Peter the Great – in Russia.

At the end of his life, Leibniz gave up a little on his plans for reviving a Republic of Christendom, but still insisted that his schemes *would* be better than a system of independent states and religious fragmentation; the tone of his last political letters is resigned and often ironic. And when he died in 1716, famous in an astounding variety of subjects, the rationalized medieval system which he tried to sustain had largely disappeared.

POLITICAL WRITINGS

It was characteristic of Leibniz to try to reconcile apparently conflicting ideas, to take from each kind of thought that which was soundest and to synthesize it with the seemingly incommensurable truths of other systems; thus he struggled throughout his life to fuse Platonism, Cartesianism, Christian voluntarism, scholasticism, Hobbesian mechanism and a number of other doctrines into a plausible whole[1] whose apex would be a *rational* theology (Leibniz used God with a relatively sparing hand, and was contemptuous of philosophers who drew him in at the first sign of intellectual difficulty). Given this desire for reconciliation, for harmony, for synthesis – which he applied to political philosophy as much as to any other philosophical question – it should come as no surprise that Leibniz wanted to establish, or rather discover, a 'universal jurisprudence', a system of law and justice common to God and man (and generally to any rational substances); both God and man existed in a 'society or universal republic of spirits' which was the 'noblest part of the universe', a moral realm within (and at the summit of) physical nature, a realm in which 'universal right is the same for God and for men'.[2]

The totality of all spirits must compose the City of God, that is to say, the most perfect state that is possible, under the most perfect of Monarchs.

This City of God, this truly universal monarchy, is a moral world in the natural world, and is the most exalted among the works of God.[3]

For Leibniz, the difference between divine and human justice was one of degree, not in kind; God's justice was simply infinitely more perfect than men's, and 'to say . . . that God's justice is different from men's is like saying that the arithmetic or the geometry of men is false in heaven.'[4] Justice had, moreover, as Leibniz observed in a commentary on Hobbes, nothing to do with the command or the power of authorities; it 'does not depend on the arbitrary laws of superiors, but on the eternal rules of wisdom and goodness, in men as well as in God'.[5] Perhaps the fullest mature statement of this view is contained in Leibniz' *Opinion on the Principles of Pufendorf:*

In the science of law . . . it is best to derive human justice, as from a spring, from the divine, in order to make it complete. Surely the idea of the just, no less than that of the true and the good, relates to God . . . And the rules which are common [to divine and human justice] certainly enter into the science [of natural law], and ought to be considered in universal jurisprudence.[6]

All of this suggests (what Leibniz actually believed), that God is not just a first cause or an 'imaginary metaphysical being, incapable of thought, will and action', but that he is 'a definite substance, a person, a mind'.[7] In God 'there is power, which is the source of all, also knowledge, whose content is the variety of the ideas, and finally will, which makes changes or products according to the principle of the best'.[8] God, then, like men, has knowledge, will and power, but Leibniz wanted to be certain that justice is not deduced out of the last two attributes alone; God will act, perfectly (as men will act, though imperfectly), in a way such that action is the issue of knowledge and volition combined. 'Wisdom', he urged in the *Meditation on the Common Concept of Justice*, 'is in the understanding, and goodness in the will. And justice as a result is in both. Power is another matter, but if it is added it transforms right into fact'.[9]

It is precisely because Leibniz usually conceived of moral activity, for both God and men, in terms of voluntary and rational *action*, that he could not reduce justice simply to a Platonic relation, or a fixed harmony; an action, rationally chosen, had to be involved. And this is why Leibniz usually defined justice as 'the charity of the wise'. 'The [proper] treatment of justice and that of charity cannot be separated', he urged in one of his earliest writings. 'Neither Moses, nor Christ, nor the Apostles nor the ancient Christians regulated justice otherwise than according to charity. . .

[and] I, too, after having tried countless definitions of justice, finally felt myself satisfied only by this one; it alone I have found universal and reciprocal.'[9a] Charity is 'a universal benevolence, which the wise man carries into execution in conformity with the measures of reason, to the end of obtaining the greatest good'.[10] Charity, a 'habit of loving' (with love defined as a 'feeling of perfection'[11] in others), necessitated voluntary action; it was to be regulated by wisdom, which would provide a knowledge of what men *deserved* through their 'perfections'. (In Leibniz' philosophy, perfection is both the *cause* of love and the *reason* which regulates that love.)

Leibniz' view of justice as charity tempered by a knowledge of what is deserved obviously suggests a more generous and benevolent idea of the just than that entertained by many philosophers; but since his full view of charity can be more happily taken up at a later point, it will perhaps be sufficient to say for the moment that he had at least three excellent reasons for conceiving justice as he did. First, in a 'universal jurisprudence' the same rules must apply to God and man. But the traditional definition of justice, resting on the idea that something is 'owed' or 'due', cannot be applied to God, who can owe no duties.[12] God can, however, love, and wisdom will show how much each rational being deserves to be loved. Since this idea can apply to men as well as to God, it is a perfect foundation for a universal jurisprudence. Second, if charity is the essence of justice, then mere power or mere command cannot be. Adopting such a universal solution is the best antidote to all legal-positivist views of justice, such as Hobbes'. And finally, charity presupposes not merely a *ius strictum* (forbearance from violence against others), and not merely rendering what is due, but an active benevolence; and Leibniz believed that if one tried to make the happiness of others his own, not only would ordinary life be happier, but disasters such as the disintegration of Christendom after the Reformation could be healed. True charity, he thought, could overcome doctrinal differences; 'charity must prevail over all other considerations in the world.'[13]

Despite the attractiveness of this view, Leibniz sometimes did try to define justice simply in terms of harmony, of proportion, of ratios as precise as any in mathematics. One of his more extreme statements in this vein (1696) urged that the

eternal truths are the fixed and immutable point on which everything turns. Such is the truth of numbers in arithmetic, and of figures in geometry...

That postulated, it is well to consider that order and harmony are also something mathematical and which consist in certain proportions: and that justice being nothing else than the order which is observed with regard to the good and evil of intelligent creatures, it follows that God, who is the sovereign substance, immutably maintains justice and the most perfect order which can be observed.[14]

Throughout his life Leibniz was tempted to assert that principles of justice, as 'eternal verities', had the same status as $A = A$ or $2 + 2 = 4$, and for an obvious reason: one of his great hopes was that of reducing all complex propositions to their simplest form, to primary and irreducible concepts whose predicates were clearly contained in their subjects, to a 'universal symbolistic' in which argument would be replaced by the use of a universal language.[15] Certainly differences over the character of justice could be obviated if, as Leibniz hoped, 'justice follows certain rules of equality and of proportion which are no less founded in the immutable nature of things, and in the ideas of the divine understanding, than the principles of arithmetic and geometry'.[16]

The reason that Leibniz could not and did not *consistently* maintain this idea of justice is that there is no voluntary act in it; a justice of harmony and proportion alone presupposes an aesthetic passivity which fails to take Christian voluntarism into account. In most Christian thought, justice is not simply a relation, but an action; and Leibniz, who grew up reading the scholastics, was aware of the transformation made in the idea of justice by philosophers such as St Thomas Aquinas:

Now justice does not aim at directing an act of the cognitive power, for we are not said to be just through knowing something aright...but since we are said to be just through doing something aright...justice must needs be in some [rational] appetitive power.[17]

That Leibniz (usually) favored this view – originally suggested by Aristotle's *Ethics*[18] and much elaborated by medieval philosophy – is perfectly clear: in an important early work he insisted that Christian virtues 'consist not only in talking and in thinking, but in thinking practically, that is, in acting';[19] and in a late letter (1706) he described justice and injustice in terms of the 'moral goodness or badness of *actions*'.[20] Justice, then, cannot be a simple proportion or harmony in Leibniz; harmony may be the product of justice, but it cannot be the essence of it. (It must be granted, however, that there is a certain tension in Leibniz' work which is caused by his working with two kinds of premises – Christian voluntarism and Platonic rationalism – simultaneously; and this makes interpretation of his thought exceedingly difficult.)

If Leibniz was, as a Christian, unavoidably a voluntarist, that does not mean that justice for him was founded on will alone; far from it. This, in fact, is what he accused Hobbes (together with Thrasymachus) of doing; and he asserted again and again that to say, *stat pro ratione voluntas*, let will take the place of reason, is properly the motto of a tyrant.[21] If will were uppermost, there would be as many kinds of justice as there were arbitrary commands;[22] if the justice of God were invented by fiat, there would be no reason to praise him.

For why praise him for what he has done if he would be equally praiseworthy in doing exactly the opposite? Where will his justice and his wisdom be found if nothing is left but a certain despotic power, if will takes the place of reason, and if, according to the definition of tyrants, that which is pleasing to the most powerful is by that very fact just?[23]

It is important to recall that, for Leibniz, God operates within limits; he chooses the best among possibilities, but he does not create ideas or essences himself. 'Wisdom and justice have their eternal theorems', he observed, and 'God does not establish them at all by his will; but he discovers them in his essence, he follows them.'[24] In an act of justice (divine or human), knowledge and volition, though separate faculties, must work together, knowledge providing the standard of what ought to be done, and will providing the purely moral element, choice. 'To will is nothing but the striving which arises from thought, or to strive for something which our thinking recognizes'.[25] Reason, or thought, or knowledge alone, is not enough for a moral action; if it were, intellectual error would be equal to moral evil.[26] The will must be *conformed* to reason, must choose the best.

Clearly, then, Leibnizian justice requires a voluntary act of charity. But if God and men are to be just, by the same standard though in differing degrees, whence evil, particularly moral evil? If God is just, why is the world full of imperfection and pain and sin (as Leibniz grants)?[27] If men are unjust because they are less perfect than God, how can they be truly responsible for their actions? In short, can both God and men be just (or, more generally, good) by the same standard – since the point of a universal jurisprudence is its equal applicability to all 'minds'? That Leibniz was aware of these difficulties is perfectly evident throughout his work, but particularly in his most famous book, the *Theodicy*, whose subtitle suggests that the author will reconcile three apparently irreconcilable problems – the justice of God, the moral freedom of men, and the origin of evil. Leibniz was unwilling to define his ideas of right and justice in narrow terms; and precisely because his conception of justice is so universal, so little 'political' in any restricted sense, an excursion into his metaphysics and theology is essential. A narrower treatment, leaving his pure philosophy to one side, would inevitably ignore what is most characteristic in his political thought. To be sure, Leibniz sometimes appears to define politics in an extremely restricted sense: 'the science of the pleasant is medicine, that of the useful is politics, and that of the just is ethics.'[28] But this is not his usual view; and, indeed, it would be more accurate to say that Leibniz tried to develop a metaphysic of perfection, of which the pleasant, the useful and the just would simply be different *aspects*. Some effort, at least, must be made to show how and why perfection is the thread which leads from metaphysics and theology to psychology and ethics – and thus to justice – in Leibniz' thought.

Divine Justice and Human Responsibility

Leibniz makes human justice turn on divine justice to avoid arbitrariness and the equation of justice with power; but he must afterwards explain the justice of God, given a visible world full of evil, not all of it apparently deserved, but all of it allowed, if not positively willed, by God. To understand the place of evil in the universe which Leibniz' God creates, a general understanding of God's mode of operation is required. The eternal verities and all essences (all possible non-self-contradictory beings) are in his understanding, not in his will or power. 'Does the will of God form the ideas which are in his understanding?' No, Leibniz says; this would involve an infinite regress of causality and would 'confuse understanding and will'.[29]* Thus 'the essences of all things are co-eternal with God'.[30] It is essential to God's moral freedom that he choose the best from a range of possibles; if this were not the case – if essence were equal to existence – then the universe would exist by a blind necessity (of the sort that Leibniz feared in Spinoza). 'If we wished absolutely to destroy such pure possibles,' he observed in a letter to Arnauld, 'we should destroy contingency and freedom, for if nothing is possible except what God has actually created, whatever God has created would be necessary.'[32] God's power only translates a portion of essence into existence; but the best is not *determined* by power. Now, God need not create the universe: eternal truths do not have a merely temporal reality, and essences can remain just that. But if God does create a universe he is restricted by the eternal verities and by possibilities: the essence of a circle is round, and it cannot have a square existence; that the sum of the angles of a triangle is equal to 180° is a function of God's understanding, not of his will. Nor does God create the essences of particular possible substances. 'God was

---

* 'In every intelligent being the acts of the will are of their nature posterior to the acts of the understanding...the eternal truths are in the divine understanding...it does not follow [however] that there is anything before God, but only that the acts of the divine understanding are prior...to the acts of the divine will.'[31]

able to create matter, a man, a circle, or leave them in nothingness, but he was not able to produce them without giving them their essential properties. He had of necessity to make man a rational animal and to give the round shape to a circle.'[33] On this point Leibniz parted company with the Cartesians, who founded even the character of truth itself on the omnipotent will of God; the Cartesian view which he was combating was well-stated by his correspondent and antagonist, Bossuet, who urged that if God chose the best it was 'not because there is a best in things which somehow precedes his will and guides it, but rather that everything he wills becomes the best, because his will is the cause of all the good and all the best which exists in nature'.[34] Leibniz devoted the opening portion of his *Meditation on the Common Concept of Justice* to a refutation of this view.

It is agreed that whatever God wills is good and just. But there remains the question whether it is good and just because God wills it or whether God wills it because it is good and just; in other words, whether justice and goodness are arbitrary or whether they belong to the necessary and eternal truths about the nature of things, as do numbers and proportions.[35]

One must, said Leibniz, hold to the second view, since, if the good were not the motive of God's will, his decisions would be only 'a certain absolute decree, without reason'.[36] Leibniz' position on this question is far from original; it stretches back at least to Plato's *Euthyphro*,[37] and had been recently re-stated by Grotius.[38] But it is essential to a fully 'natural' natural law.

God chooses for translation into existence that configuration of essences which will guarantee the greatest total perfection, pre-adjusting all substances and all of their possible relations in advance; the most perfect essences have the greatest 'claim' to existence, since 'all possible things... tend toward existence with equal right in proportion to the quantity of essence or reality, or to the degree of perfection which they involve'.[39]*

* Critics of Leibniz have pointed out that this principle – that the most perfect essences have the greatest claim to existence – seems to contradict another fundamental Leibnizian doctrine, i.e. that the universe is a *plenum*, a *continuum* with no 'gaps' or 'vacuum of forms', in which 'one of everything' exists and is separated from the substances immediately 'above' and 'below' it by the smallest possible degree of difference. (This last principle rests on the so-called 'identity of indiscernibles', which holds that no two substances can be precisely alike, since, if they were, God would have no *reason* to create either in preference to the other, and hence would create neither.) If the most perfect essences have the greatest claim to existence, then only those essences least inferior to God should be created; but Leibniz wanted to account for the whole range of existence, from 'nothing' to God. Cf. *Monadology*, props. 53 and 54.

There must be a 'sufficient reason' for God's choice of a particular universe,[40] and that reason must be the best: why the best, and not perfection itself, must be settled for, is dictated (apparently) by the fact that there can be only one God, and that everything else must be imperfect compared with him. 'God could not give the creature all without making of it a God.'[41] God acts by a moral necessity (the best) which restricts him but leaves him free in the sense that he could (conceivably) have chosen otherwise (though not as well): this is the famous distinction between metaphysical necessity, whose opposite is inconceivable, and moral necessity, whose opposite is conceivable but less good, and which 'inclines without necessitating'. 'Metaphysical necessity...admits of no choice, presenting only one object as possible...[but]...moral necessity ...constrains the wisest to choose the best.'[42] What leads to the rejection of an alternative course of action, Leibniz noted in the *Discourse on Metaphysics*, 'is not its impossibility, but its imperfection'.[43] Within the realm of morality, moral necessity is absolute in the sense that one cannot choose the lesser good and still be right; only the *possibility* of failing to choose the best is necessary for freedom (for God and men alike: God is wholly free because he always chooses the real best, while men choose the apparent best). God chooses that universe which is best on the whole; but since, for Leibniz, the simultaneous co-existence of all possibles is not itself a possibility, God will produce the best 'compossible' (compatible and possible) universe.[44] It follows that while the whole is as perfect as it can be, each individual part (including particular men) might be better in itself, if not considered in its relation to the entire system. The universe, once settled on, has a hypothetical necessity:[45] other ones are still conceivable, but in the one actually chosen everything is certain and has a moral necessity.[46]

Now, Leibniz must account for the existence of three kinds of evil – moral (sin), metaphysical (imperfection or limitation), and physical (pain)[47] – in terms of the divine mode of operation just described, and in a way which will leave both God's justice and men's moral responsibility intact. It is absolutely essential that he be able to distinguish between moral and metaphysical evil, if the idea of moral responsibility is to be maintained; if all evil is merely metaphysical (a consequence of limitation alone) then sin will be involuntary – caused, in fact, and not chosen – and thereby not a sin. Justice, as a charitable action, would be impossible for men; 'Spinozism' would reign. Generally, Leibniz avoids making God the creator of evil by giving it the same ontological status as goodness: both are essences, parts of the divine understanding – and, as will be recalled, God does not create his own understanding. 'Evil springs',

B

Leibniz said in the *Theodicy*, 'from the forms themselves in their detached state, that is, from the ideas which God has not produced by an act of his will.'[48] He insisted that God wills the good of each single created substance by an 'antecedent' will, but that the non-compossibility of all substances led to adjustments in which the overall perfection of the total scheme is uppermost;* as a result, God wills 'antecedently the good and consequently the best'.[49] Since this means that some evil had to be admitted, including evil actual men, a great strain is put on the doctrine of compossibility, a doctrine which (considering its importance) Leibniz never made very plausible.

It will be recalled that the distinctions between moral and metaphysical necessity, and between moral and metaphysical evil, are of capital importance to Leibniz; the first is the guarantor of moral freedom, the second of moral responsibility. Leibniz was certainly not prepared to do away with the latter, particularly since he admitted (rather uncritically) the idea of eternal damnation, a punishment he wanted to characterize as just.[50] But there is a serious question whether he really succeeded in upholding the distinction between moral and metaphysical evil; in the *Monadology* he claims that 'creatures receive their perfections from the influence of God but...their imperfections are due to their own nature, which is incapable of being limitless',[51] and in the *Theodicy* he insists that God could not give men 'all' without making them divine.[52] If men are necessarily imperfect (metaphysically evil), in what sense can they be held responsible for moral actions, including acts of justice? Assigning evil to the status of an essence not created by God saves him from the charge of voluntarily manufacturing evil; but it not only virtually destroys moral responsibility in human beings (who are only essences translated into existence, or substances), it also raises the question: why, if an actual universe could not be perfect throughout (a multiplication of God), and if the admission of evil was the *conditio sine qua non* of the best, did God create existence?[53] Referring to the admission of evil into the universe, Leibniz actually allowed himself to say that 'we can judge by the event (or *a posteriori*) that the permission was indispensable...sin made its way into the world; God was therefore unable to prevent it without detriment to his perfections...In God this conclusion holds good: he did this, therefore he did it well.'[54]

---

* Cf. the acid remark of Hegel, *History of Philosophy*: 'If I have some goods brought to me in the market, at some town, and say that they are certainly not perfect, but the best that are to be got, this is quite a good reason why I should content myself with them. But comprehension is a very different thing from this.'[55]

Oddly enough, Leibniz makes very little use of the idea that moral evil is inevitable if free will is an attribute of finite beings – though he does say that without sin neither grace nor Christ would be possible.[56] His more usual argument is that evil is necessary to the most perfect plan, though men (because of their limited perspective) can never know why this is so.[57] Since God is all good, all perfect, there *must* be a sufficient reason which allowed him to admit evil into existence; this is enough. Malebranche, on the other hand, who, like Leibniz, had also to account for evil, urged in his *Dialogues on Metaphysics* that 'the world as saved by Jesus Christ is of greater worth than the same universe as at first constructed, otherwise God would never have allowed his work to become corrupted'.[58] This is an interesting argument, but it is too specifically Christian for Leibniz, who made a very sparing use of Christ. He might, however, have done well to take the advice which Theodore offers to Aristes in Malebranche's ninth *Dialogue*:

Man, Aristes, is a sinner, he is not such as God made him. God, then, has allowed his work to become corrupt. Harmonize this with his wisdom, and his power, save yourself from the difficulty without the aid of the man-God, without admitting a mediator, without granting that God has had mainly in view the incarnation of his son. I defy you to do it even with the principles of the best philosophy.[59]

Leibniz' problem is fairly clear, and it casts doubt not only on his own work, but on any 'universal jurisprudence' which tries to reconcile universal justice, evil, and human freedom. He was aware that 'an inevitable necessity...would destroy the freedom of the will, so necessary to the morality of action: for justice and injustice, praise and blame, cannot attach to [metaphysically] necessary actions'.[60] His idea of moral freedom ought to have made meritorious actions and good intentions important; but his account of evil made this virtually impossible. Sometimes he makes evil (and evil men) the condition of a compossible whole, in which case men are part of a metaphysical compromise, but not free.[61] Sometimes evil men serve to 'heighten' the good of the rest, as dissonance heightens consonance in music[62] ('the glory and the perfection of the blessed may be incomparably greater than the misery and imperfection of the damned, and...here the excellence of the total good in the smaller number may exceed the total evil which is in the greater number');[63] but this is only a defense of the justice of predestination in terms of a cosmological utilitarianism. And sometimes (and most importantly) men are simply imperfect – their existences, which can be no more perfect than their essences, insure that their mistakes are the result of essential limitations of their possible knowledge of the good, not of evil will. The whole crucial distinction between metaphysical and moral evil thus appears to break down. As a result, Leibniz is forced into a position which is internally self-contradictory: 'free will is the proximate cause of the evil of punishment; although it is true that the original imperfection of creatures, which is already presented in the eternal ideas, is the first and most remote cause.'[64]

This statement comes from a late work, the *Theodicy*; but Leibniz had struggled with this problem since the beginning of his philosophical career, as a letter of 1671 makes clear: 'Pilate is condemned. Why? Because he lacks faith. Why does he lack it? Because he lacks the will to attention. Why this? Because he has not understood the neccessity of the matter...Why has he not understood it? Because the causes of understanding were lacking'[65] – that is, his metaphysical imperfection made his moral perfection impossible.

Justice, Responsibility and the Concept of 'Substance'

A brief examination of Leibniz' concept of substance may make these difficulties more clear.* When God translates a portion of essence into existence, he creates substances (or, as Leibniz called them after *c.* 1697, monads), which are characterized by 'perception' when passive and by 'force' (or activity) when active;[66] the Leibnizian substance is understood – to use a phrase of Hegel's – in terms of 'inner activity and self-movement of its own active life'.[67] While substances are always conjoined with bodies in existence, substances themselves are not material; matter can be divided and sub-divided *ad infinitum*,[68] but to account for perception ('intelligence' in the higher monads) and for action there must be a point of unity, a 'metaphysical point' or a 'formal atom'[69] (Leibniz of course rejected material atomism) which constitutes the reality of a being. Indeed, Leibniz says flatly that 'being and unity are convertible terms'.[70] He believed that thought could not be conceived as a modification of matter,† which was, for him, passive and undifferentiated;[71] a 'complete corporeal substance' (any living being having both mind and body) thus received its completeness from *two* sources, 'that is, from the active principle and from the passive principle, of which the first is called form, soul, entelechy, primitive force [or monad], and of which the second is

---

* Such an examination, in the present context, is necessarily partial and weighted in favor of those elements of the doctrine of substance with the highest potentially political content.

† This is, of course, only approximately accurate, since it can be claimed that Leibniz 'idealized' even matter itself. But this cannot be taken up here. See Loemker I, pp. 29, 54 ff.

called primary matter, solidity, resistance'.[72] (Leibniz never gave a wholly convincing account of why a material world – or a material element in a possible world – existed at all; sometimes matter, in his system, seems to be only the condition of the 'imperfection' of all substances inferior to God, since substantial perception mediated through senses is necessarily 'confused'.*)[73] Substances, then, are psychic beings, and the bodies with which they are associated are simply *phenomena bene fundata*;[74] substances, as simple unities, as 'subjects' of perception and change, are 'true things', whereas bodies – as Leibniz urged in a letter to de Volder – are 'beings by aggregation and therefore phenomena, existing, as Democritus put it, by convention and not by nature'.[75] Substances can be differentiated only intensively, or qualitatively, in terms of degrees of psychic perfection, and never extensively, or quantitatively, in terms of an 'extrinsic denomination' such as position in time or space;[†] 'it is living substance...which is truly a being, and matter, taken simply as mass, is only a phenomenon or a well-founded appearance'.[76] [‡] Substances are indestructible (except by God), and can be brought into existence only by divine creation; they are translated into being as parts of a system whose every element impinges on every other element; all substances are (so to speak) pre-modified in relation to each other, and everything that will ever happen to a substance is included in its original 'concept', much as all predicates inhere logically in a subject.[77] That Pilate would condemn Christ was thus a certainty, and had a hypothetical, though not a metaphysical necessity, since its opposite was still *conceivable*.[78] If a man undertakes a journey, this action issues out of his concept and is, hypothetically, necessary *to him*; if he did not make the journey, his concept would be altered (though no universal rule of metaphysical necessity would be overthrown).[79] (Sometimes, indeed, Leibniz defined freedom as the autonomous temporal unfolding of a substance out of its concept, unaffected by other substances: and he wavered

* Cf. *Theodicy* II, pt. 200: 'If each substance taken separately were perfect, all would be alike; which is neither fitting nor possible. If they were Gods, it would not have been possible to produce them. The best system of things will therefore not contain Gods; it will always be a system of bodies.' Cf. also Ger. VI, p. 172.
† 'I hold space to be something merely relative, as time is: I hold it to be an order of co-existences, as time is an order of successions.' Letter III to Clarke, part 4, Ger. VII, p. 363.
‡ Cf., however, the correspondence with des Bosses, in which Leibniz holds that 'no doubt there is in any body something more than phenomena...I should prefer to say that there are no substances over and above monads, but only appearances, but that these are not illusory, like a dream, or like a sword pointing at us out of a concave mirror...but that they are true phenomena'. Loemker II, pp. 978 and 1001.

between this Spinozistic conception of 'freedom' and a more traditional Christian conception based on free will.) In any case, all relations of substances are determined in advance of temporal existence; substances do not affect each other in action, but in advance, metaphysically, by being assigned a place in the pre-established harmony. 'The intercourse of substances or monads, namely, arises not from an influence but from a consensus originating in their preformation by God.'[80] There is, for Leibniz, a *continuum*[81] of substances stretching from the barely organic to God himself: bare monads have perceptions only[82] (as in the plant's 'perception' of light in the process of photo-synthesis); animals have feeling and purely empirical 'memory'; but spirits (or minds), which are characterized by self-consciousness, memory or moral personality[83] (on which responsibility, guilt and punishment depend),[84] and innate knowledge of the (logical and moral) eternal verities, are part of the City of God. Since all substances are created as parts of a compossible whole, they all have relations; and since substance is percipient, all substances express or represent all other substances with varying degrees of clarity and distinctness; 'this mutual connection or accommodation of all created things to each other and of each to all the rest causes each simple substance to have relations which express all the others and consequently to be a perpetual living mirror of the universe'.[85] Substances are perfect to the extent that they are causes *a priori* of changes in lesser substances;[86] thus the physical realm exists to serve the moral, and nature leads to grace.[87]

That Leibniz thought his concept of substance essential to an understanding of justice and morality is quite clear: 'true ethics is to metaphysics what practice is to theory, because upon the doctrine of substances in common depends the knowledge of spirits and particularly of God and the soul which gives a proper meaning to justice and virtue'.[88] But the difficulty with the theory of substance – apart from the possible meaning of such terms as 'expression' and 'representation'[89] – is that it seems to involve, in part at least, a fatalism which is incongruent with Leibniz' (Christian) idea of freedom and hence with the possibility of choosing to act charitably. On the one hand, the doctrine of substance provides for moral personality (in the higher substances); for the possibility of good and evil actions, for responsibility, guilt, punishment, and reward; for the autonomy of the mind from causal determination by physical factors; for a personal immortality in which actions can receive what they are worth. Generally, it provides for an idea of *mind* which is something more than mechanism and for an idea of *life* which is something more than motion. On the other hand, however, substance comes into existence only as part of a pattern which is 'good' as a totality: a given substance does not exist *in abstracto*, but within the constraints imposed by the principles of compossibility and pre-established harmony – both of which involve a large measure of stasis, if not of fatalism. An evil substance may be necessitated by the best, and if it 'gets better', perhaps through good actions, the order of the universe would be less fixed than Leibniz usually assumes (though he sometimes indicates that the *whole* universe may be progressing toward 'new perfections').[90] If one assumes, as Leibniz does, that evil is an essence which must be given reality if *any* world is created (and any world would be less perfect than God), then it is hard to see how all substances can attain salvation or act rightly. If this were not a sufficiently serious problem, Leibniz' rather frequent definition of freedom as the unfolding of substance according to internal laws,[91] while congruent with the concepts of compossibility and pre-established harmony, cannot be reconciled with more traditional views of moral freedom. Arnauld made Leibniz aware of some of these problems in the 1680s, and he responded, ultimately, with the distinction between moral and metaphysical necessity, as well as with the argument that men's moral actions are free because 'God has foreseen those actions in his ideas, just as they are, that is, free'.[92] But the doctrine of the metaphysical imperfection of all men overthrew the force of these distinctions, since volition is ultimately dependent on possible knowledge;* and to make matters more difficult, Leibniz admitted (a subtle form of) predestination into his system, insisting that grace and salvation were not deserved or accorded to merit.[93] If charity, however, is to be the foundation of an ethical–political system, one must grant an importance to 'good acts' which Leibniz was loath to allow (though he was also unwilling to deny their importance: 'prayers, good intentions, good actions, all are useful and sometimes even necessary, but none of it is sufficient').[94] Good acts – such as acts of justice – would necessarily involve alterations in the *relations*† of rational substances, alterations presupposing a degree of moral spontaneity which

* 'We will only what appears to the intellect. The source of all errors is precisely the same in its own way as the reason for errors which is observed in arithmetical calculation...to will is to be brought to act through a reason perceived by the intellect' (*Thoughts on the Principles of Descartes*, Loemker II, pp. 637–9). This creates terrible problems for Leibniz, who often held that goodness must be in the will, considered as a faculty which chooses among 'objects of knowledge'. The problem is even clearer in the *Mantissa* to the *Codex Iuris Gentium*, in which he says that 'even in our evil purposes we are moved by a certain perceived appearance of good or perfection'. Here the crucial distinction between error and evil breaks down altogether.

† Cf. *NE* II, xxx, pt. 4: 'Relations have a reality dependent on the mind, like truths; but not the mind of men, since there is a supreme intelligence which determines them for all time.'

important elements of the doctrine of substance seem to disallow. Individual men would have to be individually good; it would not be enough that the universe, as a totality, was good. As Leibniz' system stands, only those beneficiaries of compossibility who find themselves nearest divinity can enjoy the possibility of acting even relatively well. Ultimately, the effort to salvage God's justice by making evil an essence which might be translated into particular substances, including human beings, seriously weakened the possibility of men's responsibility and justice.* Thus, even while attempting to overthrow 'Spinozism' in the *Theodicy*, Leibniz' own logic forced him to grant that:

> often creatures lack the means of giving themselves the will they ought to have; often they even lack the will to use those means which indirectly give a good will ...This fault must be admitted...but...it is not necessary... for all rational creatures to have so great a perfection, and such as would bring them so close to the Divinity.[95]

What *would* have been more in accord with charity as the chief moral–political virtue than Leibniz' conflation of Platonism, Thomism and Calvinism, is pure Pelagianism; and this he sometimes approaches – quite inconsistently – in the *New Essays* ('for true goodness less knowledge suffices with more good will').[96] But this is not his ordinary view. The central question in Leibniz is: why did God create a *necessarily* imperfect universe? Sometimes he suggested that God created out of goodness[97] – an odd suggestion, unless plenitude and variety are better than the non-existence of evil; but more usually he treated existence as a manifestation of God's glory.[98] Substances exist to 'mirror' his perfections, to be witness to them.[99] Evidently neither of these explanations rests on 'charity' traditionally understood. At most, Leibniz is able to show that the universe as a whole is best, once a decision to create *some* universe has been made. 'Only the evil themselves have suffered any loss through sin,' he urged in the *True Theologica Mystica*, but 'the whole creation of God has not lost but gained through it.'[100] That this doctrine is destructive of individuals, Leibniz was aware without being able to do anything about it; in the *Radical Origination of Things* (1697) he said that 'just as care is taken in the

---

* The most recent defense of Leibniz' consistency on ethical questions, Nicholas Rescher's *The Philosophy of Leibniz*, holds that the distinction between moral and metaphysical necessity does in fact hold up under analysis, and that the argument about evil as imperfection (as contrasted with evil as *choice*), is unobjectionable. But Rescher does not take up an objection which Leibniz himself was willing to entertain (without, however, answering it), viz. that God could have refrained from creating *any* world. Here Russell seems to be more nearly right, though his imputation of unworthy motives to Leibniz is, as Rescher says, 'unjustifiable and unjust' (p. 147).

best-ordered commonwealth that individuals shall fare as well as possible, so the universe would not be perfect enough unless as much care is shown for individuals as is consistent with the universal harmony'.[101] It is the last phrase which is crucial, and which shows why the effort to define charity in terms of both perfection and choice becomes so problematical in a necessarily imperfect world.

Perfection

Leibniz himself observed that the relation of divine justice to the moral freedom of rational substances was a 'labyrinth' in which one could get lost;[102] and in fact he was much happier when dealing not with freedom and responsibility, but with *perfection*: it is perfection which holds the Leibnizian system together, as freedom fails to do. The 'apex of metaphysics and that of ethics are united in one' by the perfection of God.[103] Essences have a claim to existence in proportion to their perfections ('there is a struggle between all the possibles, all of them laying claim to existence, and...those which, being united, produce most reality, most perfection...carry the day.').[104]* But Leibniz did not define only his theology and his metaphysics in terms of perfection; he tried to define his ethics and psychology in the same way – or rather, he sometimes defined them in terms of perfection, sometimes in terms of will and choice. Thus love, which becomes charity when it is habitual, is a feeling of the perfection which is in others; when this charity is regulated by wisdom, which tells us how perfect men are, and thereby what they deserve, the product is justice.[105]† Leibniz' psychology is founded on perfection as well;

---

* 'Just as possibility is the principle of essence, so perfection or degree of essence is the principle of existence', *Radical Origination of Things*, Loemker II, p. 793.

† There is, obviously, a problem here: if charity is a *feeling* of perfection which becomes justice when regulated by a *knowledge* of perfection, then justice is simply perfection regulated by perfection. Leibniz avoids this difficulty (usually) by defining charity in a broad way, as tolerance, as sympathy, as generosity. But the philosophical grounds for this broadening are not well established.

In the *New Essays* I, ii, pt. 4, Leibniz complicates matters by urging that men are guided morally not only by rational perceptions of pleasure but by 'instinct' as well: 'we are prompted to acts of humanity, by instinct because it pleases us, and by reason because it is just'. But justice too is a pleasure – though a 'higher' one than instinct; as a result this distinction is confusing. In I, ii, pt. 9, he explains that 'God has given to man instincts which prompt at once and without reasoning to some portion of what reason ordains'. The difficulty in interpreting these passages lies in the fact that while Leibniz usually treats pleasure as a *continuum*, in the *New Essays* he draws a strong distinction between reason and 'le naturel'. But the *New Essays* are not always representative of the whole range of his thought.

pleasure is a feeling of perfection, pain a feeling of imperfection,[106] and 'the impulse to action arises from a striving toward perfection, the sense of which is pleasure, and there is no action or will on any other basis'.[107] There is a strong connection between Leibniz' ethics and psychology; since perfection gives pleasure, the love of other men, when regulated by what their perfections deserve, makes justice a pleasure. Because 'to love or to cherish is to be delighted by the happiness of the beloved and his perfections',[108] everyone will love other intelligent beings to the extent that they make perfection and charity *their* object.[109]*

Leibniz' most effective brief effort to link up his metaphysics, psychology and ethics through the idea of perfection is contained in his notes on *Felicity* (*c*. 1694–8), in which he says that:

1. Virtue is the habit of acting according to wisdom. It is necessary that practice accompany knowledge.
2. Wisdom is the science of felicity, [and] is what must be studied above all other things.
3. Felicity is a lasting state of pleasure. Thus it is good to abandon or moderate pleasures which can be injurious, by causing misfortunes or by blocking [the attainment of] better and more lasting pleasures.
4. Pleasure is a knowledge or feeling of perfection, not only in ourselves, but also in others, for in this way some further perfection is aroused in us.
5. To love is to find pleasure in the perfection of another.
6. Justice is charity or a habit of loving conformed to wisdom. Thus when one is inclined to justice, one tries to procure good for everybody, so far as one can, reasonably, but in proportion to the needs and merits of each: and even if one is obliged sometimes to punish evil persons, it is for the general good.[110]

In a letter to Hansch (1707), Leibniz related this highly rationalistic psychology and ethics to his theology: 'since the divine happiness is the confluence of all perfections, and pleasure is the feeling of perfection, it follows that the true happiness of a created mind is in its sense of the divine happiness'.[111] This does not mean, however, that Leibniz fell back on a world-soul, or a 'single universal spirit' (which he disliked in Spinoza);[112] rational substances are autonomous for Leibniz, and their love of others (and of God) must be an extension of their own (higher)

---

* Cf. *De Tribus Juris Naturae et Gentium Gradibus*, Mollat, p. 13. Falling back, however, on perfection did not really solve Leibniz' problem of reconciling God's justice, human freedom, and the existence of evil; in the *Radical Origination* he said that 'the law of justice...dictates that each one shall take part in the perfection of the universe...according to the measure of his own virtue and the degree to which his will is moved toward the common good'. Here again a certain moral freedom is suggested which the ideas of compossibility and pre-established harmony seem not to allow.

pleasure.* An expansion of self, not a negation of self, is required. 'To love', Leibniz said in a letter to Bossuet, 'is nothing else than finding one's pleasure (I say pleasure, and not utility or interest) in the well-being, perfection, happiness of another; and thus, while love can be disinterested, it can nonetheless never be detached from our own interest, of which pleasure is an essential part.'[113] Despite this brush with hedonism, Leibniz insisted in countless letters and memoranda that 'to contribute to the public good, and to the glory of God, is the same thing';[114] that 'the touchstone of the love of God is that which St John has given us: and when I see that a man has a true ardor for the general good, he is not far from the love of God'.[115] Men must scale the *continuum* of pleasures; near the top, just beneath the love of God, they will find love of neighbor, on which justice turns. Leibniz' most eloquent summary of this view, a letter concerning *True Piety* (1710), urged that:

one cannot love God, who is invisible, if one does not love his neighbor, who is visible. Those who...reduce justice to [mere] rigor, and who fail altogether to understand that one cannot be just without being benevolent...; in a word, not only those who look for their profit, pleasure and glory in the misery of others, but also those who are not at all anxious to procure the common good and to lift out of misery those who are in their care, and generally those who show themselves to be without enlightenment and without charity, boast in vain of a piety which they do not know at all, whatever appearance they create.[116]

Practical Justice

Charity exactly proportioned to merit would produce the most perfect human justice; but Leibniz was aware that this was too much to be hoped for in practical life. He therefore attempted to fuse his definition of justice as the charity of the wise with the three great principles of the Roman law: *neminem laedere, suum cuique tribuere, honeste vivere*. Leibniz converted the highest degree of Roman law, 'live honestly', into 'live piously', or charitably, while the *ius strictum* (whose maxim was *neminem laedere*, 'injure no one'), and which required mere forbearance from violence, became for him simply the lowest form of justice, something essential but not adequate. The middle degree of justice, *suum cuique*

---

* One must, in Leibniz' view, 'seek luminous and rational pleasures', which are to be found in 'the knowledge and in the production of order and harmony'; one must, that is, shun the 'confused pleasures of the senses' (*NE* II, xxi, pts. 35–7, 42, 53). Leibniz admired the work of Lorenzo Valla, the Renaissance scholar who, in *De Voluptate*, produced a synthesis of pleasure and Christian virtues which in some measure prefigured Leibniz' work. Cf. particularly Ernst Cassirer, *The Individual and the Cosmos in Renaissance Philosophy*, pp. 79 ff, and Gaston Grua, *La Justice Humaine selon Leibniz*, pp. 43 ff.

tribuere, rendering to each his due, made up for Leibniz the bulk of political justice.[117] In the *Codex Iuris Gentium Diplomaticus* (1693), Leibniz enlarged on these distinctions. The precept of the *ius strictum* is that no one is to be injured, 'lest if it be within the state, the person should have grounds for an action at law, or if it be without the state, he should have the right to make war'; this lowest degree of justice he also called 'commutative' (altering the sense which Aristotle gave to the term). The middle degree of justice, rendering to each his due, Leibniz sometimes called charity in a 'narrow' sense, sometimes equity, sometimes 'distributive' justice.[118] There are two important differences between the *ius strictum* and equity: first, that the *ius strictum*, which is merely preservative, treats everyone equally, whereas equity, or 'distributive' justice, looks to merit and thus treats different men differently; and second, that the *ius strictum* simply 'avoids misery' and 'has its source in the need of keeping peace', while equity 'tends to happiness, but of such a kind as falls to our mortal lot'.[119] The highest degree of justice, true charity (or piety), plays only an oblique and regulative role in politics, but is the guarantor of the goodness of men's actions in a wider sense: some men, without fear of divine justice, would not act as they should.[120]

Leibniz treated private property in relation to the three degrees of justice, though not with perfect consistency. He believed that no private property at all was best, but that such austerity was unattainable. Society, he urged, is held together by three things – friendship, political justice, and valor. 'If the first, which makes all goods common, could be observed, the second would be useless, and if men were not so far removed from justice, valor would not be needed to defend states.'[121] But 'human nature', he insisted, would not allow that society be founded on friendship alone; thus both private property and political coercion became necessary. In a perfect state, Leibniz said, 'all goods should be public property',[122] and should be publicly distributed to private persons; unfortunately, neither a sufficiently enlightened public, willing to live a 'convent-like' existence, nor sufficiently just and public-spirited administrators, could be found. As a result, men must be left to provide property for themselves (though public benevolence demands that no one actually suffer from want). Once this decision has been made, in Leibniz' view, private property must be considered to be protected by strict right: thus in respect to property men are to be treated equally, not in the sense that they all receive the same thing, but in the sense that they have an equal right to keep what they have (or can get). Redistribution of property on the basis of alleged merits and virtues is too difficult and too dangerous;[123] such a redistribution would cause an injury to private persons. The principle *suum cuique tri-*

buere, therefore, is to apply only to goods which the state has at its disposal for distribution (or to goods which private men wish to distribute out of benevolence).[124] The potential radicalism of Leibniz' theory of justice is thus socially defused; levelling is forbidden, and only a general expansion of the state's generosity is recommended.*

One of the most important things about Leibniz' theory of practical justice, when joined with the gradations of the Roman law, is that he allowed no sharp breaks between duty and benevolence: in Leibniz there is none of Kant's differentiation between 'perfect' and 'imperfect' duties to others.[125] Justice for Leibniz is a *continuum*, as everything in his philosophy tends to be: there is an unbroken continuity, with no 'gaps', between the lowest substance and God, between life and death, between rest and motion, just as there is a *continuum* between abstaining from injury and doing good. In the *Meditation on the Common Concept of Justice*, he argues persuasively that if one grants that injury ought not to be done, it is hard to deny that good should be done; 'whether one does evil or refuses to do good is a matter of degree'.[126] To this argument he added a psychological one – that if one wants to know what is just, he should put himself in the place of one who might have reason to complain of injustice. Here Leibniz came to roughly the same practical conclusion as Kant: if men did not make exceptions of themselves, they would all agree to the same rules. And this is why he urged that 'the place of others' was the soundest viewpoint from which to make moral and political judgments; 'everything which we would find unjust if we were in the place of others, must seem to us to be suspect of injustice...the sense of the principle is: do not do or do not refuse lightly that which you would not like to be done to you or which another would not refuse to you'.[127]†

Leibniz' theory of justice, then, is a complex amalgam of Christian charity, a metaphysic of Platonic perfectionism, Roman law, and transmogrified Aristotelian terminology; its relation to his pure philosophy is,

---

* Cf. *Extensive Remarks on Jurisprudence* (1676), Acad. Ed. IV, I, p. 572: 'It is sufficient that the commonwealth take care that no one becomes miserable; that men of merit can find some way to be useful; this is what is essential; for the rest, it is not very important which [citizens] possess certain things; provided that acts of violence and manifest frauds be punished and stopped.'

† Even on this point, however, Leibniz' Platonism and his Christian doctrines came into conflict: 'there is so much dissimilitude and inequality between men, that we would not reasonably demand of others that which they demand reasonably of us'. (Letter to Bierling, Dutens v, pp. 388–9). The fundamental egalitarianism of Christian moral doctrine was something that Leibniz found very difficult to reconcile with 'natural' justice resting on fixed and permanent relations.

to say the least, problematical, but taken in itself it has integrity and force. Bertrand Russell, therefore, was not altogether justified in calling Leibniz' social thought a 'mass of inconsistencies';[128] there is one central problem, to wit whether, given the ideas of substance, compossibility etc., one *could* act any better than he does, or whether one's necessarily limited knowledge will bring about imperfect charity involuntarily. In essence, the question is Spinoza's – whether it is possible to distinguish between error and evil. And on this point Leibniz was never perfectly consistent, though he tried to maintain the distinction.

Particular States and the Character of Political Rule

Leibniz' doctrine of justice as charity regulated by wisdom was rather consistently kept in view as he worked out his theory of the state: a just political order requires both benevolence and intelligence, but not the participation of all the members of society, either in forming or in sustaining the polity – least of all by a natural right. The state, in his view, is an 'unlimited unequal society' – that is, it is concerned with 'the whole life and the common good', and not simply with 'certain purposes, for example, trade and commerce, navigation, warfare, and travel';[129]* and it is founded on relations of inequality between those who rule and those who are ruled. Like Plato, Leibniz believed that it would be unjust if the best and the wisest men did *not* rule; here he fell back on justice as a relation, as a proportion, and took the Platonic view that social justice should be the most accurate possible transcript of 'nature'. In a letter to the Scottish nobleman Thomas Burnett (1699 or 1700), he sketched this position, while criticizing (with infinite circumspection) the Hobbesian/Lockean theory of equal natural rights.

I have still not had the leisure to read the entire book entitled *Two Treatises of Government*, against the principles of Mr Filmer. I did notice, however, a great justice and solidity in the reasoning. There are, nevertheless, some passages, perhaps, which demand a more ample discussion, as among others what is said of the State of Nature, and of the equality of rights of men. This equality would be certain, if all men had the same [natural] advantages, but this not being so at all, it seems that Aristotle is more correct here than Mr Hobbes. If several men found themselves in a single ship on the open sea, it would not be in the least conformable either to reason or nature, that those who understand nothing of

---

* One is reminded of a famous passage in Burke's *Reflections on the Revolution in France*: 'the state ought not to be considered as nothing better than a partnership agreement in a trade of pepper and coffee, calico, or tobacco, or some other such low concern...it is a partnership...in every virtue and in all perfection' (VII, 2 (a)).

sea-going claim to be pilots; such that, following natural reason, government belongs to the wisest.[130]

Since equal natural rights to political participation are, for Leibniz, illusory, he made very little use – at least in his mature works – of social contract theory, which presupposes a right in all contractors to found legitimate states. The legitimacy of the Leibnizian state has nothing to do with its origins. A contract, therefore, is not important; but justice, welfare, benevolence, and the promotion of the common good are. Probably Leibniz denigrated the contract precisely because Hobbes had made so much of it: in a very early work, the *Nova Methodus*, he appeared as a rather conventional contractarian;[131] but since the 'state of nature' which preceded the Hobbesian contract posited a moral vacuum in which there was no justice without positive law – a doctrine which Leibniz detested – he may have felt that contract theory was dangerous. (It also, in his view, introduced too great a measure of artifice into social relations; Hobbes, Leibniz suggested in the *New Essays*, was not aware that 'the best men, free of all malice, would unite the better to obtain their [common] end, as birds flock together to travel in company'.[132]) This aversion, however, did not prevent him from making a rather acute remark about Hobbes in his late (1712) *Remarks on Shaftesbury's Characteristics*: 'Our illustrious author [Shaftesbury] refutes with reason those who believe that there is no obligation at all in the state of nature, and outside of government; for, obligations by pacts having to form the right of government itself, according to the author of these principles, it is manifest that the obligation is anterior to the government which it must form.'[133]

Leibniz' rejection of equal natural rights and (ultimately) of contract theory did not mean, however, that he dismissed the possibility of an important 'popular' element in the state. This he made clear in his most important purely political letter (to Burnett, 1701), which is also valuable for its revelation of Leibniz' devotion to a Montesquieuean moderation and reasonability in politics.

The end of political science with regard to the doctrine of forms of commonwealths [*républiques*], must be to make the empire of reason flourish. The end of monarchy is to make a hero of eminent wisdom and virtue reign...The end of aristocracy is to give the government to the most wise and the most expert. The end of democracy, or polity, is to make the people themselves agree to what is good for them. And if one could have all [three] at once: a great hero, very wise senators, and very reasonable citizens, that would constitute a mixture of the three forms. Arbitrary power is what is directly opposed to the empire of reason. But one must realize that this arbitrary power is found not only in kings, but also in assemblies...Thus one must think in this world of laws which can serve to restrain not only kings, but also the deputies of the people, and judges.[134]

Arbitrary power, then, was wholly rejected by Leibniz; liberty was as important to him as equality was unnatural. But this love of liberty never led him to republicanism.* 'When one loves true liberty,' he observed in the same letter to Burnett, 'one is not a republican on that account, since one can find a more certain reasonable liberty when the king and the assemblies are linked by good laws, than when arbitrary power is in the king or in the multitude.'[135] If one had to choose, however, between absolutism and popular 'license', Leibniz clearly preferred the former; 'it is certain...that the absolute power of kings is more tolerable than the license of individuals, and [that] nothing is more certain to bring about tyranny than anarchy'.[136]

Leibniz, however, did not like to concentrate on power as the main attribute of rulers. In an important early work, the *Grundriss eines Bedenckens von Aufrichtung einer Societät in Deutschland* (*c.* 1671), he drew his customary sharp distinction between reason and power, and observed that a harmony of mind and power is not only the foundation of beauty and of justice, but of true statesmanship: 'if power is greater than reason, he who possesses it is either a lamb who cannot use it at all, or a wolf and a tyrant who cannot use it well.'[137] On the other hand, the man in whom reason is greater than the power to use it is 'overpowered'. Accordingly, Leibniz urged, 'those to whom God has given reason without power...have the right to be counselors', while those who have power alone 'must listen patiently, and not throw good counsels to the winds'.[138] What is ideal, however, is a union of power and reason within a single person: 'Those to whom God has given at once reason and power in a high degree, are heroes created by God to be the promoters of his will, as principal instruments.' Of the three ways of honoring God – through good words, good thoughts, and good actions – the last is best, and is accomplished (if ever) by moralists and statesmen; as 'governors of the public welfare' they 'strive not only to discover the brilliance of the beauty of God in nature', but try to imitate it. 'To praises, to thoughts, to words and to ideas, they add good works. They do not merely contemplate what he has done well,

---

* Nonetheless, Leibniz was aware of republicanism's attractions, and of the fear it produced in monarchs: 'all republics are odious in the eyes of kings... republics usually cause their neighbors to wish for comparable liberty; they tolerate all kinds of religions; the common good is the first object in their catechisms; they scarcely know corruption; they are the true seed-beds of men of genius', *Securitas Publica Interna et Externa* (1670–1), pt. II, No. 53; F de C 6, pp. 225–6.

but offer and sacrifice themselves as instruments, the better to contribute to the general good and to that of men in particular.'[139]

Power was essential, Leibniz granted, to the translation of right into 'fact', but it was the right to which he devoted his attention; power was neutral and undifferentiated, and helped evil men to carry out evil designs as readily as it helped good men to be benevolent.[140] And nothing in Leibniz is more important than benevolence. It is essential that the wise and virtuous who (ought to) rule devote all their efforts to the public welfare, not merely to prevent misery, but to promote actual improvement in both the material living conditions and the knowledge and virtue of the citizens. 'The end of politics, after virtue,' Leibniz wrote, 'is the maintenance of abundance, so that men will be in a better position to work in common concert for those solid [objects of] knowledge which cause the sovereign Author to be admired and loved.'[141] If Leibniz' insistence on liberty links him to the great English liberals of his century, his emphasis on charity and welfare separates him from them; he did not stress, as they did, rights, representation, or a Benthamite 'dislocability' of rulers, but he was much more interested in welfare and in the general improvement of men than any liberal.* This much is apparent in a strong passage from his (otherwise somewhat sanguine) *Memoir for Enlightened Persons of Good Intention*:

The greatest and most efficacious means...of augmenting the general welfare of men, while enlightening them, while turning them toward the good and while freeing them from annoying inconveniences [poverty, unemployment, maleducation] in so far as this is feasible, would be to persuade great princes and [their] principal ministers to make extraordinary efforts to procure such great goods and to allow our times to enjoy advantages which, without this [extraordinary effort] would be reserved for a distant posterity.[142]

Leibniz assures the princes who are to make these efforts that they will be working not simply for 'immortal glory' and for 'their own perfection and satisfaction', but also in their own interest: not only will they have subjects who are 'more virtuous and better-suited to serve them well', but – and here Leibniz gives more than a hint of his opinion of the general run of German aristocrats – 'persons of leisure and means, instead of amusing themselves with trifles, with criminal or ruinous pleasures, and with intrigues', will find their satisfaction in becoming virtuous.[143]

---

* Leibniz' combination of benevolent authoritarianism with welfare anticipates a good deal of later German practice; some of Bismarck's domestic policies might not have been uncongenial to him. Janet, in his *Histoire de la Science Politique* (vol. 2, p. 248), says that 'state socialism would not have frightened Leibniz very much'.

C

While English liberalism concentrated mostly on the state as a judicial authority defending natural rights (and particularly property rights), Leibniz concerned himself with social well-being; in dozens of projects which he urged on numerous princes, he advocated the setting up of economic councils which would oversee not only manufacturing and agriculture, but also public health and education ('optima respublica intelligi non potest sine optima educatione'),[144] and insisted again and again that 'it is much better to prevent poverty and misery, which is the mother of crimes, than to relieve it after it is born'.[145] His strenuous efforts to found academies of arts and sciences in a number of major capitals were successful only in Berlin; but his endeavors to interest Peter the Great of Russia, the Elector of Saxony, and the Holy Roman Emperor in such academies show how truly he was interested in making charity an important *public* virtue. Leibniz felt that many rulers made the mistake of thinking that they could be glorious through their 'destructions and desolations',[146] and that it was his function to demonstrate the superiority of constructive to destructive actions. As he noted in one of his useful poems:

> *Quel triomphe qu'on puisse obtenir par la guerre,*
> *Obliger est bien plus que conquerir la terre.*[147]

Sovereignty

Leibniz' emphasis on charity, welfare, and reasonability led, not surprisingly, to an extreme downgrading of the concept of sovereignty, which played so important a part in much other seventeenth-century theory. He did believe, with Hobbes, that the state is simply an aggregation,[148] like a herd or an army, and that its unity is found in the unity of its rulership; the doctrine of substance, of course, requires that only individuals be real, and thus on this point Leibniz' metaphysics and politics coincide exactly. A state, like a marble pavement made up of smaller stones, is only a *unum per accidens*; it is not a true unity, 'any more than would be the water of a pond with all the fish it holds, even though all the water and the fish were frozen together'.[149]* But Leibniz broke with the Hobbesian view of law as command: for him it is the content of law – its promotion of the common good and an objective justice – which matters. His treatment of sovereignty was, of course, affected by his being the official apologist for a German electorate; indeed the immediate purpose of his writing his main

---

* Thus Gierke's objection, in *Natural Law and the Theory of Society*, p. 137, that Leibniz attained to a conception of the state as a 'mere' *persona ficta* (rather than as a corporate 'personality'), is misdirected: Leibniz' metaphysics *could not* allow him to consider the state a 'real personality'.

work on sovereignty (the so-called *Caesarinus Fürstenerius*, 1677) was to show that minor German princes were as 'sovereign' as the kings of France and Spain. But he did not have to do violence to his own views of law and of rule to demonstrate this. Throughout his life Leibniz clung to the belief that the medieval *majestas* of the Empire – perhaps understood only as a court of last resort for all of the Republic of Christendom – was better than the modern states-system; and, this being so, he was quite willing to pull down what Bodin and Hobbes had built up. 'Sovereign', said Leibniz in the *Entrétiens de Philarete et d'Eugène* (a French summary, in dialogue form, of the *Caesarinus Fürstenerius*), 'is he who is master of a territory' and who is 'powerful enough to make himself considerable in Europe in time of peace and in time of war, by treaties, arms and alliances'.150 He removed the character of absolute supremacy from the concept of sovereignty, making it only a comparative rather than a super-lative standard; and, taking the fantastic morcellization and diversity of German political forms into account, urged that it did not matter whether the sovereign 'holds his lands as a fief, nor whether he recognizes the majesty of a chief, provided that he be master at home and cannot be disturbed except by arms'.151 Leibniz adhered to this merely descriptive and non-legal conception of sovereignty long after his hopes of a revived Imperial *majestas*, together with his hopes of a reunified *Respublica Christiana*, began to wane.

If Leibniz had immediate practical reasons for wanting to undermine the idea of sovereignty, he had more purely philosophical ones as well; and not surprisingly, he began with an attack on Hobbes. 'If we listen to Hobbes,' he said in the *Caesarinus Fürstenerius*, 'there will be nothing in our land [the Empire] but out and out anarchy,' for 'no people in civilized Europe is ruled by the laws that he has proposed.'152 Leibniz went on to discuss, with some accuracy, Hobbes' idea of the war of every man against every man, caused by man's natural right to all things; his conception of the transferal of these rights (save self-defense) to the state, such that (in Leibniz' words) 'each man is understood to will whatever the government or person who represents him wills'. And he faithfully described Hobbes' insistence that government be unitary and centralized, because (again in Leibniz' words) 'it is fruitless to divide the rights of supreme power among several persons or corporations [*collegia*]', since a division of power could cause disagreements and the state might be dissolved.153

Leibniz, having described Hobbes' ideas, flatly denied their accuracy. 'Hobbes' fallacy', he said, 'lies in this, that he thinks that things which can entail inconvenience should not be borne at all.' This insistence, according to Leibniz, is 'foreign to the nature of human affairs'. He admitted that 'when the supreme power is divided, many dissensions can arise; even wars, if everyone holds stubbornly to his own opinion'. But experience, he said, shows that 'men usually hold to some middle road, so as not to commit everything to hazard through their obstinacy'.154 He found examples of this moderation in Poland and in the United Provinces: 'Among the Poles, one territorial representative can dissolve the assembly by his obstinacy; in Holland, when something of great importance is being considered, such as peace, war or treaties, the disagreement of one town upsets everything.' Still, said Leibniz, because of the 'prudence and moderation of those who preside over the whole',155 most matters turn out well enough.

Leibniz then turned to an attack on Pufendorf, whom he considered an inferior German version of Hobbes, and who had called the Empire a 'political monster' in his *De Statu Imperii Germanici*. 'If this is true', Leibniz retorted, 'I would venture to say that the same monsters are being maintained by the Dutch and the Poles and the English, even by the Spanish and French.' How unreal absolute sovereignty is will be clear to those 'who know what the noble orders of the kingdom of France... once said in public assembly concerning the fundamental laws of the kingdom and the limits of royal power'. The components of the French state were not managed by 'mandates given from the plenitude of power (as they say)', but by 'demands, negotiations, and discussions'.156 'Hobbesian empires', he concluded, 'exist neither among civilized people nor among barbarians, and I consider them neither possible nor desirable – unless those who must have supreme power are gifted with angelic virtues.' Hobbes' 'demonstrations' thus 'have a place only in that state whose king is God, whom alone one can trust in all things'.157

Taking this view of sovereignty, Leibniz could not but reject the Hobbesian doctrine of law as command (hedged round by formal requirements such as promulgation and 'authentic interpretation');158 Leibniz was a natural-law theorist (though he preferred the term 'universal jurisprudence' to natural law) who held that 'the fault of those, who have made justice depend on power, is partly a consequence of their confounding right [*droit*] and law [*la loi*]. Right cannot be unjust, but law can be.'159*

While this radical distinction between positive law and natural law sometimes leads, in other theorists, to ideas of a right of revolution when the actions of rulers are 'against nature', Leibniz usually treated this subject simply as a question of prudence. 'I am of the sentiment of

---

* Cf. *NE* IV, vii, pt. 19: 'There are fundamental maxims constituting the law itself... which, when they are taught by pure reason, and do not arise from the arbitrary power of the state, constitute natural law.'

Grotius,' he wrote in 1695, 'and I believe that as a rule one must obey, the evil of revolt ordinarily being incomparably greater than that which causes it. I allow, however, that the prince can go to such an excess, and put the safety of the commonwealth in such danger, that the obligation to suffer ceases.'[160] And, indeed, if a ruler cannot provide security – here he agreed with Hobbes – 'it is permitted to subjects to swear an oath of fidelity to the enemy of their master who has conquered them, their master not being able to do anything more to insure their safety'.[161] For all his differences with Hobbes, Leibniz never denied that providing security was the first obligation of the state. 'My definition of the state, or of that which the Latins call *respublica*,' said Leibniz in 1705, 'is: that it is a large society whose end is the common security.' It is to be hoped, he went on, 'that one can obtain for men something more than security, namely happiness, and one must apply himself to this end; but security at least is essential, and without it all well-being ceases.'[162] The difference between Hobbes and Leibniz is that Leibniz concentrated on 'something more than security', namely institutionalized charity, while Hobbes, who believed that all ends other than existence were relative, contented himself with setting up a 'context'.

Before passing on to Leibniz' theory of international relations, it should be noted that, while a great many seventeenth-century theorists devoted their efforts to the (theoretical) destruction of all of the medieval *collegia* existing below the level of the state, as well as the 'universal' authorities existing above the level of the state,* Leibniz – particularly in his earlier works – tried to preserve something of the hierarchy of social forms handed down from the late Middle Ages. Thus for him the state was the 'fifth degree' of natural society: above it, as the highest natural degree, was the Church of God, comprehending both the Church *per se* and the Emperor (as head and defender of the *Respublica Christiana*); below it were four lesser degrees, of ascending (political) importance – husbands and wives, parents and children, masters and servants, and, finally, whole 'households'.[163]

If everything in the world were arranged in the most perfect way, then, first of all, parents, children, and relatives would be the best of friends, and whole families would have chosen an art of living... would abide in it and continue to perfect themselves in their art and direct their children to the same end. They would marry people of the same calling in order to be united through education from their parents. These clans would make up guilds or estates out of which cities would arise; these would enter into provinces, and all countries, finally, would stand under the Church of God.[164]

* Cf. Gierke, *The Development of Political Theory*. pp. 259 ff.

This hierarchy, reminiscent partly of Aristotle and partly of Althusius, locked the state into a system in which it had not the (for Leibniz pernicious) freedom which the Hobbesian state enjoyed. 'Natural' voluntary societies below the state level were to be negotiated with, made partners to consensual arrangements; while the universal authorities – albeit in a much restricted and rationalized form – were to preserve Europe against the immoderate appetites of any part of it.

The Republic of Christendom and International Relations

Leibniz wanted the idea of justice as charity regulated by wisdom to have not only a philosophical plausibility, and not only an effect on the internal politics of particular states, but also an impact on the international system: if charity could replace doctrinal disputation, then the greatest misfortune of Western civilization, the 'schism' between Catholics and Protestants, might be overcome. Leibniz devoted a great deal of his life to efforts aimed at healing this split, first in laboring on a vast (uncompleted) work called the *Catholic Demonstrations*,[165] which was intended to supply a Christian doctrine of sufficient imprecision to be agreeable to everyone, and later in a drawn-out correspondence with Bossuet (who apparently had greater hopes of converting Leibniz[166] than of compromising with 'heretics'.) Leibniz ransacked the history of pre-Reformation deviationism, hoping to show that if the Catholic Church re-admitted Protestants without an excessively fine-grained examination of doctrinal differences, it would be doing no more than it had when it agreed to disagree on some points with the Calixtins of Bohemia, and with the Greeks at the Council of Florence (1438).[167] He urged also that many of the differences between Catholicism and Protestantism were no wider than some of the differences within the Church itself.[168] Generally, Leibniz appealed to Bossuet to bring Christendom together on a slightly vague basis involving no apologies and no recantations; specific doctrinal disputes could be settled afterwards by genuine ecumenical councils (modelled on that of Constance, 1414–18, Leibniz' favorite). 'Would it not be better', he wrote in 1692, 'for Rome and for the general good, to regain so many nations, though one would have to remain in a state of disagreement on some points for some time...?'[169] But Leibniz and Bossuet could not agree on the status of the Council of Trent, the counter-Reformation council which was offensive to Protestants. He tried for some time to prove calmly that the Council had never been fully recognized in France; but Bossuet's continuing insistence that the questioning of one council would lead to the questioning of all finally provoked Leibniz into an uncharacteristic outburst:

> To say that you cannot consent to a new examination [of the Council of Trent], is only to renew the old equivocations: a new examination is necessary at least for the benefit of those who have a right to doubt a pretended infallible decision; and your party is deceiving itself in trying to derive any advantage from this [Council], as if it were permitted that a band of minor Italian bishops, courtesans and hangers-on from Rome (who were believed to be little-educated and little mindful of true Christianity) fabricate in a corner of the Alps, in a manner highly disapproved by the most serious men of their times, decisions which are to obligate the whole Church.[170]

Bossuet, for his part, called Leibniz 'opinionated' and even a 'heretic'; and when the Hanoverian succession to the British throne was assured, Leibniz was no longer encouraged to seek reconciliation, in view of British hostility to Catholicism. But his own views never changed. His labors in this field have sometimes been dismissed as merely politically inspired; but such a view cannot explain why – to take an example – Leibniz strove so hard, in his correspondence with the Jesuit des Bosses, to reconcile his own theory of substance with the Catholic doctrine of transubstantiation.[171] Whatever his motives, he believed that fanaticism and bloodshed could be ended throughout Europe if charity replaced theological hair-splitting.

> The essence of Catholicism is not external communion with Rome...the true and essential communion, which makes us part of the body of Jesus Christ, is charity. All those who maintain the schism by their fault, by creating obstacles to reconciliation, contrary to charity, are truly schismatics: instead of which those who are ready to do everything that can be done to re-establish external communion are Catholics in effect.[172]

Leibniz' reliance on the *Respublica Christiana* as chief defender of European concord was at its height during the 1670s, and appears most strongly in the *Caesarinus Fürstenerius*. In this most medieval of his works, he spoke of the Pope and the Holy Roman Emperor as the 'two heads' of Christendom, then went on to describe the kinds of supra-national authority which he thought these two heads ought to have. He believed:

> the Emperor is the defender or rather the chief, or if one prefers, the secular arm of the Universal Church; that all Christendom forms a species of republic, in which the Emperor has some authority, from which comes the name, Holy Empire, which should somehow extend as far as the Catholic Church; that the Emperor is...the born leader of Christians against the infidels; that it is mainly for him to destroy schisms, to bring about the meeting of [ecumenical] councils, to maintain good order ...so that the Church and the Republic of Christendom suffer no damage.[173]

At the same time, Leibniz recalled the great temporal authority which the Popes had had in the Middle Ages, urging that a good Pope had the right (by common consent, if not from God) to 'curb the tyranny and the ambition of the great, who cause so many souls to perish'.[174] And he suggested that an ecumenical council might be converted into a perpetual 'general Senate of Christendom', which would replace the insecurity and bad faith of treaties, mediations and guarantees with 'the interposition of the public authority, emanating from the heads of Christendom, the Pope and the Emperor'.[175]

By the 1690s Leibniz, older and less infatuated with medieval institutions, was placing more stress on international positive law – on the treaties and guarantees which he had earlier denigrated. In the *Codex Iuris Gentium* (1693), a collection of documents supporting the Empire's international position against French claims, he did not fail to mention the Emperor, the Pope, natural law, and Christian tradition, but mostly he insisted on the points to which France had actually agreed. In the *Codex* there was also a new emphasis on the gap between political actuality and ideality: a new 'realism' which even led Leibniz to allow that there was something in Hobbes' view that international relations were only a perpetual war. This interpretation, he said, was 'not so absurd as one might think, if the author claims to show, not that each nation has a right to destroy the others, but that prudence obliges every nation to be perpetually on guard against the others'.[176] It could be said of many princes, Leibniz went on, that 'in their palaces they play cards, and in the state with treaties'.[177] The evil designs of scheming ministers, papered over with 'specious pretexts' sometimes brought about campaigns founded on hatred and vengeance alone; sometimes a prince's 'bad night' led to the death of thousands; often a woman 'pushed' a ruler into ill-considered actions. 'History would lose some of its beauty', Leibniz concluded, 'if one always knew the true causes of events, and if it were known that the most frivolous motives...have often caused the greatest heroes to act.'[178] All of these considerations led him to play down the (still important but) diffuse and slackening restrictive power of Christendom, and to hope that historical evidence of positive agreements might be of greater utility in restraining international violence.

This does not mean that he changed his mind; he only changed the emphasis. In a very late (1715) commentary on the Abbé de St Pierre's *Project for Perpetual Peace*, Leibniz, while praising the Abbé's good intentions, urged that the medieval system, in a purified form, would be better than St Pierre's federal scheme. That system, which had been 'like a *droit des gens* among Latin Christians for several centuries', could have persisted on an even stronger footing, Leibniz maintained, had conciliar-ism ever been fully established; but the late medieval Popes, inferior to earlier ones, were afraid of councils and undermined the movement. This, he said, marked 'the beginning of their decline', and a succession of bad Popes destroyed papal authority. 'However,' he added, 'I believe that if there had been Popes with a great reputation for wisdom and virtue, who had wanted to follow the measures taken at Constance, they would have remedied the abuses, prevented the rupture, and sustained or even advanced Christian society.'[179]

In a letter of the same year, on the same subject, Leibniz' tone was both elegiac and ironic:

I have seen something of the project of M. de St Pierre, for maintaining a perpetual peace in Europe. I am reminded of a device in a cemetery, with the words: *Pax perpetua*; for the dead do not fight any longer: but the living are of another humor; and the most powerful do not respect tribunals at all. It would be necessary that these gentlemen contribute a *caution bourgeoise*, or deposit in the bank of the tribunal, a king of France, for example, a hundred million *écus*, and a king of Britain in proportion, so that the sentences of the tribunal could be executed on their money, in case they proved refractory.[180]

Leibniz suggested, in half-seriousness, that a better alternative would be to 'allow ecclesiastics to resume their old authority', so that interdictions and excommunications would 'make kings and kingdoms tremble'.* 'Here', he concluded, 'is a project which will succeed as easily as that of M. l'Abbé de St Pierre: but since it is permitted to write romances, why should we condemn the fiction which would recall the age of gold to us?'[181] At the end, Leibniz knew that some of his ideals had become impossible – without, however, being able to give them up. Hobbes, he observed in the *New Essays*, was afraid of spirits which he knew did not exist.[182]

International Relations: the Problem of French Imperialism

The main practical problem of international relations which Leibniz had to face throughout his life was that of French expansionism. Leibniz, whose life (1646–1716) coincided almost exactly with Louis XIV's

---

* Despite the lightness of his tone in this letter, the question whether a purified Church should intervene in political affairs was one which Leibniz always took quite seriously. A letter of 1706 makes his uncertainty on this point clear: 'According to the law *of nature*, ecclesiastics in the state cannot be more than counselors, following the example of doctors whose jurisdiction is purely voluntary, so to speak. But the divine law has given something more to the Church, and sometimes human laws give it even more – which I do not dis-approve absolutely' (Ger. III, pp. 310–11).

reign (1643–1715), had an ambivalent relation to France and to French culture: on the one hand, Louis' *réunions*, the seizure of Strassburg, the attack on the Empire during the Turkish siege of Vienna, the wresting of Spain away from the Hapsburgs during the War of the Spanish Succession, led Leibniz, as a German, to do what he could to shore up German defenses (and this despite his distaste for parochialism and patriotic excesses); on the other hand, Leibniz' wide-ranging interests were partly produced, partly expanded by his residence in Paris, and by his contact with leading French intellectuals whom he otherwise might not have met.[183] About Louis XIV himself, Leibniz seems to have had mixed feelings; Louis' wars produced savage pamphlets from Leibniz, but his patronage of culture he admired and praised to the end. His view seems to have been that Louis was a great king who nonetheless did inexcusable things: 'Ce roy pouvait faire les délices du gênre humain, mais il s'est tourné à des entreprises qui sont enfin devenues le fleau de l'Europe.'[184]

Leibniz' opposition to French aggression began early, with the *Consilium Aegyptiacum* (1671), which he drew up in an effort to divert an imminent French invasion of the Netherlands to a crusade against the Ottomans in Egypt. Dutch trade, he suggested, could be more effectively ruined by an attack on Egypt, sealing off middle-eastern trade routes, than through a hazardous direct assault.[185] Characteristically, he argued that a Christian prince should never make war on another Christian – though Protestant – power, and that French military force should be turned on the infidel. Conjuring up visions of the glory of medieval crusades, all of which Louis would surpass, Leibniz reached even farther back into history to hint that the Egyptian conquest might be the first act of a new Alexander. But the real object of the scheme was clear: a war within Europe would be nothing but 'that chimera of universal monarchy which it would be not only impious, but absurd to pursue in Europe at the cost of violence and carnage'; seizing a few Netherlandish towns would bring about a 'continent in arms', fear, disaffection, and an anti-French coalition.[186] (These themes remained constant in later works; the charge of a desire to set up 'universal monarchy' by force was one that Leibniz never tired of levelling, and he was always solicitous of the Netherlands and of England as the bulwarks of European liberty.)

Leibniz' most entertaining, and also most malicious, political work, the *Mars Christianissimus* (*Most Christian War-God*, 1683) a pointed satire on Louis XIV and his imperialism, was also in part a parody of Bossuet's method of arguing from scripture (particularly the Old Testament). Taking note of a resolution made in France 'to recognize no longer any judge but the sword', Leibniz observed that while treaties and moral scruples 'indeed oblige ordinary men', there was 'a certain law superior to all others, conforming nonetheless to sovereign justice, which releases the king from the obligation to observe them'.[187] In defense of the special right of Louis XIV to subjugate all Christendom, Leibniz said, he would 'lay the foundations of a new jurisprudence', of which the fundamental point was that 'all temporal matters are [to be] submitted to the eminent right of a very great and powerful king', who, because of 'destiny', should rule everybody. From this general right, he went on, could be deduced Moses' authority over the Israelites whom he 'borrowed' from the Egyptians, as well as the Israelites' authority over the Canaanites. Louis XIV, he said, was currently the beneficiary of this right, and as such was 'the true and sole vicar of the world with respect to all temporal matters'. Louis' vicarate was justified, Leibniz said, by Thrasymachus' argument, *justum est potentiori utile*, 'which agrees very well with what we have said about the right of a powerful monarch over the temporal affairs of men. The most powerful person in the world, excepting always the devil, is without doubt his Most Christian Majesty.'[188] He then proved that Louis was entitled, both by prophecy and by miracles which he had performed, to absolute control over 'the general affairs of Christendom'.[189]

Leibniz passed on to the effects of Louis' mission in Germany and Italy. The minor Catholic clergy in Germany, he said, was already singing hosannas as it saw 'the advance of its liberator'; Italian women, anxious to enjoy a *liberté française*, were impatiently awaiting a French garrison. France, said Leibniz, had powerful friends ready to receive it; 'who would dare, henceforth, to resist priests and women conspiring at the same time?'[190] Resistance was ultimately useless, in any case; 'as rivers all converge finally at the sea, whatever their detours, in the same way it is absolutely necessary that all the powers – and particularly those of Italy and Germany – be finally engulfed'.[191] England, too, would be desolated, 'as her heresy deserves'.[192] But Germans ought to be grateful, rather than resentful, since 'the most expert political analysts all agree that the Republic of Germany is so monstrous and corrupt, that it needs an absolute master to re-establish good government'. German liberty was, in any event, Leibniz added, only the 'license of frogs, who croak and jump here and there'.[193]

Leibniz was not above indulging in self-parody while writing in this vein. 'What is taken for misery is true felicity', he observed, and 'goods are always brought about through tribulations'. Germans will be happier in heaven, 'when the French shall have made you miserable on earth; you will go there more willingly, leaving without regret this vale of miseries'.[194] Louis himself, Leibniz insisted, was aware that his vicarate brought about some (merely apparent) evils; 'he himself trembles when he envisages the loss of so many thousands of souls'. But he had no choice in the matter. 'How can he resist the vocation from on high which obligates him? He sees that any other way of curing the ills of Christendom, except that which he undertakes by iron and fire, would be only a palliative; gangrene cannot be stopped except by means which involve cruelty.'[195] Leibniz concluded the *Mars Christianissimus* with a paragraph which he raised to a height of incandescent malevolence:

There will be some who will imagine that his Most Christian Majesty would do better to begin his beautiful designs by the routing of the Turks than by the affliction of the poor Christians: but these people do not reflect at all that it is the Germans and the Flemish who live on the frontiers of France, and not the Turks: that one must pass from one's neighbors to people far away, and move in these great matters by solid degrees, rather than by vain and perilous leaps. But, without looking for political reasons, here is one of conscience: which is that the king wishes to follow the rules of the New Testament, which commands that one begin with the Jews, and then orders that one turn *ad gentes;* and the king, in imitation of this, will create for himself, by the reduction of the Christians, a sure passage to go one day to the infidels.[196]

None of Leibniz' later anti-French writings is so powerful as the *Mars Christianissimus*, though he wrote many of them; the best, however, combine eloquence with barely contained fury, and are very effective tracts. About the seizure of Strassburg – which he never forgot – Leibniz was particularly bitter: 'the king needed it for the security of his kingdom; that is to say, to better maintain what he had stolen from the Empire, he had to steal more. A beautiful reason!...the appetite grows while eating.'[197] But he was perhaps even more resentful of French apologists than of French military forces. 'The noise of flatterers often extinguishes feelings of conscience in those who act,' he wrote in 1688, 'but he who undertakes the [intellectual] defense of evil actions must be able to see them at close range, and he is miserable if he has only fantasies and farfetched conjectures and even nonsense to oppose to the greatest and most real evils which a Christian and an honest man can conceive.'[198]

As Leibniz' political connections with the Empire grew closer after 1700 – he was appointed Aulic Counselor by the Emperor in 1703, and became the friend of Prince Eugene of Savoy[199] – he wrote an increasing number of political pamphlets, and may have drafted several Imperial responses to French claims. During the War of the Spanish Succession he wrote the *Manifesto for the Defense of the Rights of Charles III*, in which he attempted to show that France was hopelessly corrupt and that Spain would be ruined by Bourbon rule.[200] He wrote his last major anti-French pieces in 1712–13, when the Triple Alliance (Empire–Netherlands–

Britain), put together to counter French power, disintegrated after the Dutch and British made separate peaces with France. In his *Peace of Utrecht Inexcusable* (1713), Leibniz chided the Empire's former allies for giving up when 'universal monarchy' had nearly been brought under control, and warned that 'the house of Bourbon has come into a power which surpasses that of Charlemagne and equals that of the ancient Romans'.[201] Nevertheless, he did not despair of putting the Empire on a sounder military footing, and tried to forestall desperate measures by observing that 'one needn't cut his throat because he has lost his purse'.[202] Nor did he fail to relate his opposition to French policy to his ideas of universal justice. Condemning the *'morale à la mode'* of France, 'which thinks that the utility of the state makes everything permissible', he urged that 'it is necessary that powerful princes not do to lesser ones that which they would not want a more powerful one to do to them'.[203]

Fear of France was also the motor force – at least in part – behind some of Leibniz' other practical political schemes, notably the gaining of the throne of Great Britain for the house of Hanover, and (earlier) the raising of that house from the status of a dukedom to that of an electorate. European liberty was safe, in his opinion, only so long as the great 'northern' powers – Britain, the Netherlands, and (increasingly) Prussia – were Protestant and anti-French;[204] and he constantly warned the English against re-admitting the Stuarts, the 'creatures' of the Bourbons, to the throne.

If the wolf comes in sheep's clothing; if he pretends to accommodate himself to your laws; if bad citizens, traitors to their country, bring the people to receive him, he will ruin your liberty by degrees: no more triennial parliament, no more ancient city-charters, no more *habeas corpus*, no more judges of integrity; everything full of false testimony, juries corrupted, tramps for bishops, courtesans for jurisconsults, satellites of arbitrary power.[205]

After 1700 Leibniz wrote a number of memoranda in defense of the Hanoverian claims to the British throne, urging that everything which could be discreetly done to insure success be done. A trustworthy and zealous person, Leibniz advised, familiar with the English language and with the 'genius' of the English people, should be sent quietly to London; this envoy should make contact with 'considerable' members of the House of Commons in an effort to enlist on the Hanoverian side 'persons of merit, of reputation and of authority, whose opinions will have an effect on [other] minds, and on whose friendship one can count'.[206] The Electress (Sophie), Leibniz suggested, should modestly, but with some regularity, remind the English ruler of her claims as a Protestant and as a grand-daughter of James I; while the 'republican faction' should be convinced that a republic was too dangerous in view of the recent enlargement of French power during the War of the Spanish Succession.[207] In this affair, which he pursued for about fifteen years, Leibniz showed a great deal of tact and subtlety, and a sharp sense of what would be psychologically effective and what offensive; he skilfully blended fears of France and of Catholicism with the justice of long-standing historical claims.

This skill and political common-sense had been in evidence, too, when Leibniz, in the early 1690s, wrote a number of letters and pamphlets in an effort to raise Hanover to the dignity of an electorate. The three Rhenish electorates (Cologne, Trier and Mainz), he argued, might soon be swallowed up by France, necessitating a new electorate more securely situated in middle Germany; the balance between Catholic and Protestant forces could be made more equitable if Hanover were elevated; it was generally a good idea, politically, that important units of a political system be given power and responsibility, so as not to create 'a divorce, very prejudicial to the state, between the power of right and that of fact'.[208]* To avoid antagonizing the Catholics by the creation of a new Protestant electorate, Leibniz suggested, Hanover's cause should first be brought forward by Sweden (which, by the Treaty of Westphalia, was a marginal member of the Empire); Saxony and Brandenburg could then second the nomination, and Hanover would never have to appear excessively self-serving.[209] His detailed formulation of this plan makes plain why his services as a councilor were so highly esteemed.

The two Protestant electors [Brandenburg and Saxony] and, perhaps, the King of Sweden could write to the Emperor concerning the creation of a new Protestant electorate; the King of Sweden in rather positive terms, the two electors in a more reserved manner, as if pushed by the letters of the King of Sweden... [then]...the Emperor would write a letter to the Electoral College as the most interested [party], communicating to them the letter of the King of Sweden and of several electors, and asking for their collegial opinion. In this way the Protestant electors would give their opinions in the assembly of the Electoral College, like the others, because they would not have already taken part [openly in the process] and would not have already become demanders [of anything].[210]

If this plan were followed, Leibniz thought, success would be much more likely than if Hanover simply demanded its 'rights'. (It ought to be recalled, however – even as one enjoys Leibniz' ingenuity – that he preferred the re-unification of the *Respublica Christiana* to all of this balancing and scheming, even though he was good at it; if France were reduced, and the Church restored, Hanover could be 'merely' the *Kulturstaat* which he would have liked it to be.)

* This is an interesting, 'realistic' variation on Leibniz' usual treatment of the relation between right and fact.

Ironically and sadly enough, Leibniz' efforts on behalf of the house of Hanover brought him, not a final blaze of glory as chief counselor to the new ruler of Britain, but neglect and ingratitude: partly because George I wanted something more tangible than Leibniz' mere fame to compensate him for the salary he and his predecessors had expended, partly because the controversy with Newton over priority in the discovery of the calculus had prejudiced British opinion against him, Leibniz was obliged to remain in Hanover to complete his history of that house. He toyed with the idea of removing to Paris, the *Mars Christianissimus* notwithstanding; and in his last year, at the age of 70, produced the important exchange of letters with Samuel Clarke. When he died, on 14 November 1716, not a single member of the Hanoverian court attended the funeral; and it was left to Fontenelle, in the French Academy, to deliver a fitting *éloge*.[211] But Leibniz had already written a suitable epitaph for himself, one which expresses exactly his own view of his life and his efforts: 'Provided that something of importance is achieved, I am indifferent whether it is done in Germany or in France, for I seek the good of mankind. I am neither a phil-Hellene nor a philo-Roman, but a philanthropos.'[212] And he had, long since, summarized the whole sense of his social philosophy in a single sentence. 'Justice is...that which is useful to the community, and the public good is the supreme law – a community, however, let it be recalled, not of a few, not of a particular nation, but of all those who are part of the City of God and, so to speak, of the state of the universe'.[213]

REFERENCES

1. See particularly letter to Remond, Loemker II, p. 1064; *NE* I, i (Langley edition, pp. 66–7).
2. *Theodicy*, preliminary dissertation, pt. 35.
3. *Monadology*, props. 85 and 86.
4. Letter to Landgraf Ernst of Hesse-Rheinfels, Rommel, p. 232.
5. *Reflections on Hobbes' 'Freedom, Necessity and Chance'*, in Farrer's edition of the *Theodicy* (New Haven, 1952), p. 403.
6. *Opinion on the Principles of Pufendorf* (*Monita quaedam ad Samuelis Puffendorfii Principia*, Dutens IV, iii, pp. 278–9).
7. *Selections from Paris Notes*, Loemker I, p. 246; cf. *Dialogue sur des Sujets de Religion*, F de C II, p. 53.
8. *Monadology*, prop. 48.
9. *Meditation on the Common Concept of Justice*, Mollat, p. 62.
9a. *Elementa Iuris Naturalis*, Acad. Ed. VI, I, No. 12, p. 481.
10. Letter to Arnauld, Loemker II, p. 600.
11. *Felicity*, in *Textes Inédits*, vol. II (ed. Grua), p. 579.
12. *Meditation*, Mollat, p. 72.
13. Letter to Mme. de Brinon, Klopp VII, p. 296.
14. Letter to Electress Sophie, in *Textes Inédits*, vol. I, p. 379

15. Letter to Remond, Loemker II, p. 1063; cf. *On the General Characteristic*, Loemker I, pp. 339 ff.
16. *Opinion on...Pufendorf*, Dutens IV, iii, p. 280.
17. St Thomas Aquinas, *Summa Theologica* II, ii, Q 58, Art. 4.
18. Aristotle, *Ethics*, 1105b; 1136a – 1136b.
19. *Grundriss eines Bedenckens von Aufrichtung einer Societät in Deutschland*, F de C VII, p. 29.
20. Letter to the Duchess of Orléans, Klopp IX, p. 164.
21. *Meditation*, Mollat, p. 56.
22. *NE* II, xxviii, pt. 5.
23. *Discourse on Metaphysics*, prop. 2, Loemker I, p. 466.
24. *Dialogue sur... Religion*, F de C II, p. 532.
25. Revision note for the *Nova Methodus*, Loemker I, p. 556.
26. *Elements of Natural Law*, Loemker I, p. 210.
27. *Theodicy*, preliminary dissertation, pt. 43, and I, pts. 3–5.
28. *Elements of Natural Law*, Loemker I, p. 205.
29. *Observations on the Book 'Concerning the Origin of Evil'*, in Farrers' edition of the *Theodicy*, p. 428.
30. *Refutation of Spinoza*, Duncan, p. 264.
31. Letter to Bierling, Dutens V, p. 386.
32. Letter to Arnauld, Loemker I, p. 516.
33. *Theodicy* II, pt. 183.
34. Bossuet, *Traité du Libre Arbitre*, ch. 2 (cited in Baruzi, p. 392).
35. *Meditation*, Mollat, p. 56.
36. *On the Philosophy of Descartes*, Duncan, p. 3.
37. Plato, *Euthyphro*, lines 9E–10E.
38. Grotius, *De Jure Belli ac Pacis* I, i, X.
39. *Radical Origination of Things*, Loemker II, p. 791.
40. See Ger. VII, p. 374.
41. *Theodicy* I, pt. 31.
42. *Ibid.* III, pt. 367.
43. *Discourse on Metaphysics*, prop. 13, Loemker I, p. 478; cf. Leibniz–Clarke letters, No. V, pts. 7–9, Loemker II, pp. 1134–5.
44. Letter to Bourguet, Ger. III, p. 573; *NE* III, vi, pt. 12.
45. *Radical Origination*, Loemker II, p. 791.
46. *Ibid.* pp. 792–3.
47. *Theodicy* I, pt. 21.
48. *Ibid.* III, pt. 335.
49. *Ibid.* I, pt. 23.
50. *Theodicy* I, pts. 43, 47, 84.
51. *Monadology*, prop. 42.
52. *Theodicy* I, pt. 31.
53. This question is taken up by Leibniz in the *Discourse on Metaphysics*, prop. 30, Loemker I, pp. 495 ff.
54. *Theodicy* I, pt. 35.
55. Hegel, *History of Philosophy*, trans. Haldane and Simson, London, Kegan Paul, Trench, Trübner and Co., 1896, vol. III, p. 341.
56. *Theodicy*. I, pt. 11.
57. See particularly *Discourse on Metaphysics*, prop. 30, Loemker I, p. 497.

58. Malebranche, *Dialogues on Metaphysics*, No. 9, pt. V.
59. *Ibid.* pt. VI.
60. *Theodicy*, preface.
61. *Ibid.* III, pt. 350.
62. *Ibid. Summary of the Controversy reduced to Formal Arguments*, answer to objection V; cf. also letter to John Bernoulli, Ger. Math. III, p. 574.
63. *Theodicy, Summary of the Controversy*, answer to objection II.
64. *Ibid.* III, pt. 288.
65. Letter to Magnus Wedderkopf, Loemker I, pp. 226–7.
66. *Principles of Nature and Grace*, props. 1 and 2; *Monadology*, props. 14 and 15.
67. Hegel, *Phenomenology of Mind*, trans. Baillie, London, Allen and Unwin, 1910, p. 108.
68. *First Truths*, Loemker I, p. 416; letter to de Volder, Loemker II, pp. 873–4; letter to des Bosses, Loemker II, p. 974.
69. *New System of the Nature and Communication of Substances*, Loemker II, pp. 745 and 741.
70. Letter to des Bosses, Ger. II, p. 304.
71. *On Nature Itself*, Loemker II, pp. 818–21.
72. Letter to Burnett, Ger. III, p. 227.
73. *Reply to Thoughts on the System*, Loemker II, p. 945.
74. Letter to Burnett, Ger. III, p. 260; letter to Arnauld, Ger. II, p. 118.
75. Letter to de Volder, Loemker II, p. 864.
76. Letter to Burnett, Ger. III, p. 260; letter to Arnauld, Ger. II, p. 118.
77. *Discourse on Metaphysics*, props. 8 and 13, Loemker I, pp. 471 ff.
78. *Ibid.* prop. 30, pp. 496–7.
79. Letter to Arnauld, Ger. II, p. 52.
80. *On Nature Itself*, Loemker II, p. 817.
81. Letter to Queen Sophie-Charlotte, Klopp X, p. 193.
82. Letter to Bourguet, Loemker II, p. 1079.
83. *NE* II, xxvii, pt. 9.
84. Letter to G. Wagner, Duncan, p. 281.
85. *Monadology*, prop. 56.
86. *Monadology*, prop. 50.
87. *On Vital and Plastic Natures*, Loemker II, pp. 956 ff; *Specimen Dynamicum*, Loemker II, p. 723.
88. *NE* IV, viii, pt. 9.
89. Letter to Arnauld, Loemker I, pp. 520 ff.
90. *Radical Origination*, Loemker II, p. 798.
91. Letter to Arnauld, Loemker I, p. 519.
92. *Theodicy* III, pt. 365.
93. *Discourse on Metaphysics*, prop. 31, Loemker I, pp. 497–8; cf. Ger. I, p. 360.
94. Letter to Malebranche, Ger. I, p. 300.
95. *Theodicy* II, pt. 120.
96. *NE* II, xxi, pt. 67.
97. *Theodicy* II, pt. 228.
98. *Monadology*, prop. 86.
99. Loemker I, pp. 563–4.

D

100. *On the True Theologica Mystica*, Loemker II, p. 610.
101. *Radical Origination*, Loemker II, p. 796.
102. *Theodicy*, preface.
103. *Thoughts on the Principles of Descartes*, Loemker II, p. 676.
104. *Radical Origination*, Loemker II, p. 793.
105. *Mantissa* to the *Codex Iuris Gentium Praefatio*, Loemker II, p. 696.
106. *NE* II, xxi, pt. 42.
107. *Mantissa* to the *Codex Iuris Gentium Praefatio*, Loemker II, p. 696.
108. *Ibid.*
109. *De Tribus Juris Naturae et Gentium Gradibus*, Mollat, p. 13.
110. *Felicity*, in *Textes Inédits* (ed. Grua), vol. II, p. 579.
111. Letter to Hansch, Loemker II, p. 966.
112. Cf. *Reflections on the Doctrine of a Single Universal Spirit*, Loemker II, pp. 899 ff.
113. Letter to Bossuet, F de C II, p. 199.
114. Letter to Burnett, Ger. III, p. 261.
115. Dutens I, p. 379 (cited in Baruzi, p. 459).
116. *True Piety*, in *Textes Inédits* (ed. Grua), vol. II, p. 500.
117. *Codex Iuris Gentium*, pts. XI–XIII.
118. *Ibid.* pt. XII; cf. *Nova Methodus*, Dutens IV, iii, pp. 213 ff.
119. *Ibid.* pts, XII–XIII.
120. *NE.* IV, viii, pt. 9.
121. *Portrait of the Prince*, Klopp IV, pp. 480–1.
122. *De Tribus Juris Naturae*, Mollat, p. 14.
123. *Meditation*, Mollat, p. 81.
124. *Codex*, pts. XI–XII.
125. Kant, *The Metaphysical Elements of Justice*, Introduction, 'Division of the Metaphysics of Morals in General', pt. II.
126. *Meditation*, Mollat, p. 70.
127. *Notes on Social Life*, 'The Place of Others', in *Textes Inédits* (ed. Grua), vol. II, pp. 699–701.
128. Russell, pp. 191 ff.
129. *On Natural Law*, Loemker II, p. 705.
130. Letter to Burnett, Ger. III, p. 264.
131. *Nova Methodus*, Dutens IV, iii.
132. *NE* III, i, pt. 1.
133. Ger. III, pp. 424–5.
134. *Ibid.* p. 277.
135. *Ibid.* p. 279.
136. *Ibid.* p. 278.
137. *Grundriss*, F de C VII, p. 31.
138. *Ibid*, p. 36.
139. *Ibid*, pp. 45–6.
140. *Meditation*, Mollat, pp. 57–62.
141. Letter to Burnett, Ger. III, p. 261.
142. Klopp X, p. 14.
143. *Ibid.*
144. *De Tribus Juris Naturae*, Mollat, p. 18.
145. Klopp X, p. 23.

146. *Ibid.* p. 26.
147. Poem to Mlle. de Scudery, Klopp VI, p. 177.
148. Letter to Queen Sophie-Charlotte, Klopp X, p. 184.
149. Letter to Arnauld, Ger. II, p. 76.
150. F de C VI, p. 347.
151. *Ibid.*
152. *Caesarinus Fürstenerius (De Jure Suprematus ac Legationis)*, Acad. Ed. IV, II, p. 58 (cited hereafter as *Caes. Fürst.*).
153. *Ibid.*
154. *Ibid.* p. 59.
155. *Ibid.*
156. *Ibid.*
157. *Ibid.* p. 60.
158. Cf. Hobbes, *Leviathan*, pt. 2, ch. 26.
159. *Meditation*, Mollat, p. 61.
160. Cited in Ruck, p. 94.
161. Letter to Falaideau, Klopp IX, p. 143.
162. *Ibid.*
163. *On Natural Law*, Loemker II, pp. 702–4.
164. *Ibid.* p. 706.
165. Loemker I, pp. 86–90.
166. Cf. Klopp IX, p. 182.
167. Letters to Bossuet, F de C II, pp. 264–71.
168. *Ibid.*
169. F de C I, p. 273.
170. F de C II, pp. 258–9.
171. Cf. letters to des Bosses, Loemker II, pp. 969 ff.
172. Letter to Mme. de Brinon, F de C I, p. 163.
173. *Caes. Fürst.*, Acad. Ed. IV, II, pp. 15–16.
174. *Ibid.* pp. 16–17.
175. *Ibid.*
176. *Codex*, pt. I.
177. *Ibid.*
178. *Ibid.* pt. II.
179. F de C IV, pp. 330–1.
180. Letter No. II to Grimarest, Dutens V, pp. 65–6.
181. *Ibid.* p. 66.
182. *NE* II, xxxiii, pt. 18.
183. Cf. Loemker I, pp. 12 ff; Latta, pp. 5–10.
184. Klopp X, p. 28.
185. F de C V, pp. 5–7.
186. *Ibid.* pp. 5–6.
187. *Mars Christianissimus*, F de C III, pp. 4 and 8
188. *Ibid.* pp. 9–10.
189. *Ibid.* p. 16.
190. *Ibid.* pp. 19–22.
191. *Ibid.* p. 20.
192. *Ibid.*
193. *Ibid.* p. 23.

194. *Ibid.* p. 26.
195. *Ibid.* p. 40.
196. *Ibid.* p. 41.
197. *Remarks on a French Manifesto*, F de C III, p. 88.
198. *Ibid*, p. 84.
199. Latta, p. 15.
200. F de C III, pp. 368 ff.
201. *Peace of Utrecht Inexcusable*, F de C IV, p. 131.
202. *Considerations Relating to Peace and War*, *ibid.* p. 193.
203. F de C III, pp. 117 and 282.
204. *Considerations on the Question of the English Succession*, Klopp VIII, p. 254; *Fruits of the Campaign of the Year 1703*, Klopp IX, p. 59; *ibid.* pp. 199–200.
205. *Peace of Utrecht Inexcusable*, F de C IV, p. 134.
206. *Reflections on an English Treatise which Contains the Means which Mme. the Electress of Brunswick [Hanover] should Use to Assure the Effective Right of the English Succession for Herself and her Posterity*, F de C VIII, p. 222.
207. *Ibid.* pp. 220 ff.
208. *Treatise Composed a Few Months before the Death of the Late Elector Palatine, Touching the Creation of a Ninth Electorate in Favor of the Protestants*, Klopp VI, p. 262.
209. *Ibid.* pp. 268 ff.
210. *Ibid.*
211. Latta, pp. 15–16.
212. Letter to des Billettes, Loemker II, p. 775.
213. *Initium Institutionem Iuris Perpetui*, Mollat, p. 1.

PART I. ON JUSTICE AND NATURAL LAW

1. Meditation on the Common Concept of Justice
(*c.* 1702–3)

The *Meditation*, together with the *Opinion on the Principles of Pufendorf*, is the most important large-scale writing about justice which Leibniz produced. Though it is unfinished, and though the argument somehow never becomes quite as strong as it threatens to do from time to time, it still contains a good statement of his conviction that principles of right must be of the same kind as the 'eternal truths' of mathematics and logic, that there is a *continuum* between abstaining from evil and doing good, that divine justice must be of the same kind as human justice (differing only in the degree of its perfection), that communal property is desirable but unattainable etc. There are, in addition, passages commenting on Aristotle, Filmer, Hobbes, and others, which are of some interest; and the rejection of arguments in defense of slavery was liberal for its day. The *Meditation* must have been written, to judge from internal evidence, in *c.* 1703. (The original text is to be found in Mollat's *Rechtsphilosophisches aus Leibnizens ungedruckten Schriften*; this version omits the word 'I' [je] which comes at the end of the ms. in the Hanover library, and which would have led into a longer conclusion which, for some reason, Leibniz did not write.)

I

It is agreed that whatever God wills is good and just. But there remains the question whether it is good and just because God wills it or whether God wills it because it is good and just:[1] in other words, whether justice and goodness are arbitrary or whether they belong to the necessary and eternal truths about the nature of things, as do numbers and proportions. The former opinion has been followed by some philosophers[2] and by

[1] Leibniz' radical formulation of this question follows Plato's *Euthyphro* (9E–10E) almost literally, though Plato was dealing with 'holiness' rather than justice.
[2] To judge from his favorite targets, Leibniz probably had Descartes, Pufendorf and (perhaps) Bossuet in mind.

45

some Roman [Catholic] and Reformed theologians: but present-day Reformed [theologians] usually reject this doctrine, as do all of our theologians and most of those of the Roman Church.

Indeed it [this view] would destroy the justice of God. For why praise him because he acts according to justice, if the notion of justice, in his case, adds nothing to that of action? And to say *stat pro ratione voluntas*,[1] my will takes the place of reason, is properly the motto of a tyrant. Moreover this opinion would not sufficiently distinguish God from the devil. For if the devil, that is to say an intelligent, invisible, very great and very evil power, were the master of the world, this devil or this God would still be evil, even if it were necessary to honor him by force, as some peoples honor such imaginary gods in the hope of bringing them thereby to do less evil.

This is why certain persons, too devoted to the absolute right of God, who have believed that he could justly condemn innocent people and even that this might actually happen, have done wrong to the attributes which make God lovable, and, having destroyed the love of God, they have left only fear [behind]. Indeed those who believe (for example) that infants who die without baptism are plunged into eternal flames, must have a very weak idea of the goodness and of the justice of God, and injure thoughtlessly what is most essential to religion.

The sacred scriptures also give us an altogether different idea of this sovereign substance, in speaking so often and so clearly of the goodness of God, and presenting him as a person who justifies himself against complaints.[2] And in the story of the creation of the world the scripture says that God considered what he had done, and found it good.[3] That is to say, he was content with his work, and had reason to be. This is a human way of speaking which seems to be used explicitly to show that the goodness of the actions and productions of God do not depend on his will, but on their nature: otherwise he would only have to see what he wills and does, to find out whether it were good, and to justify himself to himself as a wise sovereign. Thus all our theologians and most of those of the Roman Church, and also most of the ancient Church Fathers and the wisest and most esteemed philosophers, have been for the second view, which holds that goodness and justice have grounds [*ont leurs raisons*] independent of will and of force.

Plato in his dialogues introduces and refutes a certain Thrasymachus, who, wishing to explain what justice is, gives a definition which would strongly recommend the position which we are combating, if it were

---

[1] Adapted from Juvenal, *Satirae* VI, 223.   [2] Job 34, 6.
[3] Genesis 1, 31.

acceptable: for that is just (says he) which is agreeable or pleasant to the most powerful.[1] If that were true, there would never be a sentence of a sovereign court, nor of a supreme judge, which would be unjust, nor would an evil but powerful man ever be blameworthy. And what is more, the same action could be just or unjust, depending on the judges who decide, which is ridiculous. It is one thing to be just and another to pass for it, and to take the place of justice.

A celebrated English philosopher named Hobbes, who is noted for his paradoxes, has wished to uphold almost the same thing as Thrasymachus: for he wants God to have the right to do everything, because he is all-powerful.[2] This is a failure to distinguish between right and fact. For what one can do is one thing, what one should do, another. It is this same Hobbes who believes (and almost for the same reason) that the true religion is that of the state and that, as a consequence, if the Emperor Claudius, who decreed in an edict that *in libera republica crepitus atque ructus liberos esse debere*, had placed the god Crepitus among the authorized gods, he would have been a real God, and worthy of worship.[3]

This is to say, in covert terms, that there is no true religion, and that it is nothing but an invention of men. Similarly, to say that 'just' is whatever pleases the most powerful is nothing else than saying that there is no certain and determined justice which keeps one from doing whatever he wants to do and can do with impunity, however evil it may be. Thus treason, assassinations, poisonings, torture of the innocent, all will be just, if they succeed. This is, indeed, to change the nature of terms and to speak a language different from that of other men; until now one has understood by justice something different than that which happens every day. It is believed that a happy man can be evil, and that an unpunished action can nevertheless be unjust; that is, that it may deserve to be punished: such that it is only a question of knowing why it deserves it, without raising the question whether the pain will actually follow or not, or whether some judge will impose it.

There were [once] two tyrants in Sicily named Denis, father and son; the father was more evil than the son, [since] he had established his tyranny by the destruction of many honest men; his son was less cruel, but more given to disorders and to luxuries: the father was happy, and maintained

---

[1] Plato, *Republic* I 338c ff.

[2] Reference to Hobbes' *De Cive* xv, 5: 'God in his natural kingdom hath a right to rule, and to punish those who break his laws, from his sole irresistible power.'

[3] From Suetonius, *Vita Claudii*, ch. 32: 'In a free state the passing of wind and belching should be free.'

himself [in power], and the son was overthrown, and finally made himself schoolmaster at Corinth, to have the pleasure of always ruling and of carrying a sort of scepter, by wielding the switches with which the children were punished. Will it be said that the actions of the first [father] were more just than those of the second, because he was happy and unpunished? And will it not be permitted at all that history condemn a happy tyrant?

One sees too every day that men, whether interested or disinterested, complain about the actions of certain powerful people, and find them unjust: thus the question is solely whether they complain with reason; and whether history can condemn with justice the inclinations and actions of a prince. This being granted one must acknowledge that men understand by justice, and by right, something else than that which pleases the powerful, and which remains unpunished if there is no judge capable of redressing [the evil].

It is true that in the entire universe or in the government of the world it happens, happily, that he who is the most powerful is just at the same time, and does nothing which one has a right to complain of: and it is necessary to hold as certain that one would find, if one understood the universal order, that it is impossible to do anything better than he does it; but power is not the formal reason which makes it just. Otherwise, if power were the formal reason of justice, all powerful persons would be just, each in proportion to his power; which is contrary to experience.

It is thus a question of finding this formal reason, that is to say, the *why* of this attribute, or this concept which should teach us what justice is, and what men mean in calling an action just or unjust. And this formal reason must be common to God and to man; otherwise one would be wrong in wanting to attribute, without equivocation, the same attribute to both: these are fundamental rules of reasoning and of discourse.[1]

I grant readily that there is a great difference between the way in which men are just and [the way] in which God is: but this difference is only one of degree. For God is perfectly and entirely just, and the justice of men is mixed with injustice, with faults and with sins, because of the imperfection of human nature. The perfections of God are infinite, and ours are limited. Thus if someone wishes to maintain that the justice and the goodness of God have entirely different rules than those of men, he must recognize at the same time that these are two different notions, and that it is either voluntary equivocation or gross self-deception to attribute justice to both. Choosing, then, which of the two notions must be taken for that of justice, it will follow that either there is no true justice in God

[1] Cf. *Theodicy*, preliminary dissertation, pts. 4 and 35.

or that there is none in men, or perhaps that there is none in either, and that in the end one doesn't know what he is saying when speaking of justice – but this would destroy it, in fact, and leave nothing but the name. As do those also who make it arbitrary and dependent on the good pleasure of a judge or of a powerful person, since the same action will appear to be just or unjust to different judges.

This is also somewhat as if someone wanted to maintain that our science, for example that of numbers, which is called arithmetic, does not agree with that of God or of the angels, or perhaps that all truth is arbitrary and depends on whim. For example 1, 4, 9, 16, 25 etc. are square numbers, that is, which are produced by multiplying 1, 2, 3, 4, 5 etc. by themselves, while saying 1 times 1 is 1, 2 times 2 is 4, 3 times 3 is 9 etc. It is discovered that the successive odd numbers are the differences between successive square numbers. For the difference between 1 and 4 is 3, the difference between 4 and 9 is 5, between 9 and 16 is 7, and so forth. This is also apparent in the cells of the square numbers noted in the margin [below], for with the exception of one square foot, the space taken up by two square feet (that is to say the space of four times one square foot) has three more cells; and the space taken up by three square feet (that is to say the space of nine times one square foot) has five cells more than the preceding one, and so forth. Now, would one have any reason to maintain that it is not thus for God and for the angels, and that they see or find in numbers the contrary of what we find? Would one not have reason to laugh at a man who maintained this, and who did not know about the difference which there is between necessary and eternal truths which must be the same everywhere, and that which is contingent and changeable or arbitrary?

1	1	1	1
3	2	2	2
5	4	3	3
7	6	5	4

0   1   4   9   16 25   etc.
  1   3   5   7   9   etc.

[This diagram (referred to above) was printed in the margin of the original text.]

The same is true of justice. If it is a fixed term which has some determined meaning; if, in a word, it is not a simple sound, without sense, like *blitiri*;[1] this term, or this word, justice, will have some definition or some intelligible notion: and from every definition one can draw certain conse-

[1] From Greek, βηίτυρι: nullity, nothingness.

quences, by using the incontestable rules of logic; and this is precisely what one does in building the necessary and demonstrative sciences which depend not at all on facts, but solely on reason, such as logic, metaphysics, arithmetic, geometry, the science of motion, and the science of right as well; which are not at all founded on experiences and facts, and serve rather to give reasons for facts and to control them in advance; which would [also] happen with respect to right, if there were no law in the world. The error of those who have made justice dependent on power comes in part from confounding right and law. Right cannot be unjust, it is a contradiction; but law can be. For it is power which gives and maintains law; and if this power lacks wisdom or good will, it can give and maintain quite evil laws: but happily for the universe, the laws of God are always just, and he is in a position to maintain them, as he does without doubt, although this has not always been done visibly and at once, for which he has, no doubt, good reasons.

It is a question, then, of determining the formal reason of justice and the measure by which we should measure actions to know whether they are just or not. After what has been said one can already foresee what this will be. Justice is nothing else than that which conforms to wisdom and goodness joined together: the end of goodness is the greatest good, but to recognize it wisdom is needed, which is nothing else than knowledge of the good. Goodness is simply the inclination to do good to everyone, and to arrest evil, at least when it is not necessary for a greater good or to arrest a greater evil. Thus wisdom is in the understanding and goodness in the will. And justice, as a consequence, is in both. Power is a different matter, but if it is used it makes right become fact, and makes what ought to be also really exist, in so far as the nature of things permits. And this is what God does in the world.

But since justice tends to the good, and [since] wisdom and goodness, which together form justice, relate to the good, one may ask what the true good is. I answer that it is nothing else than that which serves in the perfection of intelligent substances: from which it is clear that order, contentment, joy, wisdom, goodness and virtue are good things essentially and can never be evil; that power is naturally a good, that is to say in itself, because, everything being equal, it is better to have it than not to have it: but it does not become a certain good until it is joined with wisdom and goodness: for the power of an evil person serves only to plunge him farther into unhappiness sooner or later, because it gives him the means to be more evil, and to merit a greater punishment, from which he will not escape, since there is a perfectly just monarch of the universe whose infinite penetration and sovereign power one cannot avoid.

And since experience shows us that God permits, for reasons un-known to us but doubtless very wise, and founded in a greater good, that there be many evil [persons who are] happy in this life, and many good [persons who are] unhappy, which would not conform to the rules of a perfect government such as God's if it were not redressed, it follows necessarily that there will be another life, and that souls do not perish at all with the visible body; otherwise there would be unpunished crimes, and good actions without recompense, which is contrary to order.

There are, besides, demonstrative proofs of the immortality of the soul, because the principle of action and of consciousness could not come from a purely passive extended thing indifferent to all movement, such as matter is: thus action and consciousness must come from some-thing simple or immaterial [and] without extension and without parts; which is called soul: now everything which is simple or without parts, is not subject to dissolution, and as a consequence cannot be destroyed.[1] There are people who imagine that we are too small a thing in the sight of an infinite God, for him to be concerned with us; it is conceived that we are to God that which worms, which we crush without thinking, are in relation to us. But this is to imagine that God is like a man, and cannot think of everything. God, by the very fact that he is infinite, does things without working by a species of result of his will, as it results from my will and that of my friend, that we are in agreement, without needing a new action to produce the accord after our resolutions are made. But if the human race were not well governed, the universe would not be either, for the whole consists of its parts.

We also find order and marvels in the smallest whole things [*choses entières*], when we are capable of distinguishing the parts and of seeing the whole at the same time, as it appears in looking at insects and other small things in the microscope. Thus by much stronger reasons craftsmanship and harmony would be found in large things, if we were capable of seeing them as a whole. And above all they would be found in the whole economy of the governance of spirits, which are the substances most resembling God, because they are [themselves] capable of recognizing and of produc-ing order and craftsmanship. And as a consequence, one must conclude that the author of things, who is so inclined to order, will have had particular care for it with respect to those creatures who are naturally sources of order, in proportion to their perfection, and who alone are capable of imitating his craftsmanship. But it is not possible that this should seem so to us, in this small particle of life which we live here below, and which is an inconsiderable fragment of a life without bounds which no

[1] Cf. Plato, *Phaedo*, 80 ff.

spirit will lose. To consider this fragment separately is to consider things like a broken stick or like the bits of flesh torn from an animal, where the craftsmanship of its organs cannot sufficiently appear.

This is also true when one looks at the brain, which must be, without doubt, one of the greatest marvels of nature, since the most immediate organs of sense are there, although one finds there only a confused mass in which nothing singular appears, and which must, however, conceal a species of filaments of a fineness incomparably greater than that of spider-webs and which are thought to be the vessels of that very subtle fluid called the animal spirits. Now this mass of brain has too great a multitude of passages, and of passages too fine for us to escape this labyrinth with our eyes, whatever microscope one uses, because the subtlety of the spirits contained in these passages is equal to that of light-rays themselves. But our eyes and our touch show us nothing in the brain which has any extra-ordinary appearance; [and] one can say that it is the same in the government of intelligent substances under the monarchy of God, where every-thing appears confused to our eyes; but nonetheless this must be the most beautiful and the most marvelous disposition of the world, coming from an author who is the source of all perfection: but it must be too great and too beautiful, for spirits of our present range to be able to appreciate it enough so soon. And to want to see it here, is like wanting to take a novel by the tail and to pretend to decipher the plot from the first book: instead of which, the beauty of a novel is great to the degree that it finally produces more order from a greater apparent confusion. It would even be a fault in the composition, if the reader could divine the issue too soon. Now, what is only suspense and beauty in novels, which imitate, so to speak, the creation, is in addition usefulness and wisdom in this great and true poem (that is to say, word for word, work) of the universe. For the beauty and the justice of the divine government have been partly concealed from our eyes, not only because it could not be otherwise, without chang-ing the whole harmony of the world, but also because it is proper in order that there be more exercise of free virtue, of wisdom and of a non-mercenary love of God, since rewards and punishments are still out-wardly invisible and appear only to the eyes of our reason or faith: which I take here for the same thing, since true faith is founded in reason. And since the marvels of nature make us find that the operations of God are admirably beautiful, whenever we can envisage a whole in its natural context, though this beauty is not apparent in looking at things detached or torn from their wholes, we must conclude that everything which we cannot yet disentangle or envisage as a whole with all its parts must have no less of justice and of beauty. And to understand this great point well, is to have the natural foundation of faith, of hope and of the love of God, for these virtues are based on a knowledge of the divine perfections.

Now, as nothing better reconfirms the incomparable wisdom of God, than the structure of the works of nature, above all the structure which appears when looking at them more closely with a microscope; it is for this reason, as well as because of the great lights which could be thrown on bodies for the use of medicine, food, and mechanical ends, that it is most necessary that one advance knowledge with [the use of] microscopes. There are scarcely ten men in the world who are devoted to this; and if there were a hundred thousand of them, it would not be too many to discover the important marvels of this new world which makes up the interior of our own and which is capable of making our knowledge a hundred thousand times greater than it is. This is why I have more than once hoped that one could bring great princes to make arrangements for this and to support men who worked at it. Observatories are founded to look at the stars, and these structures are spectacular and require a great [deal of] apparatus, but telescopes are far from being as useful and from revealing as many beauties and varieties of knowledge, as microscopes; a man in Delft[1] has succeeded marvelously in this, and if there were many others like him, our knowledge of physics would go far beyond its present state. It is for great princes to arrange this for the public utility, in which they are the most interested. And since it is a matter of little expenditure and of little ceremony it is very easy to manage; and where one needs little more than good will and attention to succeed, one would have the less reason to neglect it. For myself, I have no other motive in recommending this research, than that of advancing the knowledge of truth and the public good, [which is] strongly interested in the augmentation of the treasure of human knowledge.

II

Most of the questions of right, but particularly of that of sovereigns and of peoples, are confused, because everyone does not agree on a common concept of justice, with the result that everyone does not understand the same thing by the same name, and this is the cause of endless dispute. Everyone will agree, perhaps, to this nominal definition, that justice is a constant will to act in such a way that no one has a reason to complain of us. But this does not suffice unless one gives the means of determining these reasons. Now I observe that some people restrict, and that others

[1] Reference to van Leuwenhoeck (1632–1723), discoverer of the existence of spermatozoa.

extend, the reasons for human complaints. There are those who believe that it is enough that no one does them harm, and that no one deprives them of anything they possess, and that one is not at all obliged to procure the good of another, or to arrest evil, even if this would cost us nothing and would not cause us any pain. Some who pass for great judges [*justiciers*] in this world, keep themselves within these limits; they content themselves with not harming anybody, but they are not at all of a humor to improve people's conditions [*rendre les gens bien aisés*]; they believe, in a word, that one can be just, without being charitable.

There are others who have larger and finer views, who would not wish that anyone complain of their lack of goodness; they would approve what I have put in my preface to the *Codex Iuris Gentium*, that justice is nothing else than the charity of the wise, that is to say goodness toward others which is conformed to wisdom. And wisdom, in my sense, is nothing else than the science of felicity. It is permitted that men vary in their use of terms, and if someone wishes to insist on limiting the term *just* to oppose it to that of *charitable*, there is no way of forcing him to change his language, since names are arbitrary. However, it is permitted that we inform ourselves of the reasons which he has for being what he calls just, in order to see whether the same reasons will not bring him also to be good, and to do good.

One will agree, I believe, that those who are charged with the conduct of another, like tutors, directors of societies and certain magistrates, are obligated not only to prevent evil, but also to procure the good. But one will perhaps wish to doubt whether a man free of commitments or a sovereign of a state has these same obligations, the first in relation to all the others in a given situation, and the second in relation to his subjects. In addition I shall ask that whoever can maintain another person not do evil to others. One can give more than one reason for this: the most pressing will be the fear that someone will do the same to us. But has one not reason to fear as well, that men will hate us if we refuse them aid which does not inconvenience us at all, and if we fail to arrest an evil which is going to overwhelm them? Someone will say: I am content that others do not harm me, I do not ask at all their aid or their beneficence and I do not want to do or to claim more. But can one hold to this language sincerely? Let him ask himself what he would say and hope for if he should find himself actually on the point of falling into an evil, which another could make him avoid by a turn of his hand. Would one not hold him for a bad man and even for an enemy, if he did not want to save us in this situation? I have read in a travelog of the East Indies that a man being chased by an elephant was saved, because another man in a neighboring house beat on a drum, which stopped the beast; supposing that the former had cried to the other to beat [the drum], and that he had not wanted to out of pure inhumanity: would he not have had the right to complain?

One will grant to me, then, that one must prevent evil for another, if one can conveniently, but one will perhaps not agree that justice orders us to do positive good to others. I then ask whether one is not obliged at least to relieve their ills? And I return again to the proof, that is to say to the rule, *quod tibi non vis fieri*.[1] Suppose that you were plunged into misery; would you not complain of him who did not help you at all, if he could do it easily? You have fallen into the water; he does not wish to throw you a rope to give you a means of getting out: would you not judge that he is an evil man, and even an enemy? Let us suppose that you are suffering from violent pains, and that another person had in his house, under lock and key, a healing-fountain capable of relieving your ills: what would you not say and what would you not do, if he refused to give you some glasses of [this] water?

Led by degrees, one will agree not only that men should abstain from wrongdoing, but also that they should prevent evil from happening and even relieve it, when it is done; at least in so far as they can without inconveniencing themselves (and I do not examine now how far this inconvenience may go). However, some will perhaps still doubt whether one is obliged to secure the good of another, even if one can do it without difficulty. Someone will say: I am not obliged to help you get ahead; each for himself, God for us all. But I wish again to propose an intermediate case. A great good is going to come to you; an impediment appears; I can remove that impediment without pain: would you not believe yourself to have a right to ask it of me, and to remind me that I would ask it of you, if I were in a similar position? If you grant me this point, as you can hardly help doing, how will you refuse the only remaining request, that is, to secure a great good for me, when you can do it without inconveniencing yourself in any way, and without being able to allege any reason for not doing it, except for a simple 'I don't want to'? You could make me happy and you do not do it: I complain; you would complain in the same situation; thus I complain with justice.

This gradation makes it clear that the same reasons of complaint subsist always; whether one does evil or refuses to do good is a matter of degree, but that does not change the species and the nature of the thing. One can also say that the absence of good is an evil and that the absence of evil is a general good. Someone makes a request of you, be it to do or to omit something. If you refuse the request, he has reason to complain,

[1] 'What you do not wish to have done to you.'

since he can judge that you would make the same request if you were in the place of him who makes it. And it is the principle of equity, or, what is the same thing, of the equality or of the identity of reasons [*de la même raison*], which holds that one should grant [to others] whatever one would wish in a similar situation, without claiming to be privileged, against reason, or [without claiming] to be able to allege one's will as a reason.

Perhaps one can say, then, that not to do evil to another, *neminem laedere*, is the precept of law which is called *ius strictum*, but that equity demands that one do good as well, when it is fitting, and that it is in this that the precept consists which orders that we give each his due: *suum cuique tribuere*. But this fitness, or what is due, is determined by the rule of equity or of equality: *quod tibi non vis fieri, aut quod tibi vis fieri, neque aliis facito aut negato*.[1] This is the rule[2] of reason and of our Master. Put yourself in the place of another, and you will have the true point of view for judging what is just or not.

Some objections have been made against this great rule, but they come from the fact that it is not applied universally. It is objected, for example, that a criminal can claim, by virtue of this maxim, a pardon from the sovereign judge, because the judge would wish the same thing, if he were in a similar position. The reply is easy: the judge must put himself not only in the place of the criminal, but also in that of others, who are interested that the crime be punished. And the balance of good (in which the lesser evil is included) must determine it [the case]. The same is true of this objection, that distributive justice demands inequality among men, that in a society one must divide gains in proportion to that which each has contributed, and that one must pay attention to merit and to lack of merit. The reply again is easy: put yourself in the place of all, and suppose that they are well-informed and enlightened; you will gather this conclusion from their votes, that they judge it fitting to their own interest, that distinctions be made between one another. For example, if profits were not divided proportionally in a commercial society, people would either not enter it at all, or they would leave it quite soon, which is contrary to the interest of the whole society.

One can say, then, that justice, at least among men, is the constant will to act, so far as possible, in a way such that no one can complain of us, if

[1] 'What you do not wish to have done to you, or what you do wish to have done to you, do not do to others, or do not deny to others.' Cf. Matthew 7. 12; Luke 6. 31.

[2] Leibniz' original manuscript, preserved in the Niedersächsische Landesbibliothek, has 'rule' written in over 'precept' (which is scratched out) at this point. Apparently Leibniz wanted to re-enforce the point that God, as well as men, acted according to moral rules; 'precept' is a weaker-sounding word.

we would not complain of others in a similar case. From which it is evident that, since it is impossible to act so that the whole world is content, one must try to content people as much as possible, and thus that whatever is just, conforms to the charity of the wise.

Wisdom, which is the knowledge of our own good, brings us to justice, that is to a reasonable advancement of the good of others; for this we have already alleged one reason, which is the fear that others will harm us, if we do otherwise: but there is still the hope that others will do the same for us; nothing is more certain than these proverbs, *homo homini deus, homo homini lupus*.[1] And nothing can contribute more to the happiness or the misery of man than men. If they were all wise, and knew how to treat each other, they would all be happy, so far as happiness can be attained by human reason.

But to enter better into the nature of things, it is permitted to use fictions. Let us imagine a person who has nothing to fear from others, such as would be, in relation to men, a superior power, some higher spirit, some substance which the pagans would have called a divinity, some immortal, invulnerable, invincible man: a person, in fine, who can neither hope for nor fear anything from us. Shall we say that this person is obligated nonetheless to do us no evil and even to do us good? Mr Hobbes will say no: he will even add that this person will have an absolute right over us after he conquers us [*en nous faisant sa conqueste*], since one cannot complain of this conqueror for the reasons which we have just pointed out, since there is another condition which exempts him from all consideration for us. But without needing a fiction, what shall we say of the supreme divinity, whom reason makes us recognize? Christians agree, and others should agree, that this great God is sovereignly just and sovereignly good; but it is not for his own repose nor to maintain peace with us, that he shows us so much goodness; for we could not make war against him. What, then, will be the principle of his justice, and what will be its rule? It will not be that equity, or that equality, which obtains among men and which makes them envisage the common end of the human condition [in terms of the maxim], to do unto others as we would have them do unto us.

One cannot envisage in God any other motive than that of perfection, or, if you like, of his pleasure; supposing (according to my definition) that pleasure is nothing but a feeling of perfection, he has nothing to consider outside himself; on the contrary everything depends on him. But his goodness would not be supreme, if he did not aim at the good and at perfection so far as is possible. But what will one say, if I show that this same motive has a place in truly virtuous and generous men, whose

[1] Symmachus, *Epistolae* IX, 114; Plautus, *Asinaria* II, 88.

E

supreme function [*degré*] is to imitate divinity, in so far as human nature is capable of it? The earlier reasons of fear and of hope can bring men to be just in public, and when their interest demands it. They will even obligate them to exercise themselves from childhood to practice the rules of justice, in order to acquire the habit of doing so, for fear of betraying themselves too easily, and of thereby harming themselves along with others. However, this will be merely political at bottom, if there is no other motive. And if some man, just by this standard, shall find an occasion to make a great fortune by means of a great crime which will be unknown or at least unpunished, he will say, like Julius Caesar, following Euripides:[1] *Si violandum est jus, regnandi gratia violandum est.*[2] But he whose justice is proof against such a temptation, cannot have any other motive than that of his inclination, acquired by birth or by exercise and regulated by reason, which makes him find so much pleasure in the exercise of justice and so much ugliness in unjust actions, that other pleasures and displeasures are obliged to give way.

One can say that this serenity of spirit, which would find the greatest pleasure in virtue and the greatest evil in vice, that is, in the perfection or imperfection of the will, would be the greatest good of which man is capable here below, even if he had nothing to expect beyond this life, for what can one prefer to this interior harmony, to this continual pleasure of the purest and greatest things, of which one is always the master, and which one could not abandon? But it must also be admitted that it is difficult to arrive at this spiritual disposition, that the number of those who have attained it is small, and that the majority of men are insensible to this motive, great and beautiful as it is. This is why it seems that the Siamese believed that those who attained this degree of perfection received divinity as a reward. The goodness of the author of things has thus provided for it by [supplying] a motive more within the reach of all men, by making himself known to the human race, as he has done through the eternal light of reason which he has given us, and through the wonderful effects of his power, of his wisdom and of his infinite goodness, which he has placed before our eyes. This knowledge should make us envisage God as the sovereign monarch of the universe whose government is the most perfect State that one can conceive, where nothing is neglected, where every hair on our head is counted, where all right becomes fact, either by itself or in some equivalent form, such that justice is something which coincides with the good pleasure of God, and that a divorce between the honest and

---

[1] Euripides, *Phoenissae*, v. 524–5: 'If wrong e'er be right, for a throne's sake were wrong most right.' (Way's translation, cited in Loemker II, p. 1196.
[2] Cicero, *De Officiis*, III, 21, 82.

the useful does not arise. After this, it must be imprudent not to be just, because no one will fail to derive good or evil from what he will have done, according as it is just or unjust.

But there is something still more beautiful than all of this in the government of God. What Cicero said allegorically of ideal justice is really true in relation to this substantial justice: that if we could see this justice, we would be inflamed by its beauty.[1] One can compare the divine monarchy to a kingdom whose sovereign would be a queen more spiritual and more wise than Queen Elizabeth; more judicious, more happy and, in a word, greater than Queen Anne; more clever, more wise, and more beautiful than the Queen of Prussia:[2] in short, as accomplished as it is possible to be. Let us imagine that the perfections of this queen make such an impression on the minds of her subjects, that they take the greatest pleasure in obeying her and in pleasing her: in this case everyone would be virtuous and just by inclination. It is this which happens literally, and beyond everything one can describe, with respect to God and those who know him. It is in him that wisdom, virtue, justice, and greatness are accompanied by sovereign beauty. One cannot know God as one ought without loving him above all things, and one cannot love him thus without willing what he wills. His perfections are infinite and cannot end, and this is why the pleasure which consists in the feeling of his perfections is the greatest and most durable which can exist. That is, the greatest happiness, which causes one to love him, causes one to be happy and virtuous at the same time.

After this one can say absolutely that justice is goodness conformed to wisdom, even in those who have not attained to this wisdom. For, apart from God, the majority of those who act according to justice in all things, even against their own interest, do in effect what a wise man would demand who found his pleasure in the general good; but in certain cases they will not act as sages themselves, not being sensible of the pleasure of virtue. And in these cases, where their disinterestedness would not be compensated either by praises or honors, nor by fortune, nor otherwise, they would not have acted in a way most conforming to prudence. But as soon as they consider that justice conforms to the will of a sage whose wisdom is infinite and whose power is proportioned to it, they find that they would not be wise at all (that is, prudent) if they did not conform themselves to the will of such a sage.

This shows that justice can be taken in different ways. One can oppose it to charity, and then it is only the *ius strictum*. One can oppose it to the

[1] Cicero, *De Officiis* III, 6, 28, and III, 17, 69.
[2] The references are to Elizabeth I of England, Anne of Great Britain and Sophia Charlotte of Prussia.

wisdom of him who must exercise justice, and then it conforms to the general good, although there will be certain cases in which the particular good will not appear in it. God and immortality would not enter into account. But when one considers them, one always finds his own good in the general good.

And while justice is only a particular virtue, when one leaves out of consideration God or a government which imitates that of God; and while this limited virtue comprises only what are called commutative and distributive justice; one can also say that as soon as it is founded on God or on the imitation of God, it becomes universal justice, and contains all the virtues. For when we are vicious, we harm not only ourselves, but we diminish, so far as it depends on us, the perfection of the great state whose monarch is God as well; and although the evil is redressed by the wisdom of the sovereign master, it is partly through our punishment. And universal justice is stamped with the supreme precept: *honeste* (*hoc est probe, pie*) *vivere*, just as *suum cuique tribuere* was in conformity to particular justice, whether in general or (taking it more narrowly) as distributive justice (which distinguishes men); and as *neminem laedere* stood for commutative justice, or for the *ius strictum* as opposed to equity, according as one takes the terms [in different ways].

It is true that Aristotle has recognized this universal justice,[1] although he did not relate it to God; and I find it beautiful of him to have had nonetheless so high an idea of it. But this is because a well-formed government or state, for him, took the place of God on earth, and this government will do what it can to oblige men to be virtuous. But as I have already said, one cannot oblige men always to be virtuous by the sole principle of [self-] interest in this life, any more than one can find the rare secret of elevating them such that virtue constitutes their greatest pleasure, as I have said before; this is what Aristotle seems to have hoped for more than shown. However, I do not find it impossible that there be times and places where one attains this, especially if piety is added.

When it is a question of the rights of sovereigns and of peoples, one can still distinguish the *ius strictum*, equity, and piety. Hobbes and Filmer seem to have considered only the *ius strictum*. The Roman jurisconsults also adhere sometimes to this [degree of] right alone. One can even say that piety and equity regularly demand the *ius strictum*, whenever they provide no exceptions. But in insisting on the *ius strictum* one must always understand [*sousentendre*], 'except for equity and piety'; otherwise this proverb would hold: *summum ius summa est injuria.*[2]

---

[1] Aristotle, *Nicomachean Ethics* V, 1, 19 (1130a and 1135a).
[2] 'The more law, the more injustice there is.' Cf. Cicero, *De Officiis* I, 10, 33.

In examining the *ius strictum*, it is important to consider the origin of kingdoms or states. Hobbes seems to conceive that men were something like beasts at first; that little by little they became more tractable, but that so far as they were free, they were in a state of war of all against all and that there was thus no *ius strictum*, each having a *ius in omnia* and being able to seize without injustice the possessions of his neighbor, as he judged appropriate; because there was then no security or judge at all, and everyone had a right to forestall those from whom one had everything to fear. But as this state of rude nature was a state of misery, men agreed upon the means to obtain their security, by transferring their right of judging to the person of the state, represented by a single man or by some assembly.[1] Nonetheless, Hobbes recognizes somewhere that a man has not thereby lost the right to judge of what suits him best and that it is permitted that a criminal do what he can to save himself,[2] but that his fellow-citizens must restrain themselves according to the judgment of the state. The same author will also be obliged to recognize, however, that these same citizens, not having lost their judgment either, cannot allow their security to be endangered, when some of them are mistreated, such that at bottom, whatever Hobbes says, each has retained his right and his liberty regardless of the transfer made to the state, which will be limited and provisional, that is, it will last as long as we believe that our security lasts. And the reasons which this illustrious author gives to stop subjects from resisting the sovereign are only plausible considerations [*des persuasions*] based on the very true principle that ordinarily such a remedy is worse than the evil; but what is ordinarily the case is not so absolutely. The one is like the *ius strictum*, the other like equity.

It seems to me also that this author is wrong to confuse right with its effect. He who has acquired a good, who has built a house, who has forged a sword, is the proprietary master of it, although another, in time of war, has the right to drive him from his house and to deprive him of his sword. And although there are cases, where one cannot exercise his rights for lack of a judge and of enforcement, the right does not cease to exist. And it is confusing matters if one tries to destroy it because there is no present means of verifying and exercising it.

Filmer seems to me to have recognized, and with reason, that there is a right, and even a *ius strictum*, before the foundation of states.[3] He who produces something new or who comes into possession of something already extant, but which no one has heretofore possessed, and who

---

[1] Hobbes, *De Cive* v, 8.
[2] *Ibid.* VI, 13; stated more fully in *Leviathan*, ch. 21.
[3] Filmer, *Patriarcha* I, 8.

improves it and makes it fit for his own use, cannot ordinarily be deprived of it without injustice. It is the same of him who acquires it directly or indirectly from such a possessor. This right of acquisition is a *ius strictum* which even equity approves. Hobbes believes that by virtue of this right, children are the property of the mother unless society orders differently,[1] and Filmer, supposing the superiority of the father, accords to him the proprietary right over his children, as well as over those of his slaves.[2] And as all men up to the present, according to sacred scripture, are descended from Adam and also from Noah, it follows, according to him, that if Noah were living he would have the right of an absolute monarch over all men. In his absence fathers always are and must be the sovereign masters of their posterity. And this paternal power is the origin of kings, who are finally put in the place of the progenitors, be it by force or by consent. And since the power of fathers is absolute, that of kings is as well.[3]

This view should not be completely condemned, though I believe one can say that it has been pushed too far. One must admit that a father or a mother acquires a great power over children by their generation and education. But I do not think that one can draw this consequence from it, that children are the property of their progenitor, as are horses or dogs which are born to us, and [as are] the works which we create. It will be objected against me, that we can acquire slaves and that the children of our slaves are slaves also: now according to the law of nations [*droit des gens*] slaves are the property of their masters, and no reason can be seen why the children whom we have produced and formed by education are not our slaves by an even juster title than those whom we have bought or captured.

I reply that, [even] if I granted that there is a right of slavery among men which conforms to natural reason, and that according to the *ius strictum* the bodies of slaves and of their children are under the power of their masters, it will always be true that another stronger right is opposed to the abuse of this right. This is the right of rational souls which are naturally and inalienably free; it is the right of God, who is the sovereign master of bodies and of souls, and under whom masters are the fellow-citizens of their slaves, since the latter have the right of citizenship in the kingdom of God as well as their masters. One can say, then, that the body of a man belongs to his soul, and cannot be taken away from him while he is living; now, the soul not being able to be acquired, the ownership of his body can only be like what is called a servitude to another, or like a species of usu-

---

[1] Hobbes, *De Cive* IX, 3.

[2] Filmer, *Observations on Mr Hob's Leviathan*, XI.

[3] Filmer, *Patriarcha* I, 7–9.

fruct; but usufruct has its limits: it must be exercised *salva re*,[1] so that this right cannot go to the point of making a slave bad or unhappy.

But if I were to grant, contrary to the nature of things, that an enslaved man is the property of another man, the right of the master, however strict, would be limited by equity, which requires that a man take care of another man in the way that he would wish that others take care of him in a similar case, and by charity, which ordains that one work for the happiness of others. And these obligations are perfected by piety, that is, by what one owes to God. And if we wanted to stop merely at the *ius strictum*, the American cannibals would have a right to eat their prisoners. There are some among them who go even farther: they use their prisoners to have children, and then they fatten and eat these children, and finally the mother, when she produces no more. Such are the consequences of the pretended absolute right of masters over slaves, or of fathers over children.

If the law of decency or of good order is opposed to strict right with respect to slaves, it is still further opposed to it with respect to children. Aristotle has treated this right very well. Looking, as I do, for the principle of justice in the good, he regulates decency by [the rule of] the best, that is by that which would suit the best government (*quod optimae Reipublicae conveniret*), so that natural right, according to this author, is that which is most conducive to order.[2] From which it follows that according to the nature of things, no one should be the slave of another, unless he deserves to be a slave, that is, unless he is incapable of conducting himself well. But as for the children of the father of a family, a free man with noble feelings, one must presume that they will be like their parents, that they will have a natural goodness and a liberal education; and that the father will work to make them the inheritors not only of his goods, but also of his virtue, in order to administer these goods properly one day. This is why Aristotle has distinguished kinds of kingdoms, saying that there is a *regnum paternum et regnum herile*, that is, a paternal rule like that of a father over his children, and a despotic rule like that of a master over his slaves.[3] The former tends to make subjects happy and virtuous, but the aim of the latter is only the preservation of a condition which makes them fit to work for their master. But it seems that when one can make men happy and virtuous, one should never leave virtue out, although virtue has its degrees, and the same virtues are not necessary to [men in] all conditions, to make a man happy.

[1] Without damage to the thing in question, i.e. the slave's body.
[2] This rather vague account of Aristotle seems to apply to various passages in books III and VII of the *Politics*.
[3] Aristotle, *Nicomachean Ethics* V, 8 (1134b).

It must be granted, however, that there is a difference between the right of property (*strictum ius*) and that of some convenience, and that often the former is preferable. But it is because of a greater convenience. For it is not permitted to deprive the rich of their goods to accommodate the poor, nor to deprive a man of his coat which does not suit his size in order to give it to another whose size is better suited to it. This is because the disorder which would be born of it would cause more general evil and inconvenience, than this particular inconvenience. Moreover, it is necessary to maintain possessions, and since the state cannot care for all of men's domestic affairs, it must preserve the ownership of goods so that each will have his own sphere which he can enhance and put into good order, *Spartam quam ornet*, emulation being useful, in general; otherwise, if everything were commonly owned, it would be neglected by individuals, [unless]¹ it were arranged [as it is] among the members of religious orders, which would be difficult in these times. Thus the state must maintain the possessions of individuals; it can, nonetheless, make tolerable breaches in this policy for the common security, and even for a great common good: from which comes what is called *dominium Eminens*, and imposts, and what is called [taxation for] war-expenses.

I...²

2. *Opinion on the Principles of Pufendorf*
(1706)

This work, originally written in the form of a letter (see n. 1) became fairly well known in the early eighteenth century because Barbeyrac translated most of it and appended it to his translation of Pufendorf's *De Officio Hominis*; he also provided an able defense of Pufendorf, and castigated Leibniz for not writing

¹ At this point Leibniz' manuscript becomes illegible, owing to the fact that the present passage is a marginal addition whose paper has crumbled away. I have added the single word 'unless', which makes the passage intelligible; there may have been a longer phrase here.

² The last leaf of the manuscript says only 'I' ['Je'], then leaves the rest of the sheet blank. What Leibniz would have gone on to say is not clear; the *Meditation*, in any case, ends rather lamely.

the definitive book on natural law which he (Leibniz) criticized Pufendorf for not writing. Though the argument in this piece is similar to that found in the *Meditation on the Common Concept of Justice*, pt. IV, particularly, is more rigorous than anything that Leibniz wrote on natural law, and the references to Descartes are of particular interest. Throughout the *Opinion* it is evident that Leibniz is really attacking Hobbes, or rather all legal positivists, as much as he is criticizing Pufendorf. (The original Latin text is to be found in vol. IV of Dutens' edition; the Barbeyrac translation is appended to the French version of Pufendorf published at Amsterdam in 1718.)

I

You have asked me on behalf of a friend, most eminent man,[1] whether in my opinion the book entitled *De Officio Hominis et Civis*, [written] by a man long renowned for his merit, Samuel Pufendorf,[2] is suitable as a topic of instruction for the young. I have re-examined this work, which I had not consulted for a long time, and I have ascertained that its principles suffer from no small weaknesses. However, since the greater part of the thoughts expounded in the course of the work are not consistent with the principles, and are not logically deduced from them, but rather are borrowed elsewhere, from good authors, nothing keeps this little book from containing many good things, and from serving usefully as a compendium of natural law for those who are satisfied with a superficial smattering (as are the majority of readers), without looking for sound learning. I could wish, nonetheless, that something more solid and effective existed, which would give clear and fruitful definitions, which would draw its conclusions from correct principles as if by a thread [of logic], which would establish in order the fundamental principles of all actions and exceptions valid by nature, which would, finally, afford students of the science [of natural law] a sure way to supply for themselves that which is left out, and to decide the questions which are submitted to them on their own by a fixed method. This, indeed, must be expected of a scientific instruction which is complete and well-conveyed. The discernment and erudition of the incomparable Grotius, or the profound genius

[1] The 'most eminent man', Leibniz' friend Gerhardt Walter van den Muelen (or Molanus, 1633–1722), Abbot of Loccum, requested Leibniz' opinion of Pufendorf's *De Officio Hominis* on behalf of his relative, J. Christoph Boehmer, a professor at Helmstadt.

[2] Samuel Freiherr von Pufendorf (1632–94), German jurist and historian, author of *De Officio Hominis et Civis juxta Legem Naturalem* (1673), translated by F. G. Moore, Oxford University Press, New York, 1927. (Leibniz' long citation of Pufendorf's text in part V of the *Opinion* is given here in the Moore translation.)

of Hobbes, would have been capable of something like this, if the former
had not been distracted by many other concerns, and the latter had not
lain down truly wicked principles, and adhered to them with too much
fidelity. Something better and more complete than the usual works could
have been produced by Selden,[1] if he had wished to apply his ability and
his erudition to this work with more zeal. It would be of the greatest use,
moreover, for parallels to be drawn from the civil law, as accepted by men,
particularly the Roman, and from the divine law itself. Theologians and
jurisconsults would thereby be more willing to make use of the natural
law, which at present is more celebrated by words than applied to affairs.
In the meantime, since a work such as we desire does not exist, and since
Pufendorf's epitome is more widely known than any other, I think that it is
at least advisable to give readers or auditors some warning, particularly
about the principles which are most subject to distortion. The most
important of these fall under these main headings, that the author seems
to have correctly identified neither the end, the object, nor the efficient
cause of natural law.

II

Concerning the end [of natural law], he speaks eloquently in part 8 of his
preface thus, that: 'The end of the science of natural law is bounded by
the limit of this life alone.' And, foreseeing the objection that it is possible
to demonstrate the immortality of the soul by natural reason, and that,
therefore, the consequences which result from this, with respect to law
and justice, apply to the theory of law as understood by means of natural
reason, he answers in the same passage that it is true, indeed, that the
spirit of man yearns ardently for immortality and is strongly opposed to
its own destruction, as a result of which the persuasion has become fixed
among most peoples that the soul continues to exist after being separated
from the body, and that all goes well for good people, and badly for the
wicked; but that, in any case, such a belief about these matters, to which
the human mind can adhere with complete faith, can be derived only
from divine revelation. Thus far the author. But indeed, supposing it
were as true as it is [in fact] false, that natural reason cannot by itself
provide a full demonstration of the immortality of the soul; nevertheless,

---

[1] John Selden (1584–1654), English jurist. Mathieu notes that Grotius called
Selden 'the glory of England', and that in his work *De Jure Naturali et
Gentium juxta Disciplinam Hebraeorum* (1640), Selden attempted to derive a
complete natural law doctrine from the Old Testament, leaving out everything
relative to the Hebrew people alone.

it would be enough for a wise man that the arguments at least have a great weight, and that they give to good people a glorious hope for a better life and instill in the wicked a proper fear of a dire punishment to follow. Indeed, even a small reason for fearing, not to mention a great probability, ought to excite one's care in avoiding it. Nor can one disregard either the agreement of almost all people [on this point], or their innate desire for immortality. But an argument which is certain and evident to all (omitting for now the other more subtle ones) is offered by the very recognition of the divinity which our author rightly accepts and deservedly places among the very foundations of natural law. One cannot doubt, in fact, that the ruler of the universe, at once most wise and most powerful, has allotted rewards for the good and punishments for the wicked, and that his plan will be put into effect in a future life, since in present life many crimes remain without punishment and without recompense. Therefore, to set aside here the consideration of the future life, which is inseparably connected to divine providence, and to be content with an inferior degree of natural law, which can even be valid for atheists (as I have explained elsewhere), would mean cutting off the best part of the science [of law], and suppressing many duties in this life as well. Why, indeed, would someone risk riches, honors and his very existence on behalf of his dear ones, of his country or of justice, when, by the ruin of others, he could think only of himself, and live amidst honors and riches? Indeed, to put off [the enjoyment of] actual and tangible goods simply for the immortality of one's name and for posthumous fame – for the voices of those whom one can no longer hear – what would this be if not magnificent folly? More sublime and perfect is the theory of natural law according to Christian doctrine (concerning which Prasch has written),[1] or rather of the true philosophers, [namely] that not everything should be measured by the goods of this life. In fact, unless someone is born or educated to find an intense pleasure in virtue, and pain in vice (which is not true of everybody), there will be no more arguments which can dissuade him from committing great crimes, which can gain very great goods for him with impunity:

Sit spes fallendi, miscebit sacra profanis.[2]

But no one will escape the divine vengeance, which is deferred to the future life; and this is a solid reason by which men may understand the

---

[1] Johann Ludwig Prasch (1637–1702), author of *Designatio Juris Naturae ex Disciplina Christianorum* (1688), to which Leibniz is apparently referring.

[2] Horace, *Epistolae* I, 16, v. 54: 'So long as there is hope of successful deceit, he will mix sacred with profane.'

duty to conduct themselves according to justice, if they want to provide for themselves.

III

It should not be admitted, therefore, as our author urges, that that which remains hidden in the soul, and does not appear externally, is not pertinent to natural law; it is clear here that, in consequence of the [sudden] cutting off of the end of natural law, its object also is too restricted. Shortly after having said, indeed, at the end of part 8, that the maxims of natural law are applicable only to the human forum, which does not reach outside of this life, in part 9 it is now maintained that the human forum is concerned only with the external actions of man, but does not penetrate to those which remain shut up in the soul and do not produce external signs or effects, and hence is not concerned with them. What is beyond [external human actions] he eloquently ascribes to moral theology, whose principle, as he teaches in part 4, is revelation, and which informs Christian man, [as in] part 8, where he adds that it is wrong in many cases to apply natural law to the divine forum, which is above all the concern of the theologian. Thus (says part 9), it is not enough for moral theology to make the external conduct of men conform to propriety (as if this sufficed for a moral philosopher or for a teacher of natural law); it must especially endeavor to make the internal movements of the soul conform to the desire of God, and to reprove those actions which appear perfectly correct externally, but which nonetheless arise from an impure soul. The author claims all of this for the theologians alone, though it is well known that not only Christian philosophers treated this matter, but also the ancient pagans, whose philosophy was so wise, so grave and sublime. For which reasons I am astonished that a man so renowned for his scholarship could have said such things, [which are] no less absurd than paradoxical. It was taught by the Platonists, and by the Stoics, and indeed in the works of the poets, that the gods must be imitated, that to them one must offer:

> *Compositum jus fasque animi, sanctosque recessus,*
> *Mentis, et inoctum generoso pectus honesto.*[1]

And it was not the philosopher, but the civil lawyer, that Cicero directed to rest contented with external actions; teaching in fact that the laws are concerned with physical objects, philosophers with what can be learned by reason and intelligence.[2] To what level, then, will philosophy sink under

---

[1] Persius, *Satirae* II, 73: 'Well-ordered law and justice of the soul, and of the sacred recesses of the mind, and a spirit pervaded with noble honor.'
[2] Cicero, *De Officiis* IV, 17, 88.

the Christians, which was once, under the pagans, so holy and noble!
Many of the ancients complained of the [moral] laxity of Aristotle; but
he, nonetheless, was much more elevated [than Pufendorf], and the
Schools did well to follow him on this point. Indeed, Aristotelian philosophy bases all of the virtues splendidly on universal justice; and we owe
it not only to ourselves, but also to society, above all to that in which we
find ourselves with God, by the natural law written in our hearts, that we
have a soul imbued with free thoughts, and a will which tends constantly
toward the just. Nor is it clear what place oaths (whose efficacy the author
thinks to be very great) can have in natural law, if this law does not concern itself with what is internal. Therefore he who has control of the
education or instruction of others is obligated, by natural law, to form
minds with eminent precepts, and to take care that the practice of virtue,
almost like a second nature, guides the will toward the good. This is the
most trustworthy method of education because, according to Aristotle's
fine saying, customs [*mores*] are stronger than laws.[1] And while it is
possible that someone, by hope or by fear, will repress wicked thoughts,
so that they do no harm (a thing which is, however, hard to attain),
nonetheless he will never succeed in making them useful. Therefore whoever is not well-intentioned will often sin, at least by omission. Thus the
author's hypothesis about a soul which is internally corrupt and outwardly
innocent is not very safe and not very probable. And those scholars are
truly to be praised who, though following Pufendorfian theory on other
points, correct this excessively hard and objectionable doctrine, and
assuredly deny to natural law all concern with what is internal, but at least
restore it to moral philosophy and to natural theology. But since nobody
can deny that law, duty, sins in relation to God, and good actions are also
naturally located in the interior, where – I ask them – shall we consider
these topics, which certainly pertain to law and to natural justice, if not
in the science of natural law? (Unless one wants to construct another
universal jurisprudence, to include natural law not only in relation to men,
but also to God; something which appears vain and superfluous to
everybody.) In the science of law, rather, it is best to derive human
justice, as from a spring, from the divine, to make it complete. Surely the
idea of the just, no less than that of the true and the good, relates to God,
and above all to God, who is the measure of all things. And the rules
which are common [to divine and human justice] certainly enter into the
science [of natural law], and ought to be considered in universal jurisprudence, whose precepts natural theology will use as well. Therefore we
cannot agree with those who, contrary to truth, restrict the natural law;

[1] Aristotle, *Nicomachean Ethics* x, 9 (1180b).

although this error is not dangerous provided that one reserves the consideration of internal probity for another part of philosophy, and not simply for the precepts of revealed religion.

IV

So much for what regards the end and the object [of natural law]; it remains now to treat the efficient cause of this law, which our author does not correctly establish. He, indeed, does not find it in the nature of things and in the precepts of right reason which conform to it, which emanate from the divine understanding, but (what will appear to be strange and contradictory) in the command of a superior. Indeed, Book I, chapter I, part I, defines duty as 'the human action exactly conforming to the prescriptions of the laws in virtue of an obligation'. And soon chapter II, part 2, defines law as 'a command by which the superior obliges the subject to conform his actions to what the law itself prescribes'. If we admit this, no one will do his duty spontaneously; also, there will be no duty when there is no superior to compel its observance; nor will there be any duties for those who do not have a superior. And since, according to the author, duty and acts prescribed by justice coincide (because his whole natural jurisprudence is contained in the doctrine of duty), it follows that all law is prescribed by a superior. This paradox, brought out by Hobbes above all, who seemed to deny to the state of nature, that is [a condition] in which there are no superiors, all binding justice whatsoever (although even he is inconsistent), is a view to which I am astonished that anyone could have adhered. Now, then, will he who is invested with the supreme power do nothing against justice if he proceeds tyrannically against his subjects; who arbitrarily despoils his subjects, torments them, and kills them under torture; who makes war on others without cause? On the basis of this principle several learned followers of our author do not allow any voluntary law of nations whatever, for the reason, among others, that peoples cannot bring about a law by reciprocal pacts, not having the obligation rendered valid by any superior. With this argument too much is proved, namely that men cannot set up any superior for themselves by consent and agreement: which is contrary to what [even] Hobbes admits. It is true that it seems that one can give some remedy for this doctrine by considering God as the superior of all, which is precisely what our author does afterwards. Indeed, someone will say, this proposition [of Pufendorf's] is only apparently scandalous, but that, if one looks at it thoroughly, one can perceive nothing reprehensible in it, since it corrects itself and carries its own remedy with it. In truth, a condition of existence without any superiors can be imagined by somebody for a didactic purpose, but cannot really exist, everybody being by nature subordinated to God. Thus agreements among men, as much as international treaties, establish a law, whose validity God will assure. It is without doubt most true, that God is by nature superior to all; all the same the doctrine itself, which makes all law derivative from the command of a superior, is not freed of scandal and errors, however one justifies it. Indeed, not to mention that which Grotius justly observed, namely that there would be a natural obligation even on the hypothesis – which is impossible – that God does not exist,[1] or if one but left the divine existence out of consideration; since care for one's own preservation and well-being certainly lays on men many requirements about taking care of others, as even Hobbes perceives in part (and this obligatory tie bands of brigands confirm by their example, who, while they are enemies of others, are obliged to respect certain duties among themselves[2] – although, as I have observed, a natural law based on this source alone would be very imperfect); to pass over all this, one must pay attention to this fact: that God is praised because he is just. There must be, then, a certain justice – or rather a supreme justice – in God, even though no one is superior to him, and he, by the spontaneity of his excellent nature, accomplishes all things well, such that no one can reasonably complain of him. Neither the norm of conduct itself, nor the essence of the just, depends on his free decision, but rather on eternal truths, objects of the divine intellect, which constitute, so to speak, the essence of divinity itself; and it is right that our author is reproached by theologians when he maintains the contrary; because, I believe, he had not seen the wicked consequences which arise from it. Justice, indeed, would not be an essential attribute of God, if he himself established justice and law by his free will. And, indeed, justice follows certain rules of equality and of proportion [which are] no less founded in the immutable nature of things, and in the divine ideas, than are the principles of arithmetic and of geometry. So that no one will maintain that justice and goodness originate in the divine will, without at the same time maintaining that truth originates in it as well: an unheard-of paradox by which Descartes showed how great can be the errors of great men;[3] as if the reason that a triangle has three

[1] Grotius, De Jure Belli ac Pacis, Prolegomena, section 11.
[2] Cf. Plato, Republic I (351c–d).
[3] Descartes, Reply to the Six Objections, pt. 6. In this work, Descartes urges that 'it is self-contradictory that the will of God should not have been from eternity indifferent to all that has come to pass or that will ever occur, because we can form no conception of anything good or true, or anything to be believed or to be performed or to be omitted, the idea of which existed in the divine understanding before God's will determined him so to act as to bring it to

sides, or that two contrary propositions are incompatible, or that God himself exists, is that God has willed it so. It would follow from this, too, that which some people have imprudently said, that God could with justice condemn an innocent person, since he could make it such that precisely this would constitute justice. Doubtless those who attain to such aberrations do not distinguish justice from unaccountability [ἀνιπε-υθυνία]. God, because of his supreme power over all things, cannot be made to submit his accounts [ἀνυπεύθυνος], inasmuch as he can be neither constrained nor punished, nor is he required to give reasons to anyone whomsoever; but, because of his justice, he accomplishes all things in a way which satisfies every wise man, and above all himself. This has also not a little relevance for the practice of true piety: it is not enough, indeed, that we be subject to God just as we would obey a tyrant; nor must he be only feared because of his greatness, but also loved because of his goodness: which right reason teaches, no less than the Scriptures. To this lead the best principles of universal jurisprudence, which collaborate also with wise theology and bring about true virtue. Thus he who acts well, not out of hope or fear, but by an inclination of his soul, is so far from not behaving justly that, on the contrary, he acts more justly than all others, imitating, in a certain way, as a man, divine justice. Whoever, indeed, does good out of love for God or of his neighbor, takes pleasure precisely in the action itself (such being the nature of love) and does not need any other incitement, or the command of a superior; for that man the saying that the law is not made for the just is valid.[1] To such a degree is it repugnant to reason to say that only the law or constraint make a man just; although it must be conceded that those who have not reached this point of spiritual perfection are only susceptible of obligation by hope or by fear; and that the prospect of divine vengeance, which one cannot escape even by death,

pass...Thus, to illustrate, God did not will...the three angles of a triangle to be equal to two right angles because he knew that they could not be otherwise. On the contrary,...it is because he willed the three angles of a triangle to be necessarily equal to two right angles that this is true and cannot be otherwise...To one who pays attention to God's immensity, it is clear that nothing at all can exist which does not depend on him. This is true not only of everything that subsists, but of all order, of every law, and of every reason of truth and goodness...For if any reason for what is good had preceded his pre-ordination, it would have determined him towards that which it was best to bring about; but on the contrary because he determined himself towards these things which ought to be accomplished, for that reason, as it stands in Genesis, they are very good; that is to say, the reason for their goodness is the fact that he wished to create them so.' (English edition of R. M. Eaton, Charles Scribner's Sons, New York, 1927, pp. 264–6.)

[1] I Timothy I. 9; also in St Thomas Aquinas, *Summa Theologica* II, I, Q 96, art. 5.

can better than anything else make apparent to them the absolute and universal necessity to respect law and justice [*juris et aequi*].

V

From this one can infer of how much interest it is to youth, and much more to the state, that better principles of juridical science be established. Nor is chapter ii, part 4, correct in saying that he who recognizes no superior cannot be constrained by necessity: as if the very nature of things and care for one's own happiness and safety did not have their own requirements; and many things which are ordained by reason itself in order that, following the guidance of our best nature, we will not attract evil to ourselves, or come to lose the good. This precept of reason, since it considers others as well, to whose advantage it is, is a part of justice. And, in truth, however much some people understand duty in a broader sense, extending it to every act required by virtue, even when others are not concerned by it, or the interest of others is not taken into consideration (and in this sense it can be said that our duties include even courage and temperance, or, for example, the matter of caring for our health, in as much as, if people do not do it, a fault is imputed to them), nonetheless I do not reject the use which our author makes of this word, restricting duty to that which is prescribed by law. But my analysis of this is scarcely recognized by our author, [namely] that in a universal society governed by God every virtue, as has already been said many times, is comprehended among the obligations of universal justice; and not only external acts, but also all of our sentiments are regulated by a certain rule of law; thus those who are worthy of being philosophers of law [must] consider not only concord among men [*humanae tranquilitatis*], but also friendship with God, the possession of which assures us of an enduring felicity. We are not born for ourselves alone, but a part of us is claimed by our neighbors, and by God the whole. Nor do I see how the author, acute as he is, could easily be absolved of the contradiction into which he falls, when he makes all juridical obligations derivative from the command of a superior (which we have shown through citations of him), while afterwards in Book I, chapter ii, part 5, he states that in order that one have a superior it is necessary that they [superiors] possess not only the force [necessary] to exercise coercion, but also that they have a just cause to justify their power over my person. Consequently the justice of the cause is antecedent to this same superior, contrary to what had been asserted. Well, then, if the source of law is the will of a superior and, inversely, a justifying cause of law is necessary in order to have a superior, a circle is created, than which none was ever

more manifest. From what will the justice of the cause derive, if there is
not yet a superior, from whom, supposedly, the law may emanate? And it
would be strange that so acute a person could take such measures against
himself, if we did not know that to those who undertake to maintain
paradoxes it happens easily that, when good sense prevails in them, they
forget their own doctrines. It is useful to record the words of the author
himself, so that it will not be thought that we are falsifying the sense of
them:

Obligation is properly introduced into the mind of a man by a superior, that is,
a person who has not only the power to bring harm at once upon those who
resist, but also just grounds for his claim that the freedom of our will should be
limited at his discretion. For when these conditions are found in anyone, he has
only to intimate his wish, and there must arise in men's minds a fear that is
tempered with respect...for whoever is unable to assign any other reason why
he wishes to impose an obligation upon me against my will, except mere power,
can indeed frighten me into thinking it better for a time to obey him, to avoid a
greater evil; but, once that fear is removed, nothing further remains to prevent
my acting according to my will rather than his. Conversely, if he has indeed the
reasons which make it my duty to obey him, but lacks the power of inflicting
any harm on me, I may with impunity neglect his commands, unless a more
powerful person comes to assert the authority upon which I have trampled. Now
the reasons why one may rightly demand that another obey him are: in case some
conspicuous benefits have come to the latter from the former; or if it be proved
that he wishes the other well, and is also better able than the man himself to
provide for him, and at the same time actually claims control over the other; and
finally, if a man has willingly subjected himself to another and agreed to his
control.

These are the author's words.

But whoever examines carefully what he says, will not fail to notice that
he is neither consistent, nor resolves the difficulty. Indeed, if neither
coercion without reasons, nor the latter without force is sufficient, why
– I ask – when force ceases and reason alone remains, shall I not return to
that liberty which it is said I had when, before the application of force,
reason alone was present? What the author says, in fact – that, failing
fear, no one can stop me from behaving according to my own will rather
than according to someone else's – would be valid even if reasons existed.
On the other hand, if reasons restrain even by themselves, why did they
not already restrain by themselves, before fear arose? And what force, I
pray you, can fear give to reasons, except itself – which it would not
itself provide even without reasons? Or will this not very durable sentiment impress some indelible character on unwilling minds? Suppose that
a man who owes obedience to another solely in virtue of reasons, is afterwards also constrained by force on the part of the other, and that he

persists nonetheless in his soul's original disposition, by which he does not want to obey any more than he is constrained [to do]; I do not see why, once constrained, he ought to remain in submission in perpetuity. Supposing, for example, that a Christian who is ill falls into the power of a Turkish doctor, by whom he is made to practice hygienic precepts that he already knew [to be efficacious] for some time, but which are now imposed on him coercively; when, afterwards, he is offered an occasion to escape, would he be obliged to [observe] temperance more than he had before his imprisonment? One or the other, then: either reasons oblige prior to force, or they do not obligate any longer when force fails.

The things [which I have indicated] show sufficiently that the author is lacking sound principles on which to found the true reasons for laws, about which he himself has arbitrarily supposed principles which cannot be maintained. For the rest, the foundations of jurisprudence, whether common to all law (even to that which is derived solely from equity),[1] or proper to law in a narrow sense (which involves a superior), have been indicated by us elsewhere. To summarize, we shall say in general that: the end of natural law is the good of those who observe it; its object, all that which concerns others and is in our power; finally, its efficient cause in us is the light of eternal reason, kindled in our minds by the divinity. These principles, so plain and simple, have, I believe, appeared too obvious to certain acute men, and for this reason they have thought up others which are more paradoxical, capable of attracting [attention] by the appearance of novelty, because neither the fruitfulness of the former [plain and simple principles] nor the imperfection of the latter [paradoxical and novel principles] has been adequately recognized.

This, most eminent man, I have believed worth writing to you, so that it will be clear that Pufendorf's work, although it is not to be despised, has nonetheless need of many corrections in its very principles. For the rest, there is no time to go into particulars.

---

[1] Cf. Aristotle, *Nicomachean Ethics* 1137a, for the idea that equity is more comprehensive than merely legal justice.

3. On Natural Law

This short piece shows, perhaps more clearly than any other, how much some of Leibniz' political views remained medieval, how much force the ideas of hierarchy and natural subordination still had for him. It relates Leibniz to some of his German predecessors – particularly Althusius – and makes clear the gap which separates him from, e.g. the great English theorists of the seventeenth century. (The present translation follows the German text to be found in Guhrauer's *Deutsche Schriften*.)

I

Justice is a social duty [*Tugend*], or a duty which preserves society.

A society [*Gemeinschaft*] is a union of different men for a common purpose.

A natural society is one which is demanded by nature [*so die Natur haben will*].

The signs by which one can conclude that nature demands something, are that nature has given us a desire and the powers or force to fulfill it: for nature does nothing in vain.

Above all, when the matter involves a necessity or a permanent [*beständigen*] utility: for nature everywhere achieves the best.

The most perfect society is that whose purpose is the general and supreme happiness [*Glückseligkeit*].

Natural law is that which preserves or promotes natural societies.

The first natural society is between man and wife, for it is necessary to preserve the human race.

The second [is] between parents and children; it arises at once out of the former; for when children are once created, or freely adopted, they must be reared, that is, governed and nourished. In return they owe their parents obedience and help after they are raised. For [it] is in hope of such gratitude [that] such societies are preserved and promoted, though nature demands them primarily for the sake of children. For they may one day

77

reach perfection. Parents, then, exist primarily for the sake of children, [and] the present, which does not last long, for the future.

The third natural society is between master and servant [*Herr und Knecht*], which is conformable to nature when a person lacks understanding but does not lack the strength to nourish himself. For such a person is a servant by nature who must work as another directs him, and [who] derives therefrom his livelihood; the rest is for the master. For everything that the servant is, he is on account of his master, since all other powers exist only for the sake of the understanding [*Verstand*]. In this case the understanding is in the master, but all other powers are in the servant.[1] Since such a servant exists for the sake of the master, his master owes him only his maintenance, for his [the master's] sake, in order that he not ruin him.

It is to be understood [that this would be true] if there were no hope that the servant might attain understanding, for otherwise the master would be responsible for promoting his servant's freedom through education, [at least] in so far as this is necessary to the happiness of the servant. To admit the truth alone, I doubt whether an example of such a servitude can be found, in which the servant exists entirely for the sake of the master; especially because souls are immortal and hence can sometimes attain understanding and the happiness of that life [which is] based on it. In my opinion, therefore, this society exists only between men and cattle. For [even] if a man were born quite stupid and incapable of any education, we would still not have the right to martyr, to kill or to sell him to the barbarians. But if souls were mortal, then this servitude could exist among whole peoples, which are almost as dumb as cattle, and so could be kept in this stupidity for the benefit of their masters – at least, certainly, to the extent that children can be reared not to advance beyond cattle. Now, since the general rules of justice [*Gerechtigkeit*] are taught, which even atheists [*Gottlose*] must accept, it seems that one can deal with the natural servants of men, in the case that such men exist. Even if such servitude is not to be suffered in all its sharpness among men, there is still something which is similar and comes close to it, which is sometimes conformable to nature. To summarize, natural servitude takes place among unintelligent men, in so far as it is not restricted by the rules concerning the fear of God.

The fourth natural society is the household, which is composed of all the above-mentioned societies – some or all. Its purpose is [the satisfaction of] daily needs.

[1] Cf. Aristotle, *Politics* I, v, 1254a; here Leibniz follows Aristotle rather closely. Cf. also Hegel, *Phenomenology*, 'Master and Servant'.

The fifth natural society is the civil [*bürgerliche*] society. If it is small, it is called a city; a province is a society of different cities, and a kingdom or a large dominion is a society of different provinces – all to attain happiness for to be secure in it – whose members sometimes live together in a city sometimes spread out over the land. Its purpose is temporal welfare.

The sixth natural society is the Church of God, which would probably have existed among men even without revelation [*Offenbarung*], and been preserved and spread by pious and holy men. Its purpose is eternal happiness. And it is no wonder that I call it a natural society, since there is a natural religion and a desire for immortality planted in us. This society of the saints [*Heiligen*] is catholic or universal, and binds the whole human race together. If revelation is added, this bond is not torn, but strengthened.[1]

II

CLASSIFICATION OF SOCIETIES OR COMMUNITIES (*DIVISIO SOCIETATUM*)

Every society is equal [*gleich*] or unequal. [It is] equal when one has as much power in it as another, unequal when one rules another.

Every society is either unlimited [*unbeschränkt*] or limited. An unlimited society concerns the whole life and the common good [*gemeine Beste*]. A limited society concerns certain subjects, for example trade and commerce, navigation, warfare and travel.[2]

An unlimited equal society exists between true friends. And such [a society] exists particularly between man and wife, between parents and grown children, between masters and freedmen, and in general between all intelligent men who are adequately acquainted with each other.

An unlimited unequal society exists between rulers and subjects. Such rule happens for the sake either of improvement or of conservation. If it is for the sake of improvement, it really takes place between parents and children, and also between us and those whom we accept in place of children, or whom we raise so that they receive their welfare from us, and are under our sole rule. This has no place between teacher and student, since the latter is subject [to the former] only in a certain degree or way; here,

---

[1] Leibniz' fifth and sixth degrees of natural society are grafted onto Aristotelian distinctions, and appear to be derived from Johannes Althusius' *Politicae Methodice Digesta* (1603), ch. 5 ff.

[2] Cf. Burke, *Reflections on the Revolution in France* VII, 2a (passage cited in introduction, p. 22n).

however, we are speaking of unlimited society which involves the whole of life and welfare. Stupid men are grown children. But if such rule [*Regierung*] is for the sake of conservation, it exists between master and servant and consists in this, that the master makes the servant's welfare secure, while the latter submits to the rule of the former.

All of these societies are simple or composite [*zusammengesetzt*], and also [exist] between a few or many men. Accordingly all unlimited or comprehensive societies [*Lebensgesellschaften*] can be reduced to certain points, namely to education and instruction, rule and obedience, friendship or co-operation, *adjutorium*, etc.

Children, in so far as they have been reared, already owe obedience as far as their powers permit, [and] as they attain understanding, friendship and assistance to the master as well, although their education is not completed.

Man and wife are bound by nature to friendship and mutual assistance in a brotherly way. In the same way parents and children, and also relatives and members of a community [*Gemeine*] must have an understanding of each other; for understanding belongs to friendship.

One can educate, who is himself being educated, and also rule, while he is being ruled. But there must be subordination in this case.

All unlimited societies do indeed aim at welfare, but they do not all attain it; hence more men have had to unite to create greater and stronger communities. Thus households, clans, villages, monasteries, orders, cities, provinces, and finally the whole human race, which also constitutes a community under the rule of God, [have united].

If everything in the world were arranged in the most perfect way, then, first of all, parents, children and relatives would be the best of friends, and whole families would have chosen an art of living, would have arranged everything that they have to this end, would abide in it and continue to perfect themselves in their art and direct their children to the same end, and would marry people of the same calling [*Beruf*] in order to be united through education from their parents. These clans would make up guilds or castes out of which cities would arise; these would enter into provinces and all countries, finally, would stand under the church of God.[1]

---

[1] Leibniz' views on this point did not change very much in later life, as, e.g. his letter to Peter the Great (1716) shows. See *Projet d'un Mémoire de Leibniz au Czar en vue des Progrès des Arts et des Sciences et des Écoles dans l'Empire Russe*, in *Leibniz et Pierre le Grand*, by A. Foucher de Careil, Paris, 1874.

4. Notes on Social Life

This short work, which is undated, is somewhat surprising in the use Leibniz makes of the Golden Rule, which he turns into a prudential political maxim. (The present translation omits a few passages which refer to writers who are no longer read at all; the original text is to be found in vol. II of Grua's *Textes Inédits*.)

The place of others is the true point of perspective in politics as well as in morality. And the precept of Jesus Christ to put oneself in another's place serves not only the object of which our Lord spoke, that is to say morality, in order to know our duties toward our neighbor, but also in politics, in order to know the intentions which our neighbor may have against us.[1] One will never understand these [intentions] better than by putting himself in his place, or when one imagines oneself councilor and minister of state of an enemy or suspect prince. One thinks then what he could think or undertake, and what one could advise him to do. This fiction excites our thoughts, and has served me more than once in properly divining what was to be done. It may be, in truth, that one's neighbor is neither so mal-intentioned, nor so clear-sighted as I make him out; but the surest thing is to imagine things at their worst in politics, that is when it is a question of being careful and of being defensive, just as it is necessary to imagine [things] at their best in morality, when it is a question of harming and offending others. However, morality itself permits this [kind of] politics, when the evil that one fears is great, that is, when the taking of security measures does not cause a greater number of greater evils than the evil [itself], and there is an *actio damni infecti* in natural law...[2]

Thus one can say that the place of others, in morality as in politics, is a place proper to help us discover considerations which would not otherwise come to us; and that everything which we would find unjust if we were in the place of others, must seem to us to be suspect of injustice. And, moreover, everything which we would not wish if we were in this place must make us stop and examine it [what would not be wished] more closely.

[1] Leibniz' turning of this moral maxim into an expedient of political utility is rather surprising – but no more so than the concluding paragraph, which turns on a cynicism which one does not ordinarily associate with Leibniz.

[2] See note 2 to the *Codex Iuris Gentium* (below, p. 166n).

Thus the sense of the principle is: do not do or do not refuse lightly that which you would not like to be done to you or which one would not refuse to you.[1] Think about it more carefully, after putting yourself in the other's place, which will furnish you with considerations proper to a better knowledge of what to do. One can still distinguish the will which one would have while in the place of another, which can be unjust (as in not wishing to pay at all), and the judgment which one would make himself, as one will always be obliged to avow that one must pay...[2]

One should always look at people from their good side, except when one is obliged to embark with them on some affair; for then it is reasonable to take precautions.

We should guard against demanding useless things of people, giving superfluous instructions, explaining with excessive minuteness that which a person himself should decide: in doing this, indeed, one disheartens him, making him believe that he cannot do anything except that which is explicitly and completely determined by his assignment.

It is sometimes useful that we allow someone to do us an injury in a matter of little consequence, for if some great man is involved in it, it will give him some inclination (if he is good-natured) to do us good in some other situation; and one can handle the affair so that the second [situation] is more important to us than the first.

5. Felicity
(*c.* 1694-8?)

In this brief piece, probably written during the 1690s, Leibniz attempted to connect his theory of justice as the charity of the wise man with his psychology and his theology. (There are two versions of this work, both contained in vol. II

[1] Leibniz formulates the Golden Rule negatively in this case, as does Hobbes in *Leviathan* 14-15; cf. *Meditation on the Common Concept of Justice* (above, pp. 55ff) in which Leibniz argues that there is a *continuum* between abstaining from harm and doing good.

[2] Cf. Kant, *The Metaphysical Elements of Justice*, sect. 49, E, 'The Penal Law and the Law of Pardon': 'No one suffers punishment because he has willed the punishment, but because he has willed a punishable action' (J. Ladd trans., Library of Liberal Arts, New York 1965, p. 105).

of Grua's *Textes Inédits*; the present translation is of the first version, which is shorter and simpler than the second. A comparison of the two versions is most instructive, particularly since Grua prints, in brackets, all the phrases and sentences excised by Leibniz in the final version.)

1. Virtue is the habit of acting according to wisdom. It is necessary that practice accompany knowledge.

2. Wisdom is the science of felicity, [and] is what must be studied above all other things.

3. Felicity is a lasting state of pleasure. Thus it is good to abandon or moderate pleasures which can be injurious, by causing misfortunes or by blocking [the attainment of] better and more lasting pleasures.

4. Pleasure is a knowledge or feeling of perfection, not only in ourselves, but also in others, for in this way some further perfection is aroused in us.

5. To love is to find pleasure in the perfection of another.

6. Justice is charity or a habit of loving conformed to wisdom. Thus when one is inclined to justice, one tries to procure good for everybody, so far as one can, reasonably, but in proportion to the needs and merits of each: and even if one is obliged sometimes to punish evil persons, it is for the general good.

6a. Now it is necessary to explain the feeling or the knowledge of perfection. The confused perception of some perfection constitutes the pleasure of sense, but this pleasure can be [productive] of greater imperfections which are born of it, as a fruit with a good taste and a good odor can conceal a poison. This is why one must shun the pleasures of sense, as one shuns a stranger, or, sooner, a flattering enemy.

7. Knowledge is of two kinds, that of facts and that of reasons. That of facts is perception, that of reasons is intelligence.

8. Knowledge of reasons perfects us because it teaches us universal and eternal truths, which are manifested in the perfect Being. But knowledge of facts is like that of the streets of a town, which serves us while we stay there, [but] after [leaving] which we don't wish to burden our memory any longer.

8a. The pleasures of sense which most closely approach pleasures of the mind, and are the most pure and the most certain, are that of music and that of symmetry, the former [being pleasure] of the ears, the latter of the eyes; for it is easy to understand the principles [*raisons*] of harmony, this perfection which gives us pleasure. The sole thing to be feared in this respect is to use it too often.

9. One need not shun at all pleasures which are born of intelligence or

of reasons, as one penetrates the reason of the reason of perfections, that is to say as one sees them flow from their source, which is the absolutely perfect Being.

10. The perfect Being is called God. He is the ultimate reason of things, and the cause of causes. Being the sovereign wisdom and the sovereign power, he has always chosen the best and acts always in an orderly way.

11. One is happy when he loves God, and God, who has done everything perfectly, cannot fail to arrange everything thus, to elevate created beings to the perfection of which they are capable through union with him, which can subsist only through the spirit.

12. But one cannot love God without knowing his perfections, or his beauty. And since we can know him only in his emanations, these are two means of seeing his beauty, namely in the knowledge of eternal truths (which explain [their own] reasons in themselves), and in the knowledge of the Harmony of the Universe (in applying reasons to facts). That is to say, one must know the marvels of reason and the marvels of nature.

13. The marvels of reason and of eternal truths which our mind discovers in itself [are essential] in the sciences of reasoning about numbers, about figures, about good and evil, about justice and injustice.

14. The marvels of physical nature are the system of the universe, the structure of the bodies of animals, the causes of the rainbow, of magnetism, of the ebb and flow [of the tides], and a thousand other similar things.

15. One must hold as certain that the more a mind desires to know order, reason, the beauty of things which God has produced, and the more he is moved to imitate this order in the things which God has left to his direction, the happier he will be.

16. It is most true, as a result, that one cannot know God without loving one's brother, that one cannot have wisdom without having charity (which is the real touchstone of virtue), and that one even advances one's own good in working for that of others: for it is an eternal law of reason and of the harmony of things that the works of each [person] will follow it. Thus the sovereign wisdom has so well regulated all things that our duty must also be our happiness, that all virtue produces its [own] reward, and that all crime punishes itself, sooner or later.

6. Portrait of the Prince
(1679)

This relatively early work (1679) was written for George Frederick of Hanover (d. 1679) in the 'mirror of princes' style. Modelled partly on Pliny's *Panegyricus*, written for Trajan, the more fulsome and extravagant praises of Duke George are offset by a number of interesting passages on the proper education of princes, on the kinds of virtues which they ought to cultivate, which become particularly important when one recalls that Leibniz favored relatively absolute concentrated power and had to rely on princely virtue as the only check to arbitrary rule. The *Portrait* reveals Leibniz' extraordinarily wide acquaintance with classical writers, and contains a passage on the nature of justice which is, in many ways, his most radical pronouncement on that subject. (The original text is contained in vol. IV of Klopp's edition.)

Since the order of states is founded on the authority of those who govern them, and on the dependence of peoples, nature, which destines men for civil life, causes them to be born with different qualities, some to command, others to obey,[1] so that the power of sovereigns in monarchies, and the inequality of those who command and those who obey in republics, are founded no less in nature than in law, and in virtue than in fortune: thus princes must be above their subjects by their virtue, and by their natural qualities, as they are above them by the authority which the laws give them to reign according to natural law and civil law – just as the first kings of the world, who, having been elevated to the governance of peoples through their virtue and their intellectual advantages, commanded as much by nature as by law, and by merit as by fortune.

It may happen, however, that though nature wishes that those to whom she has given many great qualities and who have the most virtue always rule over others, the laws of many states ordain, on the contrary, that children be the heirs of the goods and of the power of their fathers, because, as a result of the prudence of legislators and of human weakness, the civil law is often contrary to natural law; but the empire of great princes has always been founded on the advantages of nature and of fortune, on the authority of virtue and on the power of law.

Indeed, one cannot question the authority which virtue and merit give to even those men [who are] without position and without [official]

[1] Cf. Aristotle, *Politics* I, 1252a ff.

dignity in a republic. Scipio is a fine example of this. In the city of Rome he was without employment after the glory of so many triumphs, and nonetheless he had more authority in the Senate and among the people than the consuls, tribunes and praetors, because the prudence and the valor of so great a captain struggled in the hearts of the Romans against the rights of those who exercised the sovereign magistracies.[1] And if goodness had not restrained him, he could have from that time made the Romans feel the cruel fury of Sylla and of Marius; instead of which he preferred to leave his ungrateful country forever. Thus Scipio would have enjoyed a power to which his eminent virtues entitled him in Rome, if the laws of the republic had not disposed differently of the sovereign and legitimate authority.

No one is unaware, either, of the force of laws which have caused so many bad princes to reign, without any other support than that of the laws. One must, for all that, grant that the struggle of nature against the laws and of virtue against fortune, has often troubled the calm of their states, and caused revolutions in monarchies. It deprived Saul of his crown, to give it to David.[2] It caused Charlemagne to supersede the posterity of Clovis,[3] and it gave the same crown of France to King Hugh Capet and his descendants:[4] providence and destiny having thus arranged human affairs to make it clear that virtue is no less powerful than fortune.

It is necessary, then, that the dominance of princes be equally based on the advantages of nature, on virtue, and on the laws, to bring to an end the struggle of virtue and of merit against the laws and against fortune, in order to assure the public tranquility, and to avoid being exposed to the effects of the power of virtue, which has so often triumphed over legitimate power. This is the advantage which is visible in the person of Your Most Serene Highness.[5] His authority is doubly legitimate: it is based on the law of nature, which requires that the most perfect command the others, since he is above his subjects by his virtue and by his natural qualities; it is established by the civil law, since he was born the son of a Prince in an hereditary state; it is based on the divine law which commands peoples to obey their sovereigns. And I might add that it is founded on a particular providence of God, who has added to so many illustrious advantages the high position which they merit, and who has seen fit to make widely-known his piety and his zeal for religion, which is the

---

[1] The reference is to P. Cornelius Scipio Africanus (237–183 B.C.), the great general who retired to the countryside rather than overthrow the Roman state.
[2] I Kings 28. 17.
[3] Partly through the efforts of his father, Pipin.
[4] In 987, after the death of Louis V, last of the Carolingians.
[5] Leibniz' *Portrait of the Prince* was written for George Frederick of Brunswick-Lüneburg (1625–79), ruler of Hanover.

most certain foundation of sovereigns and which restrains subjects by hope and by fear, which are the two principles which move men to the good and which keep them away from evil; such that one should not be surprised if his government has brought him so much glory and [good] reputation, and if the obedience of his peoples is accompanied by admiration and respect.

But because the great virtues come from nature, from nobility and from education, and because these last two advantages depend on fortune, the greatness of princes is the work of nature, of fortune, and of virtue.

Nature must give them, as she has to Your Most Serene Highness, all the [appropriate] dispositions toward great qualities and heroic virtues: a great mind [*esprit*], a solid judgment, an invincible courage, an extraordinary goodness, and a strong inclination towards virtue and glory.

The mind is the principle of virtue and of learning [*science*] which disposes men toward great actions and to the important tasks in life. The one and the other have need of the lights of nature; for true virtue cannot be exercised without knowledge, and learning can only be acquired by reasoning, and being always proportioned to natural dispositions, it cannot be perfect, if it does not suppose a great source of mental power.

If the men who are above others through their positions and their dignities, are obliged to possess more learning and virtue because they must instruct them and serve as an example to them, it is also necessary that they surpass them in greatness of mind. Such that kings and princes who are so highly placed that they see nothing above them in the world must have an eminent mind, capable of knowing the interests of their states, of thinking through public matters, and of finding the means which can lead them to their goal – which must always be the public good, the glory and the repose of peoples. Your Most Serene Highness possesses this advantage in an admirable way; for if nature and fortune have destined him for commanding, which is of all actions the most exalted and the most difficult, nature has given him a mind which is quick, penetrating, and of an extraordinary breadth and force.

But it is not sufficient that princes have a mind which is capable of deliberation [*consultation*] and which can discover, as a result of [its] quickness and imaginativeness, many means to make their plans succeed; it is [also] necessary that nature give them a solid judgment to make a choice between them, to make appropriate decisions, to manage promptly the matters which arise in peace and in war, and to make a just assessment of persons and of things, [which is] so necessary to dispose sovereigns to prudence. Learning can indeed provide some maxims for conduct, but it is for the judgment to apply them, to make up for a lack of means, to delimit in practice those which are general and indeterminate, to take notice of those which lead to certain collisions, and, in fine, to make particular rules for itself, on the occasions when those of morality and of politics are lacking – which happens often, because these maxims are limited, while [possible] occurrences are infinite because of the diversity of circumstances which arise.

Such are the results of judgment which appear marvellously in all the actions of Your Most Serene Highness, in his decisions, in the choice of means, and in his admirable discernment of men and of things. We should grant that it is the principal part of the human mind, that which most serves particular conduct, and which is all the more necessary to princes because it is infinitely more difficult to control oneself and to govern so many peoples. Moreover, since sovereigns are the images of the Divinity, they must be able, like Your Most Serene Highness, to regulate their interests by themselves and to make use of ministers [merely] for the execution of business, as God uses creatures to carry out the things which he alone has established and ordained. The mind and the judgment are not only necessary to princes to acquire heroic virtues: it is essential that nature give them the courage which is at the root of them, in order to combat the inclination which attaches men to pleasure and to life, to sustain great plans, and to resist the difficulties that accompany moderation, valor, and generosity, which come from nature rather than from habit.

There is a great difference between courageous men, and those to whom this name is given. In an army some fight for money, others for glory, some for fear of being punished or by the rigor of discipline, others by a natural impulsion, some because of the love which they have for the fatherland, or out of apprehension over shame and reproaches, others for their safety (who, seeing themselves pressed by extreme danger, do violence to themselves and to the enemies who are attacking them, drawing thereby confidence out of fear and hope out of despair). But the courage of sovereigns and of princes must come from nature, because it must be great to resist within themselves so many attachments to pleasure, and so many reasons to love life. It must be natural, because it must be constant, to serve as an example to subjects; and it must never measure itself by age or experience, because it must always be invincible, like that of Your Most Serene Highness, who shows by his fortitude in dangerous situations, and in his resolutions, and by his efforts in the burden of [public] affairs, that he fears death not at all, because the glory which is the sole remedy against this fate will make him live always in the memory of men and of all posterity.

It is not enough that princes have the mind, the judgment and the courage which dispose them toward [good] conduct and great actions. It is necessary that they have goodness, which is a natural penchant for those things which contribute to the life, to the reputation and to the fortune of men. It is a quality which comes from nature, for since cruelty is natural to wild beasts, man, who is directly opposed to them, must have naturally a contrary quality, which can only be goodness. It must be extraordinary in princes, because, having the power to do evil without punishment and without fear, they can be restrained only by a great goodness. It is that which disposes them toward justice, liberality, and clemency, which is the particular virtue of kings and princes. It is the source of their glory, the greatest security and the most faithful guardian of their persons, and the cause of the goodness of their reign. That of Trajan was so happy, thanks to his goodness, that he earned from the Senate and from the Roman people the nickname of 'Very Good' and 'Very Great'.[1] This Emperor was so persuaded that goodness is necessary to princes that, when he put his constable in possession of his office, by giving him his sword, he said to him that he ought to use it to defend himself, if he lived as a good prince, but that if he lived otherwise, he ought to use it on himself.[2] And Pliny said of him that, if he was the greatest of Romans, it was because he was the best of men.[3]

Indeed goodness is so admirable that it is even more excellent than virtue, since God, who is goodness itself, has no virtue. And Seneca even dared to say, according to the principles of his philosophy, that it is something greater to be able, and not to want to do evil, as a man, than not to be able and not to want to do evil, as God.[4]

In short it is certain that, if there are few generous men, it is because there are few who have natural goodness, which is ordinarily found only in persons of [good] birth – if we must believe history on this point, which, speaking of great men who were not of high rank, accuses them almost always of infidelity, of malice and cruelty: as Marius, the bravest and most valiant of Romans, who as a result of many fine actions obtained the seventh consulate, is condemned for his perfidies and for his peculations. But this quality is so admirable in Your Most Serene Highness that all those who have the honor to approach his person are amazed to see so rare a thing, so great a goodness with so much enlightenment and discernment. They are surprised to see so obliging a manner and so much mildness

[1] Pliny the Younger, *Panegyricus* II, 7, 322, 29.
[2] Sextus Aurelius Vittorius, *Liber de Caesaribus* 13, 9.
[3] Pliny the Younger, *Panegyricus* II, 4, 322, 14–17.
[4] Probably a reference to Seneca's *De Providentia* VI, 6.

G

[combined] with the grand bearing which nature has given him, and they never leave his presence but with the respect and affection which the one and the other inspire. People admire in Your Most Serene Highness the pains which he takes to lighten the load of his peoples, the goodness with which he maintains and protects his domestics and servants, and the small disposition which he has to believe and to listen to remarks which damage reputations. This is a sign of an excellent nature; for one must have inclinations [which are] completely devoted to the good, in order not to believe evil easily; one must be aware of those men who are pleased to establish their glory on the ruins of that of others, and it is essential to lack completely the weaknesses of human nature, in order not to take pleasure, by a secret comparison, in putting oneself above those whose defects one publicizes, and whose honor or reputation one blackens. It is a quality which all princes ought to have, like Your Most Serene Highness, in order to end the disorders which bad offices cause in courts, [and] in order to render useless the efforts of jealousy, and to disarm the envy which most often has an effect in these places in proportion as one abuses the credulity of kings and princes. Thus the government of Your Most Serene Highness, being founded on goodness, like that of Trajan, one must hope that he will always be happy; and if the Senate and the people of Rome hoped in earlier times for new Emperors of the goodness of Trajan and the felicity of Augustus, I dare say that one will have reason to hope for Your Most Serene Highness' goodness and happiness in his successors.

In fine nature must give to princes a strong inclination for virtue and for glory, because one cannot be truly virtuous, without taking pleasure in doing virtuous actions, and one is pleased only by things which one loves. Moreover the virtue of princes must serve as an example to peoples; this is why they must also love glory and have a particular inclination for honor, which makes virtue, which is the greatest of all external goods, and the only one which, in the created universe, can touch divinity, shine in this world. But since the glory of God is based on his goodness, his power, his justice, and his mercifulness, which shine in his works, and since he has no wish other than the good of men, it is also necessary that princes, who are portraits of him, not wish for honor except for the advancement of their subjects, and that they derive it always from virtue, of which it is the finest and the most worthy reward. It is for this reason that the Romans, having built temples [dedicated] to glory and to virtue, arranged them in such a way that it was necessary to pass through the temple of virtue to enter into that of glory. Virtue is difficult, but glory is agreeable, such that it is often glory which leads men to virtue, which animates them and sustains them in the dangers to which [the pursuit of] virtue exposes them. Indeed the magnificent pomp of the Roman triumphs caused them to fight with so great a valor that they won as many victories as they initiated battles. When Alexander passed the Hydaspes after so many dangers, he told the Athenians in his army that he exposed himself thus to earn their esteem;[1] and Cambysus, speaking to Cyrus, his son, told him that he should not at all fear to take part in the work and the hardships of the camp, and that the whole army would have its eyes turned on him to mitigate the pains that he would take and the difficulties which go along with virtue by the pleasure of this glory.[2] Such that there are few examples of virtue which have not been animated by glory or by fortune, unhappy virtue always having had few followers, and bringing about sympathy sooner than envy. But princes must love virtue for itself, and glory for virtue's sake, that is, as an example; because all praises and all the signs of honor and of glory are beneath virtue. This was the feeling of Fabius Maximus, who preferred the safety of the Roman republic to the applause of the people, and [preferred] virtue [which was] disapproved to ill-established glory[3] [*la vertu blamée à la gloire mal fondée*]. But to acquire virtue and glory, one must love hard work, dangers and pain, like Your Most Serene Highness, who dreads hardships not at all, who has no attachment to pleasures, and who fears not to mingle the sweat of his brow with the dust, as Pliny said of Trajan;[4] and one must be his own follower, like Your Most Serene Highness, who always intends to surmount his past glory by a new glory which is ever greater and better, as Plutarch said of Caesar.[5]

Nature having given princes mind, judgment, courage, and the love of virtue and of glory, it is essential that fortune be favorable to all these endowments, and that she second all of these fine dispositions by birth and by education.

Nobility is a great motive for cultivating these excellent natural qualities; for, without saying that the propensities of fathers, being as if imprinted in the blood, are often passed on to children, it is certain that men guide themselves by example, which can often have a greater effect on their minds than reason, and that inclination brings them to imitate domestic sooner then foreign examples: such that nobility, being nothing else than a succession of illustrious men in a single family, excites [men] to virtue by the force of the examples which it puts forward. One sees signs of this in history. A great Greek prince, getting himself ready for

---

[1] Plutarch, *Vita Alexandri* LX, 2 (698e).
[2] Xenophon, *Cyropaedia* I, VI.   [3] Livy, XXII, 15, 1.
[4] Pliny the Younger, *Panegyricus* XV, 4, 333, 30.
[5] Plutarch, *Vita Caesaris* LVIII, 2 (735a).

battle, said that he was animated by the glory of his ancestors,[1] and when a tribune of the Roman people accused the consul Posthumius of cowardice because of the disorder of his army, he asked him where the greatness of patrician courage was, since he was from those great Roman houses which were called patrician.[2] Which makes it clear that nobility brings about so great an obligation to virtue, by the examples which it sets, that one cannot free oneself from following them without [being subject to] reproach. It is for this reason that the noble houses have always been so honored. Among the Greeks the families which had provided many heroes had the reputation of being of divine origin, while those who had not this advantage were thought to come from men. This is why Herodotus, speaking of a prince of Samos, said that he was of the human race, that is, of a house which had not provided illustrious men, and which as a result could not attract to itself the respect and veneration of the people.[3]

But because nobility incites [men] to virtue the more as she is able to offer more examples of it, and because the glory of ancestors is more elevated and more striking, the birth of princes must enjoy equally these two endowments, antiquity and splendor, like the house of Your Most Serene Majesty, which is among the most ancient and illustrious in the world, and which for so many centuries has provided kings and the most renowned Emperors for Germany, and so many great princes for the Empire and for Italy. Its establishment in these two places, its riches and its great power have conserved for it such fine proofs of its purity, its antiquity and its splendor, that it is certain that there are few houses in Europe which can show so many certain signs of it, or which can be compared with the Most Serene House of Brunswick and of Lüneburg.

The [high] birth of princes must be accompanied by education, which gives the first impressions of virtue and of good habits, which forms the mind and the judgment through various kinds of knowledge and through good conduct, courage by bearing of arms and by exercises, goodness by the care [which one takes] not to do anyone a disservice, and to serve everyone, and love of virtue and of glory through good actions, through praises and through hatred of vice.

It is not necessary that princes possess all the varieties of knowledge: it is enough that they know those which are most useful for action and for government, like geography, moral science and political science, [those which are] the most honorable in respect to glory, such as [a knowledge of]

---

[1] Cf. Homer, *Iliad* VII, v. 198–9, and Leibniz' own marginal note: 'Ajax against Hector'.

[2] Sallust, *De Bello Jugurthino* LXXXV, 16.

[3] Herodotus III, 122–8; the reference is to Polycrates and Oroetes.

fortification and everything relating to war, and [those which are] the most agreeable in conversation, such as a knowledge of languages, of foreign courts, of *mores*, of the endowments and curiosities of [different] countries. Those kinds of knowledge which are the ornament of arms-bearing or of good birth can be learned by reflection and by reading, but princes ought to learn them sooner by conversation than by study, more in the world than in books, and more by practice than by theory. Reflection about themselves, and observation of the good conduct of others, experience and conversation with enlightened persons concerning matters which happen in different countries, the government and the example of great princes – [all of these] make more of an impression and instruct far better than the reasonings and the general maxims of politics, which often deceive in particular application, when the mind and the judgment have not been formed and exercised in practical affairs. Such that it is always necessary to combine practice with theory, and usage with precepts, in morality, in politics, and in the science of war. It is thus that Your Most Serene Majesty has learned all of these sciences more in the world than in books, and that, thanks to the pains of the late Most Serene Highness the Duke George,[1] his father of glorious memory, one of the greatest princes of the century, the most warlike and the most politic in the Empire, he has been raised in a way of living so far removed from softness that one ought not to be surprised if at present he is altogether tireless. But one can judge of the advantages of his education by [considering] the countries in which he was raised: in Germany, which possesses the glory of the title 'Roman Empire', which has carried its name throughout Europe and into a part of Africa, and which maintained its liberty against the Romans, of whom one can say that they learned to conquer the world, by developing their valor [fighting] against the Germans; in Italy, which made herself mistress of the whole world, and which surpassed all the other nations in learning, in virtue and in good laws; and in France, of which Sallust said that the Romans fought other peoples for glory, but the Gauls for life itself,[2] and that the Romans granted to the Greeks the prize for eloquence, and to the Gauls [that for] glory and the honor of arms. Your Most Serene Highness has happily united in his person all the endowments of these three nations, Italian phlegm, German melancholy and French bile, which form an heroic temperament by the mixture of fire and earth. Fire provides activity, brilliance, elevation, while melancholy, which partakes of the nature of the earth, [supplies] firmness, moderation, and restraint. Fire gives courage to undertake [great enterprises] in politics, and phlegm

---

[1] George of Brunswick-Lüneburg (1582–1641).

[2] Sallust, *De Bello Jugurthino* CXIV, 2.

the constancy requisite to these enterprises: the one causes one to attack vigorously in war, and the other causes one to keep up the same amount of force. The solidity and the judgment of the Germans; the artfulness, the delicacy of mind, the circumspection, and the politeness of the Italians; the openness, the pleasantness, the vivacity and the freedom of the French, moderated by this union [of all three national characters], attract the respect and affection of everyone, are useful in public affairs and for commanding, and make conversation solid, agreeable and worthy of a prince.

In fine if the inclination of the Germans and the Italians has brought them to devote themselves to only one kind of learning, and if the curiosity of the French [has caused them] to apply themselves to all, the union of these three geniuses is useful in making learning universal and singular, as is that of Your Most Serene Highness, who has made his main study those elements of knowledge which are worthy of him, who is so enlightened in religion that one can say that it is supported no less by the knowledge he has of it, than by his birth and his authority, and who is possessed of other sciences in a way which is no less surprising than the knowledge which he has of the languages of the three nations. He speaks them so perfectly that he makes it quite evident that, if a prince ought to be above others on account of his generous views and his great thoughts, it is also necessary that he surpass them in eloquence and in the fittingness of his expression, in order not to be less influential over minds through words, than over bodies by arms. Such that one ought not to be surprised, if Your Most Serene Highness, for the common good and because of particular utility, has chosen Germans, Italians and Frenchmen to have the honor of serving him. He has determined that their combination could be based on a mutual communication of the advantages which they possess, and that this is the means of joining pride with mildness, the circumspection of the Italians with the gallantry of the French, the reserve of the former with the sincerity of the latter, the sentiments of honor and of glory of the Germans with the bearing and the detachment of the French, and that by tempering all of these qualities, he can form a court which would be no less illustrious on account of the merit of those who compose it than on account of its magnificence.

The fine dispositions of princes being cultivated by reason of [good] birth and by the pains taken with education, virtue, which is an honorable habit, is formed finally in the mind and in the will, prudence to guide the judgment, and courage, moderation, justice, clemency, liberality, magnificence and generosity to regulate their passions and their actions. Prudence is the first of all the virtues, because it is she who ordains the manner in which one must act in all sorts of circumstances. She must be the more enlightened in princes, as their virtues must be greater, as their actions are more exposed to the view of everyone, and as matters of government require more lights. They must know the inclinations of the people, the laws, the power of their states and of their neighbors, the advantages of religion, of the arts, of commerce, of alliances, of peace and of war; [they must] know how to make a [proper] choice of ministers and of generals, and be able to judge of future events by the memory of things past, and by the consideration of things present, noticing the connection and the relationship which they have together.[1] Which demands a strong imagination, a good memory, and a great knowledge of history, which is the greatest aid to prudence.[2] This virtue appears so strongly in all of Your Most Serene Highness' actions, that one can say that he owes to her the greatest glory, and that reputation which he has acquired for himself throughout Europe. His conduct and the decisions he has made on the appropriate occasions, the calm of his state and of the Empire, the pains which he takes with general business, with particular matters, with natives and with foreigners, the choice of ministers which he has made, the great circumspection which appears in his utterances and in his conversations, the way of speaking about things, [which is] always so fitting, the regulation of everything pertaining to his house, his court, his troops, his estates, his domestics and his servants, and the places which he is now having fortified – [all of these] are certain signs of it. Your Most Serene Highness knows that the time of peace is the time to prepare oneself for war. But if the Romans made more conquests, and if they maintained them more by the conduct of their consuls than by the valor of their legions, as Titus Livius says,[3] and if there is no less glory in vanquishing one's enemies by talking than by arms, as Caesar says,[4] I daresay that the felicity of his peoples will subsist forever, more because of his prudence than of his fortresses, however unassailable they may be; that Your Most Serene Highness will always conquer as much by his conduct as by his armed forces, however considerable they may be in terms of numbers and of the valor of his finest troops; and that one must expect [to follow from] so many fine beginnings of his government a progression always more advantageous to his subjects, and an ever more admirable greatness for his person.

[1] Cf. Hobbes, *Leviathan*, ch. 8.
[2] Cf. Machiavelli's introduction to *The Prince*.
[3] A recurrent theme in Livy; picked up (in part) by Machiavelli in *Discourses* III, chs. 19–20.
[4] Caesar, *Civil Wars* III, 107.

If prudence guides all the virtues, she must first of all guide valor, which rules courage and the natural inclination for life, the strongest passion which can turn men away from virtue. The valiant is between the timid and the temerarious, in such a way, however, that it is closer to temerity than to timidity; the temerarious [man] does not know and does not fear dangers at all, [while] the courageous [man] knows them, like the timid one; but one cannot say that he does not fear them at all, like the temerarious one. The latter often exposes himself to perils without reason, uselessly, and without measure. The timid [man] always flees from them, and gets away from them even against his duty; but the courageous [man] exposes himself to dangers and stays there as much and as long as reason and prudence demand.

These are the results of the ordinary valor which moderates fear and boldness; but the valor of great princes has other attributes. If the valiant man scorns life, sorrows and death, the valiant prince sets no value on delights, pleasures and joys. If the former holds firm and is pleased in the midst of dangers, the valiant prince loves them, desires them and seeks them out. If the valiant man obeys to the death the command of his sovereign or of his general, the valiant prince always exposes himself of his own accord and voluntarily. If the former rests and enjoys pleasures at his ease, the valiant prince cannot remain in idleness, nor enjoy any but secret pleasures. Finally, if the valiant man wants not to be reproached, the valiant prince wants to acquire honor. These are the particular signs and the natures of the valor of Your Most Serene Highness, who has sought out war in foreign countries, not being able to find it in Germany, who is intrepid in the midst of dangers, and always busied with the cares of public business, who is [always to be found] in the perils of the sea and in the hardships of his journeys, while the others enjoy pleasures in security and repose, and who has so great a firmness that in his encounters the difficulties of his great plans have served only to augment his courage. But this should not be surprising, since his valor is sustained by his prudence, and since the one and the other have moved him to those great decisions which have brought so much glory and reputation to him, and which can come only from himself; for it is not for everyone to advise princes on these occasions, because everyone does not have the sentiments which birth inspires in them. In fine if princes, who are above others, must be continuously in action, as the highest created things in the world, the stars and the heavens, are in perpetual motion; and if the valor of Caesar was accompanied by an extraordinary activity, if in four days he went from Lucca to Narbonne, and afterwards in four days to the middle of the Auvergne with his legions, if in the theatre he busied himself writing and dispatching the most important business, and if in his leisure hours he conversed with wise persons, one can say that Your Most Serene Highness practices no less diligence than he in his journeys, that he is no less careful in his care for business, spending whole days writing, arranging and regulating everything with respect to the execution of those things which his admirable prudence causes him to resolve, and that all of his amusements are either uncommon or are always mixed with some business or with conversations about *belles sciences*.

It is not only love of life which can deflect men from virtue; the love of pleasures often has the same effect, and the natural penchant toward passion needs to be restrained. This is why moderation is necessary to regulate legitimate likings, to oppose itself to those which are forbidden, to moderate the use of those things which preserve life, and to reprimand passion. This virtue has the greater glory in princes and in sovereigns since, their power being absolute, it is more difficult for them to avoid excesses, to keep themselves within the bounds of honorable passions, of moderate resentment, and of just anger, which animate virtue in the difficulties which accompany it. One must grant, too, that it contributes much toward making them reign happily, that it is extremely useful in public business, and in negotiations, and that the immoderate pleasures of princes, their fury and their cruel and immoderate resentments, have caused revolutions in their states no less than the criminal ambition of subjects. The disgrace of the Tarquins, the death of the Emperor Valentinian III, the establishment of the Moors in Spain, and the Sicilian Vespers, are examples of it. But the moderation of Trajan and of Antoninus Pius was the safeguard of their persons, whereas the majority of the other Emperors drew on themselves, because of their licentiousness, a violent death in their youth, and [brought about] the misery of the people during their lives. This virtue is the more admirable in Your Most Serene Highness, as there are few examples in Germany and in Europe who have a way of life as sober as his, so moderate, so far removed from immoderate pleasures and rages. Such that I could say to Your Most Serene Highness that which Pliny once said to the Emperor Trajan: that the more power he has, the less license he practices,[1] because if it is happiness to be able to do whatever one wants, it is virtue to want only what one may do, that is to want only what one ought to do.

Princes must not only have the virtues which perfect a man with regard to himself, such as moderation and valor. They must also have those which will dispose them to do, with respect to others and to the people, everything which pertains to the duty, the glory and the greatness of

[1] Pliny the Younger, *Panegyricus* LXV, 1, 2.

sovereigns, such as justice, clemency, liberality, magnificence and generosity.

Justice is, of all these virtues, the most necessary to princes. The others are the ornaments of his glory, but this is essential, being in states what reason is in nature. For if reason, which is in God to direct his power, is the cause of the natural disposition of creatures, and if it conserves the admirable harmony of the universe, justice establishes the political order, and allows the union of men in monarchies and republics to subsist. It is the social tie which can only be established by these three political virtues: friendship, justice, and valor. If the first, which makes goods common, could be observed, the second would be useless; and if men did not always estrange themselves from justice, valor would not be necessary to defend states. But the weakness of human nature not being able to suffer that civil life be founded solely on friendship, it was necessary to arrive at a division of goods, common by nature, and to conserve it through [legal] justice, which must be applied by force against those who dare to violate the laws. And because princes are the depositories of this power, they must cause the justice which philosophers call commutative to be observed in commerce, which is the source of abundance, and [must] themselves administer distributive justice, which mixes rewards and punishments for the felicity and the security of subjects. Finally sovereigns and peoples must be restrained by respect for the laws, and since the peace of states with neighbors is ordinarily maintained by the motive of mutual fear, it is necessary that princes rule equally by it and by the laws, like Your Most Serene Highness, who has so much solicitude for justice that he wishes that it be rendered without exception of persons and without drawing a distinction between subjects and foreigners. It was thus that the Romans, by the reputation of their justice, and by letting persons from every kind of nation partake of their goods and their honors, having regard only for merit, peopled Italy with honorable men from all the countries of the world. It was thus that they drew commerce to the Empire, and that they made themselves masters of the whole world, as Titus Livius says. And if nature and reason are the two primary rules of justice, those two things are so admirable in Your Most Serene Highness that one can say that his state is no less secure because of the care which he always takes to protect the laws and because of the fame of his prudence, than because of his military forces and of the discipline of his arms.

But just as justice ought not to be so attached to the laws that, on those occasions on which it would seem unreasonable and too severe, the equitable judge would not be able to interpret them suitably, and judge of their sense more by reason, which is the sovereign law, than by words, and by the spirit sooner than by the letter;[1] so too princes ought not to be so exact in their punishment of crimes that they not sometimes give signs of their clemency, which is in sovereigns what equity is in judges. They ought to exercise this virtue to make their authority more striking, to make it evident that they are above the laws, and that they dispose equally of graces and of pains, sometimes by *raison d'état*, and often because it happens that men are more unfortunate than guilty. Thus this virtue has need of all the enlightenment of prudence, in order to draw distinctions appropriate to the times, to persons, to places and to crimes. For a too-great goodness is as dangerous (because of the bad consequences of impunity), as well-aimed clemency is glorious to princes. The former takes away fear, which keeps almost all men in their duty, and the latter attracts the affection of peoples, and makes it clear that sovereigns are truly the images of divinity, since they, like God, can exercise justice and clemency over the evil. Moreover cruelty and excessive rigor are always signs of weakness and of fear, and it is for this reason that clemency has always triumphed in generous princes. Julius Caesar offered so many proofs of this that the Romans built a temple to virtue on his account, and Henry the Great, King of France, showed how clement he was by pardoning those princes, nobles and cities who had fought for so long against his fortune, against his crown and against his life. Your Most Serene Highness has also given signs of this virtue, and one cannot doubt that it will always shine even more brightly in the progression of his government. For Your Most Serene Highness is not unaware that, if other virtues bring honor to princes, their ministers, their officers and their soldiers often share in them, but that they are always alone in enjoying the glory which clemency brings them.

Princes must not only render to each that which belongs to him, by justice, and pardon sometimes by clemency: they must also distribute their riches by liberality, which is a virtue between avarice and prodigality, in such a way nonetheless that it approaches prodigality more nearly than avarice.[2] For the liberal man takes less than he is entitled to receive and gives more than he is obliged to give, maintaining between this 'more' and this 'less' a just and reasonable mean. Liberality follows the nature of the good which it is itself communicating: the sun its light, the earth its fruits, the sea its fish, and its conveniences, and the most sterile mountains the gold and the silver which they contain. Such that this virtue is the more worthy of princes as they have more goods and are richer than others. But since it loses its force by exercise, since it destroys itself, and since princes cannot give without receiving, it is essential that they

[1] Cf. Aristotle, *Nicomachean Ethics* V, 1137b.   [2] *Ibid.* II, 7, 4 (1107b).

measure their liberalities by their revenues, and that they always have a reserve fund for the security of their state, and for the reputation of their [armed] forces. Moreover, in giving they must keep this in mind, to give to persons of merit and virtue, to men who do badly in business sooner than to the rich, and to persons of rank and of quality sooner than to persons of lower birth. This is the means of drawing more honor from their liberality, which often creates more adherents and which gives them more faithful servants and more partisans of their glory, than do their power and their merit, because interest and obligation ordinarily have more force on the minds of men than have esteem and respect. All great princes have exercised this virtue. Alexander, on his return from the conquest of India, had ten millions in gold placed on tables set up in his camp, to pay the debts of all the soldiers in his army. Caesar said that after the victory at Pharsala he had heard no sound more agreeable to his ears than a request; Sylla, that no one had ever done more good for his friends than he, nor more evil to his enemies;[1] Antoninus, that nothing would remain to him after being conquered except the good that he had done, having spent in Asia or given away 200 millions in gold in three years; and the Emperor Titus, that he counted as lost a day on which he had undertaken no liberalities,[2] believing that princes cannot reign better than by giving, nor in a way more agreeable and more worthy of their character, which represents that divinity who takes pleasure in communicating himself, and whose government is accompanied with so many continual gifts and graces. But those who know that Alexander found 120 millions in Darius' coffers after the defeat of that king, and that others possessed or shared the revenues of the Empire, which amounted to 200 millions in gold, according to the count of Justus Lipsius,[3] will not be surprised at the extraordinary effects of the liberality which ought always to be proportioned to the revenues of a prince, so as not to fall into extravagance, which is an extreme more dangerous than avarice for subjects and for sovereigns. It is thus that Your Most Serene Highness disposes of his favors and of his interests, always causing his liberality and his conduct to be equally admired. He takes care to establish and to insure his affairs in order to proportion his liberalities to the great revenues of a state which is one of the most beautiful in the Empire, one of the most powerful because of its situation, and one of the most pleasant because of the diversity of its meadows, its valleys, its hills and its mountains, which is the most abundant in all things and which holds no less riches in its famous mines, the finest in Europe, than it shows in the great fertility of its lands.

[1] Cf. Plutarch, *Vita Sillae*, 38, 5 (475e).   [2] Suetonius, VIII (239, 10)
[3] Justus Lipsius (1547–1606), philologist and writer.

If liberality regulates the gifts of princes, magnificence arranges their great expenditures. This virtue is useful, in order to draw to themselves by that external show which marks their greatness, the respect and veneration of the people, who are influenced by appearances, and more by the senses than by the mind. It serves also to preserve their names for posterity, as the temple of Solomon, the walls and gardens of Babylon, the great pyramids of Egypt, the statue of Jupiter in Greece, the Mausoleum and the Colossus of Rhodes preserved in history the names of the princes and rulers who built them. And the superb building of the Escorial, and the celebrated library of His Most Serene Highness, Prince Augustus, Duke of Brunswick and Lüneburg,[1] the greatest in Europe, will be eternal monuments to their memory: such that great princes have always taken pleasure in exercising this virtue, in order to be above others no less by expenditures than by the glory of their actions. Your Most Serene Highness, who makes his magnificence appear on all occasions by means of his fine court, who spares nothing to make resound the greatness of religion and the relationship between heaven and earth in the celebration of these mysteries with the most beautiful music in the Empire, has wished to follow this example, but with this difference, that however many superb works serve only as ornaments, his greatest expenditures are useful to his state, because his magnificence, like all his other virtues, look to the good and the advantage of his peoples. Everyone is not capable of reading history, where the great actions of Your Most Serene Highness are written, but everyone will be able to see the magnificent fortifications that he caused to be built, which will be illustrious monuments of the affection he bears his subjects, and of his zeal for the security and for the reputation of his state.

Finally, princes must have the generosity which is the ornament of all the virtues, because it makes something great out of every virtue. If prudence prescribes many maxims for war and for politics, the generous prince does not choose [all] those which are permitted, but always the most honorable ones, like Alexander, who refused to fight in the destruction of Issus, saying that he wanted no secret victory.[2] If the valiant [man] scorns life and the pleasures which make men timid, the generous [man] scorns the riches and honors which bring about so many base actions in courts, like Germanicus, who refused the Empire that his army offered to him;[3] or, if he accepts them, it is in order to assure that they not be given to persons unworthy of possessing them, as the Emperor Trajan

---

[1] Augustus of Brunswick (1578–1666), collected about 180,000 books for the library at Wolffenbüttel.

[2] Cf. Plutarch, *Vita Alexandri*.   [3] Cf. Tacitus, *Annales* I, 31.

said that he accepted the position of prince for fear it would be occupied by a tyrant.[1] If the moderate prince abstains from forbidden pleasures, the generous prince denies himself those which are allowed, like Alexander, who abandoned the delights of Persia to go into the snows of Scythia, and to suffer the burning heats of India. If the just man observes exactly the proportion and the equality which must subsist between what he gives and what he receives, between a thing and its price, the generous prince always gives more than he owes, and is satisfied with far less than what is owed to him. He rewards merit even more, and the punishments which he ordains are always less than the crimes, like the Emperor Augustus, who, after having made himself master of the Empire, gave the first positions to those who had served him, and contented himself with banishing the greatest enemies of his glory. If the liberal [man] makes ordinary presents, the generous [man] makes none which are not great, like Alexander, who, after his arrival in Asia, distributed all his money among his soldiers, reserving only hope for himself.[2] If the clement prince pardons offenses done to others, the generous prince pardons the conspiracies made against his person, like Caesar, who preferred to expose himself to the danger of being killed in the Senate than to secure his life by the death of the citizens who were conspiring against him.[3] If the magnificent prince makes great expenditures for his [own] satisfaction, the generous prince makes them for the public good, like Alexander, who built the superb Pharos of Alexandria, to light the way, at night and at great distances, for the ships which arrived at the port of the city. In fine the generous [man] is above praises, and always the same in good and bad fortune, like the ancient Romans, of whom Titus Livius said that their courage was neither raised by victories nor lowered by the loss of battles, and that triumph did not make them insolent, nor defeat more submissive. But if generosity shows itself in this equality of feelings, can one see a greater example of it than in Your Most Serene Highness, who has been able to change his condition without changing his disposition and inclinations, who has no less goodness for having more power, and who can live amidst a great fortune as if in a mediocre one? And if this virtue detaches men from their own interest and causes them always to seek the advantage and the good of others, everyone knows that when Your Most Serene Highness has given signs of his clemency, it has always been more to pardon the faults which injured him than those which harmed others, and that when he exercises justice, it is always to ordain rewards which surpass merit, and to impose pains which are less than crimes. But if the generosity of princes appears

[1] Pliny the Younger, *Panegyricus* v, 5–6, 325, 11–15.
[2] Plutarch xv, 2 (672b).   [3] *Ibid.* LXII, 1 (737b).

principally in the things which most favor the public, for which they must take care, rather than individuals, one can say that all the actions of Your Most Serene Highness are signs of it. If, to make his prudence more enlightened, he has wished to join to the many endowments which nature has given him the great range of knowledge which he has acquired in foreign countries, and if his valor has caused him to seek out war beyond the Empire, it is in order to make himself more capable of a rule which is more useful and more glorious for his peoples. If by an extraordinary moderation he has no attachment to pleasures, it is in order to apply himself entirely to affairs of state. If he distributes his riches by his liberality, and if, finally, his magnificence causes him to make great expenditures, it is in order to make them serve security, glory, and the public utility.

7. *Memoir for Enlightened Persons of Good Intention*
(mid 1690s)

This piece, probably written during the 1690s (to judge from internal evidence), is one of the fullest statements of Leibniz' general purposes as a statesman, scholar, scientist, etc. Though some of the earlier paragraphs are a bit simple and 'optimistic' in the bad sense of the word, the *Memoir* improves markedly as it moves on; and toward the end there are trenchant attacks on sectarianism, and good statements of Leibniz' belief that working for the common good is the highest human duty. (The present translation follows the text in vol. x of Klopp's edition of Leibniz.)

1. It is uncommon to meet persons to whom this memoir is suited. There are still some of them, for all that, and perhaps more than one thinks, though one does not always have the occasion to know them. And it is for them that I have drawn it up.

2. I find that even enlightened men of good intention usually let themselves be carried away by the torrent of general corruption, and do not think with enough skill about the means to pull themselves out of it and do some good.

3. Two things are the cause of this: the want of attention or of application, and the want of intelligence or of information. For one is diverted by the ordinary cares of life, and even when one has enough skill or enough mental energy to see what he ought to do, one finds only rarely people with whom one dares to be open. Men dream ordinarily only of trifles, and it is so *hors d'usage* to think of anything serious that it passes for ridiculous.

4. This memoir is written to demonstrate how one could remedy these two defects of application and of information, and I even think that one could hope for success in this, if one had the good fortune of meeting persons who took what is most important and most solid to heart.

5. I maintain, then, that men could be incomparably happier than they are, and that they could, in a short time, make great progress in increasing their happiness, if they were willing to set about it as they should. We have in hand excellent means to do in ten years more than could be done in several centuries without them, if we apply ourselves to making the most of them, and do nothing else except what must be done.

6. Indeed, there is nothing so easy as contributing to the solid well-being of men; and without waiting for universal peace or for the assistance of princes and of states, even individuals already have the means to do it in part. One need only will; and the common saying, *in magnis et voluisse sat est*,[1] is still more true than is vulgarly thought. For sincere and ardent good will suffices not only in fulfilling one's duty and in being excusable, when one does not succeed, but even in really succeeding. It is true that to achieve this it would be best that this will exist in several [persons] with whom one deals. Nothing is stronger than association.

7. I grant that people speak often enough of our misfortunes, or shortcomings, and of their remedies. But this is ordinarily only a manner of speaking and a diversion, or [is done] by habit and without the slightest intention of taking effective measures to remedy them. And this is, nonetheless, what should be the object of all our cares, in order not to lose the precious time of our life in impotent wishes and useless complaints.

8. I find that the main cause of this negligence, besides natural levity and the inconstancy of the human mind, is despair of succeeding, in which scepticism is comprised. For as the desire to remedy our misfortunes and to contribute to the common good can spring up only in minds which are above the ordinary, it is unhappily the case that the majority of these minds, by dint of thinking about the difficulties and about the vanity of human things, begin to despair of the discovery of the truth and the acquisition of solid happiness. Thus, contenting themselves

---

[1] Propertius, *Elegiarum* II, 10: 'In great enterprises it is enough to have attempted.'

with following an easy way of life, they laugh at everything, and let things go. This results from the fact that they have enough intellect and penetration to perceive defects and difficulties, but not enough application to find means to surmount them.

9. As for me, I put forward the great principle of metaphysics as well as of morality, that the world is governed by the most perfect intelligence which is possible, which means that one must consider it as a universal monarchy whose head is all-powerful and sovereignly wise, and whose subjects are all minds [*esprits*], that is, substances capable of relations or society with God; and that all the rest is only the instrument of the glory of God and of the felicity of minds, and that as a result the entire universe is made for minds, such that it can contribute to their happiness as much as possible.[1]

10. From this follows another principle which is purely practical – which is that the more minds have good will and are brought to contribute to the glory of God, or (what is the same thing) to the common good, the more they will participate in this happiness themselves. And if they fail to do so, they will doubtless be punished. For in a perfectly governed monarchy or city it is essential that there be no good action, internal or external, which does not have its proportionate reward, and no bad one, which does not have its punishment. We cannot explain the details of this with the help of reason alone, nor say how this is to be achieved, above all in another life; but in general it must be sufficient for us that this is so, and that it is something certain and indubitable.

11. This being established, every enlightened person must judge that the true means of guaranteeing forever his own individual happiness is to seek his satisfaction in occupations which tend toward the general good; for the love of God, above all, and the necessary enlightenment, will not be denied to a mind which is animated in this way, God never refusing his grace to those who seek it with a good heart. Now this general good, in so far as we can contribute to it, is the advancement toward perfection of men, as much by enlightening them so that they can know the marvels of the sovereign substance, as by helping them to remove the obstacles which stop the progress of our enlightenment...

12. To contribute truly to the happiness of men, one must enlighten their understanding; one must fortify their will in the exercise of virtues, that is, in the habit of acting according to reason; and one must, finally, try to remove the obstacles which keep them from finding truth and following true goods.

---

[1] Cf. *Monadology*, props. 83–90.

H

13. To enlighten the understanding, one must perfect the art of reasoning, that is, the method of judging and inventing which is that true logic that is the source of all objects of knowledge. In addition, one must cause to be recorded, as if in a general inventory, the truths of consequence which have already been discovered, and which are to be found not only in books, but also among men of all sorts of professions. And one must, finally, take measures suited to insure the carrying out of research and experimentation in order to advance toward the future as much as is possible. Each of these points merits an individual explanation, and I have thought enough about this to be able to enter into great detail, if this were the place to do it.

14. To improve men's will, one can put forward good precepts; but it is only under [the aegis of] the public authority that one can put them into practice. The great point is the reform of education, which ought to consist in making virtue agreeable, and in making it a second nature. But if someone has lacked this in his youth, he must have recourse to good company and to examples, to a lively representation of good and evil in order to love the one and hate the other, to the examination of his conscience and to frequent reflection, saying often to himself: *dic cur hic; hoc age; respice finem*,[1] with respect to certain rules that one makes for himself, and which have a relation to others. Finally, one must have recourse to punishment and reward, which are the ultimate remedies and the least fit to bring about solid virtue. They are necessary, nonetheless, to bring it about.

15. The obstacles to our happiness (that is, to reason and virtue) which come from the mind alone, cease by [use of] the remedies already noted; but the impediments which lie outside our mind, come from our body or from fortune. And to make men as happy as possible, one must seek the means of preserving their health, and of giving them the conveniences of life.[2] Thus one must inquire into the nature of bodies in the universe, as

---

[1] 'Say why [you are] here; do this; look to the end.' The last phrase appears in Plutarch's *Life of Solon*, ch. 28, and also in Epictetus.

[2] Cf. Leibniz' *Moyens*, F de C IV, pp. 150-1: 'Above everything else one must seek means of obviating public misery. Conscience, honor, duty and interest equally oblige one to do it. For extreme poverty is the mother of crimes and also the source of sicknesses: plague and famine can come of it, and these are, when joined with war, the three principal scourges of God, intimately bound together, which come from the malice or from the imprudence of men, and are the punishment of them. From which it follows that one must furnish the poor with the means of earning their livelihood, not only by using charity and [charitable] foundations to this end, but also by taking an interest in agriculture, by furnishing to artisans materials and a market, by educating them

much to recognize therein the marvelous traces of divine wisdom, as to notice the respects in which they can be useful to our preservation and even to our greater perfection. Thus the advancement of natural science and of the fine arts is of great importance.

16. But besides natural history it is also important to know human history, and the arts and sciences which depend on it. It comprehends the universal history of time, the geography of places, the recovery of antiquities and of ancient records, such as medals, inscriptions, manuscripts etc.; the knowledge of languages and what is called philology (which also includes etymological origins); I would add literary history, which teaches us about the progress of our knowledge, and what we owe to the studies of others, as well as the means of finding in these authors an account of what there is which one can use profitably in the work of others.

17. I even hold that human history includes that of customs and of positive laws, of which the main ones are the Roman laws, which serve as the foundation of the private and public jurisprudence in use today; besides the fundamental laws of states, with the heraldry, genealogies and the well-known controversies or pretensions of princes, about which it is well to be informed – not so much because these things are significant in themselves, as because they cause great revolutions which envelop us and which interest the societies of which we are part.

18. Finally, I include [in human history] the history of religions, and above all that of the true revealed religion, together with ecclesiastical history. Since this history of religion is most important for our salvation, in order to know what God has revealed or not, one can say with reason that the greatest function of the knowledge of ancient things and of dead languages, is that which one derives from them for [use in] theology...

19. The greatest and most efficacious means of attaining all these things, and of augmenting the general welfare of men, while enlightening them, while turning them toward the good and while freeing them from annoying inconveniences, in so far as this is feasible, would be to persuade great princes and [their] principal ministers to make extraordinary efforts to procure such great goods and to allow our times to enjoy advantages which, without this [extraordinary effort], would be reserved for a distant posterity.[1] And it is certain that besides immortal glory, they will derive

to make their productions better, and finally by putting an end to idleness and to abusive practices in manufactures and in commerce.'

[1] G. W. Leibniz, *Einige Patriotische Gedanken* (1697), in *Politische Schriften*, ed. H. H. Holz, vol. I (Frankfurt, 1966), p. 90: 'Since almost all important things which concern the common good consist in exact inquiry, it is better to deal with one leader [*Haupt*] and a few high officials than with a community, which is incapable of reflection.

great utility from this, and will be working even for their own perfection and satisfaction; for nothing is more worthy of great souls than the knowledge and the execution of that which produces human happiness,[1] and which displays the greatness of God, which gives us admiration and love for him. But besides this, great men, by these means, will have subjects who are more virtuous and better suited to serve them well; and persons of leisure and means, instead of amusing themselves with trifles, with criminal or ruinous pleasures, and with intrigues, will find their satisfaction in being curious [about things which promote the common good], or what are called *virtuosi*. And the great themselves, or their children and relatives, would often be saved from dangerous sicknesses, and delivered from a number of evils, which now appear invincible to us because of the scant attention which is still devoted to the advancement of medicine and of practical physics. If, in fine, the great contributed as much as they can to the increasing of knowledge and of the true good of the human race, the arts of peace and war would flourish marvelously in their states, as much to resist enemies by land and by sea, as to cultivate and populate the country by navigation and commerce – not to mention missions and colonies, [which are] suited to bring piety, reason and virtue to the barbarians and the infidels.

20. But while waiting for a favorable time to interest the public in these worthy plans, individuals must carry out their own; and each must fulfil his duty without reference to others. For one is obligated in conscience to act in such a way that one can give an accounting to God of the time and powers he has lent us. Thus the time which remains to us, beyond what is necessary for business and the relaxation which our health requires, must be used in occupations which are useful, not only to us, but also to others. And those who are in a position to afford considerable expenditures, should not limit themselves to the views of pleasure, honor and interest alone, but should apply a part to whatever can procure solid advantages for the public. For this is [a kind of] charity which is worth as much as, and often much more than, the alms which are only for a small number of individuals.

21. And as for intellectuals capable of contributing to the increase of

'Since only in a few places does power remain in the hands of the community at present, those who intend to do good have only to see how they can win over the rulers [*die Obrigkeit*].

'This, too, is a better and easier way, for just as Caligula, as an enemy of mankind, wished that the entire Roman people might have only one neck, so that he might cut it with a single stroke of the axe, so when an entire people has only one head all may be helped and served by one person.'

[1] Cf. Leibniz' *Von der Weisheit*, Guhrauer *DS* I, pp. 420 ff.

our knowledge, they must think of projects which serve not only to make them known and applauded, but also to produce some new knowledge... For to write for writing's sake is only a bad habit, and to write merely to make people talk about us, is wicked vanity, which even does harm to others, by making them lose their time in useless reading.

22. It is not the case that I condemn compilations when they are done on good subjects, and in a way which is suited to repay our efforts. For I said above that I would hope for good inventories of our knowledge. I even approve books for amusement, such as tales, poetry, speeches, elegies, satires, and *pièces galantes*. For if able men and virtuous persons have a hand in it, they can make use of them to make virtue esteemed and vice hated and ridiculous; to immortalize some fine thought by turning it into a well-made epigram; and even to teach the arts and sciences in a way which excites the memory pleasantly, following the method of the ancients, which was to put forward important precepts in songs or verses. ... But I could wish that all this be done in a way which benefits us, without making us lose time, and without crushing us under an infinity of bad books, which finally suffocate the good ones, and lead us back to barbarism.

23. But although individuals of merit and good intention can give us quite fine and quite useful things, it is still true that they could do infinitely better if there were a great deal of understanding and communication between them. For when each person thinks by himself, it happens that different people do the same thing, which is so much time wasted; it happens that those who undertake some project lack knowledge, materials and other aids which able or educated persons could provide for them. And, what is most important, a thousand things can be done by two or three or by several [people] who understand each other, which will never be done, or never be well done, if they work without communicating...

25. The peculiarity [of an individual intellectual] also has the bad effect of providing occasions for sects and for the wilfulness of false glory, which arrest progress. An intellectual will have some opinions which he thinks great and fine. Thereupon he wants to turn himself into the head of a sect.[1] He will work to ruin the reputation of others. He will make himself a learned magician's book, to which his disciples will so accustom themselves as to be unable to reason without it. For him, it is easy to dazzle them, in order to have the glory of being their sole leader. The public, however, will lose everything that the good minds which can come

[1] Here Leibniz is thinking particularly of Descartes and the Cartesians, as a number of his letters show.

together in a sect could have done, if they had kept the liberty and the diligence that they lack now, in the belief that what they learned from their master is enough for them. Good understanding and communication destroys this wilfulness. Then one recognizes easily that he should not limit himself to [the doctrines of] his master, and that a single man counts for little compared with the union of several. Thus one will render to each the justice that he merits, in proportion to what he contributes to the common good.

26. Our century has seen fine societies born, and it has derived great benefits from them; but things could go much beyond this...[1]

27. There is one important thing which all of these societies lack (except the Royal Academy of Sciences at Paris), and that is that they do not have the means to pay fairly large expenses. Thus they cannot attempt enterprises capable of having a great effect in a short time. And yet this is the main thing which one must prop up. For time is the most precious of all the things we have: it is life, indeed. Thus if we amuse ourselves by walking with little steps, we shall never perceive our progress. And other centuries (perhaps quite far off) will scarcely begin to profit, finally, from our work. I grant that we must work for posterity. One often builds houses in which one will not live; one plants trees whose fruits one will not eat. But when one can himself enjoy his effort, it is a great imprudence to neglect it.

---

[1] At this point Leibniz enumerates a large number of learned societies, many of them more odd than significant.

8. Caesarinus Fürstenerius (De Suprematu Principum Germaniae)
(1677)

Leibniz' main purpose in writing this extremely long work, of which only a few excerpts are reproduced here, was the redefinition of the concept of sovereignty in a way which would allow the minor German princes to be treated as sovereigns in international negotiations. In his effort to weaken the idea of sovereignty, and to make it consistent with, e.g., the allegiance which a 'sovereign' might owe to a 'universal' power such as the Holy Roman Empire or (perhaps) the Papacy, Leibniz mounted an interesting attack on Hobbes – this passage is translated in full – and defended at length the value of the medieval 'Republic of Christendom'. In the *Caesarinus Fürstenerius* he was attempting to maintain a delicate balance between medieval and more modern ideas. (The original Latin text is to be found in the Academy, Dutens, and Klopp editions of Leibniz' works.)

PREFACE TO THE READER (EXCERPT)

The position of the [Holy Roman] Emperor is a little more elevated than one commonly thinks; Caesar is the defender, or rather the chief, or if one prefers the secular arm of the universal Church. All Christendom forms a species of republic, in which Caesar has some authority – from which comes the name, Holy Empire, which should somehow extend as far as the Catholic Church. Caesar is the commander [*Imperator*], that is, the born leader of Christians against the infidels: it is mainly for him to destroy schisms, to bring about the meeting of [ecumenical] Councils, to maintain good order, in short to act through the authority of his position so that the Church and the Republic of Christendom suffer no harm. It is established that several princes are feudatories or vassals of the Roman Empire, or at least of the Roman Church; that some kings and dukes have been created by the Emperor or by the Pope; and that the others are not sacred kings, without making homage to Jesus Christ, to whose Church they promise fidelity, when they receive unction from the hands of the bishop. And it is thus that the saying, *Christus regnat, vincit, imperat*,[1] is verified; since all histories show that most of the peoples of the West submitted themselves to the Church with as much eagerness as piety.

I do not inquire whether all these things are done by divine law. That which is established is that they have been done with unanimous consent, that they have been gotten used to, that they are not opposed to the common good of Christendom; for often the salvation of souls and the public good are the object of the same attentions. And I do not know whether the scepters of kings are not subject, like their consciences, to the universal church – not to diminish the consideration which is due them, nor to tie princely hands which must always be free to administer justice and to govern peoples happily; but to constrain, by a greater authority, those turbulent men who, without regard to what is permitted and what is not, are disposed to sacrifice the blood of the innocent to their particular ambition, and often push princes into criminal actions: to constrain them, by the authority which I believe resides somehow in the universal Church, and in the Holy Empire, and in its two heads, the Emperor and a legitimate Pope, using his power legitimately. Thus, if it is a question of what is right [*si jure agendum est*], one cannot refuse to Caesar some authority in a great part of Europe, and a species of primacy analogous to the ecclesiastical primacy [of the Pope]; and just as in our Empire there are general rules which concern the maintenance of public peace, the raising of subsidies [to be used] against the infidels, the administration of justice between the princes themselves, we know too that the universal Church has often judged the causes of princes, that the princes have appealed to Councils, that in the Councils their rank and bearing have been decided, that the Councils have, in the name of all Christendom, declared war against the enemies of the Christian name. And if the Council were perpetual, or if there existed a general Senate of Christendom established by its authority, that which is done today by treaties and, as is said, by mediations and guarantees, would be done by the interposition of the public authority, emanating from the heads of Christendom, the Pope and the Emperor – by friendly agreement, it is true, but with much more solidity than that which all treaties and all guarantees have today...

[I know that it is open to doubt whether the Pope has the power to depose kings, and to absolve subjects of their oaths of fidelity; and the arguments of Bellarmine, who, from the supposition that the Popes have the spiritual jurisdiction, infers that they have at least an indirect temporal

---

[1] 'Christ reigns, conquers, commands.'

jurisdiction,[1] did not seem contemptible even to Hobbes himself.[2] Indeed it is certain that he who has received the full power from God to procure the salvation of souls has the power to curb the tyranny and the ambition of the great, who cause so many souls to perish. One can doubt, I grant, whether the Pope has received such a power from God; but no one doubts, at least among those who follow Roman doctrine, that this power resides in the universal Church, to which all consciences are submitted. Philip the Fair, King of France, seemed to be persuaded of it, when he appealed the judgment of Boniface VIII, which excommunicated him and deprived him of his kingdom, to a universal Council...][3]

CHAPTER IX

...In explaining the concept of sovereignty, I confess that I must enter into – and this is remarkable, dealing as it does with so important and common a concept – a field which is thorny and little-cultivated. The reason for this is that, because of a deplorable mania, those who undertake to write [on sovereignty] have eyes only for what is ancient, [and] of which vestiges scarcely survive, while they are not interested in more modern things. Among vulgar jurisconsults this does not surprise me; for them, all wisdom appears collected in the tomes of Roman law alone. Their experience of human things – supposing that they have any – does not go beyond the gates of the tribunals ... But what has always made me marvel is that persons who are famous for their merit, for feats accomplished and for learning, have preferred, when they took the trouble to write, to give proofs of their erudition rather than of their experience and capacity to judge ... they guard against producing documents or maxims which cannot be supported by the authority of some orator or poet, [and] the examples they adduce must be drawn exclusively from ancient history ...

Certainly one must admit that Hugo Grotius, that excellent man, took

---

[1] R. Bellarmine, *Disputationes de Controversiis Christianae Fidei*, and particularly *De Summo Pontifice*, lib. v, ch. 6.
[2] Here Leibniz can mean only that Hobbes went to a great deal of trouble to examine Bellarmine's doctrines, for chapter 42 of *Leviathan* completely repudiates the idea of indirect temporal authority in the Papacy. Hobbes refutes Bellarmine by a minute examination of the scriptural examples on which the Cardinal rested his case, and concludes with a blast at 'the champion of the Papacy against all other Christian Princes and States' (Oakeshott's edition, Basil Blackwell, Oxford, 1957, p. 383).
[3] This interpolated passage comes from chapter xxxi of the same work, and is inserted here because it completes – or at least extends – the argument.

into greater account things which are actually in use;[1] and that his examples, which draw on all of history and [on] ancient records seem to be adapted in an excellent way to establish rules which can serve even today. Nonetheless, he could have written a more useful work if... he had explained [things] in a more familiar way to us ...

In conclusion, no one should be surprised that whoever wants to treat of the *jure suprematus*, commonly called sovereignty, lacks the aid of good writers ...

CHAPTER X

Before speaking of supremacy, it is necessary for me to touch upon what a state is, what a commonwealth [*respublica*], what freedom, what the highest power; what *regalia* are, what the right of territorial hegemony, what are reserved things [*reservata*], what is the union of several governments. A state would seem to be a fairly large gathering of men, begun in the hope of mutual defense against a large [external] force, such as is usually feared, with the intention of living together, including the foundation of some administration of common affairs. A family, or rather a hamlet or village composed of several families, lacks the size. Armies, or some large fortuitous company such as caravans in Asiatic journeys, lack the intention of living together. Those whose custom it is to use the language of Aristotle today, call entire kingdoms *civitates*. I am not sure that this conforms to the thought of Aristotle himself, who, I believe, would not have called the kingdom of the Persians a *polis*; and who did not call Babylon one, because of its size, but a nation.[2] A city [*civitas*] would seem to require cohabitation such that the citizens can easily assemble when the call goes out. A *civitas* is either self-sufficient or not. A dominion is an area of inhabited land served by a common administration. A larger dominion is called a region, and when a region is part of another still larger dominion it is said to be a province. Territory is a name common to a state or a dominion or a tract of land. But in addition to its fundamental meaning, it also expresses the aggregate of laws and rights, so that just as inheritance and patrimony involve the whole of the things and rights in some family or dwelling, so territory signifies the whole of laws and rights which can come to obtain in an inhabited portion of the earth. Hence there arises what German jurists call territorial hegemony, or the right of territory. But the Italians preceded them [in this], and one remembers the

---

[1] Grotius, *De Jure Belli ac Pacis*, particularly II, xviii.

[2] Aristotle, *Politics* III, ch. 3 (1276a). But Aristotle admits that this point is somewhat dubious.

dictum of Baldus, who used to say that hegemony inhered in a territory as the mist to a swamp.[1] In this right, moreover, in addition to jurisdiction and the mild power of coercion, there is also contained the right of military might. The more closely all these [elements] are mixed together, the more accurately it is necessary to distinguish them. For the lord of the jurisdiction and the lord of the territory are two different things. I call jurisdiction the right of deciding cases or of handing down judgments, and of coercing obstinate private persons. I say that the right of coercing (which the ancient jurists called *imperium*) lies in being able, when necessary, to use force on stubborn people. But the right of military might is something far higher than the power of coercion. For one may coerce stubborn private persons by using a few officers of justice, or even, if necessary, by calling citizens together for help. But I call it the right of military might when it is in the power of the one holding this right to assemble a military force which is sufficient for keeping the whole dominion in its duty. Thus the lord of some village or burg can have all jurisdiction, can impose capital punishment, can restore to order a number of obstinate persons by using marshals and, if necessary, by means of a collected group of citizens or people from the countryside. But conscribe soldiers, or employ the larger engines of war, or do other things whereby the entire land might be brought under his command – these things he cannot do. Therefore in that case, where force must be readied not against a few stubborn persons, but against an entire community, he will call upon the lord of the territory. He who considers these things with care will see that territorial hegemony consists in the highest right of forcing or coercing, which differs as much from the simple faculty of coercing as does public force [*vis publica*] from private [*vis privata*] in Roman law. It should, still, be noted that this right can be retained even without soldiers, merely by men's opinion, that is by their obedient reverence, by the dignity [of the ruler], which can accomplish just as much, and often more, than force itself – so long as the common opinion of the subjects is that one ought to obey. For then it is enough that a small force of men be on hand, which can be opposed to the revolt of a few excited men. In the meantime it is sufficient to have the power of using great force when necessary. This right, in turn, belongs not only to the princes of the Empire, but also to the counts. For a long time there was doubt concerning [the right of] the free cities [to exercise a similar right], but recently, especially by the monastic peace, the question seems to have been settled.[2] And what we call territorial hegemony seems to be identical to what the

---

[1] P. Baldus, *Super Feudis*, ch. 'De Allodiis', 7.

[2] Cf. *Instrumentum Pacis Caesareo-Gallicum*, sec. 65, Mainz, 1648.

French call *la souverainété*, in a slightly looser sense: such as *la souverainété de Neufchatel de M. de Longueville* . . . [1] Once it is understood that territorial hegemony consists in the highest right of coercing subjects it is obvious, first, that there is contained in it full discretion to command all other things, so far as these are not expressly excepted, or reserved to another; whence, as I said above, territorial right consists in an entirety of rights. Next, it is clear that many regal rights [*regalia*] are excepted, either by express pacts, or oaths, or by provincial custom, and that the territorial hegemony remains intact nonetheless. Thus it can happen that another in our territory has the right of hunting, the right of mining, of hiring, of taxes; perhaps even the right of supreme jurisdiction or the right of judging capital crimes and exacting the penalty from condemned men, or even what is called the right of last instance, or the right to be appealed to over [the head of] him who has territorial hegemony. Furthermore, the lord of the territory can lack the right of coinage, the right of imposing tribute at will, the right of erecting fortifications, and many others. It is essential only that he have in readiness the power to obtain from his subjects, either by his dignity or, when necessary, by *force majeure*, whatever rights do remain his. For even if all other rights or royalties are taken from him, it is enough that there remain sufficient jurisdiction to preserve his authority over his subjects, and enough revenue to sustain his household, in keeping with his rank, and to support the ministers of his power.

In addition, although smaller territories of this kind are customarily called *souverainétés*, the term in its more usual sense is somewhat more narrowly restricted, and those persons only are called sovereigns or potentates who hold a larger territory and can lead out an army. And this it is, finally, which I call supremacy. The French too, I think, when they are discussing matters concerning the law of nations [*ius gentium*] – peace, war, treaties – and call some persons sovereigns, are not speaking of free cities, or of lords of tiny territories which even a wealthy merchant might easily buy for himself, but of those larger powers which can wage war, sustain it, survive somehow by their own power, make treaties, take part with authority in the affairs of other peoples: [in short], powers which are somehow exempt from the commerce of private persons and which, as human affairs now stand, cannot easily fall to lower persons, or persons of lesser standing (excepting the election of ecclesiastical princes). Thus it is that those who occupy this summit are honored by the other major powers, and by the lords of lands and peoples and the masters of human affairs, as brothers and persons of equal condition (although, perhaps, of

[1] Other examples, which followed here, have been omitted.

lesser power by a considerable degree), and are considered to differ from those men by the degree, not the nature, of their rank. When, finally, that right [of sovereignty] subsists in a family, it comes about that the family is seen to exceed the lot of other men, and its members are deemed sacred and inviolable, which privilege is not only the right of him who is the head of the house, whom they call the ruler, but is somehow communicated to the others, who have the sole hope of the succession, and are said to be *princes d'une maison souveraine.*

CHAPTER XI

Several territories, moreover, can unite into one body, with the territorial hegemony of each preserved intact. We have ready examples of this in the Empire, in the Swiss body, and in the United Provinces. For if the individual regions each have their own right of maintaining soldiers for keeping their subjects in their duty, the right of territory is unchanged. If, further, they can each make treaties with foreigners, and conscribe armies, and maintain arms by which they can gain sway with their neighbors – and the German princes can do all of these – it is clear that, the union notwithstanding, there still remains in each region that which I have defined as supremacy. But there is a great difference between confederation and union, just as between society and company. Several persons form a society, when the individuals' substance is shared by all and the profits divided among all. But in a corporation or company, a new civil person is formed, and what is brought into the common treasury belongs not to the individuals, but to the corporation itself. Nor are profits distributed except by the will of all or of the majority. A confederation is entered into by words alone and, if necessary, forces are joined. For a union, it is necessary that a certain administration be formed, with some power over the members; which power obtains as a matter of ordinary right, in matters of greater moment, and those which concern the public welfare. Here I say there exists a state. The learned men, therefore, who have treated this subject, have exceeded the bounds in both directions: some, admitting the unity of the state, have believed that liberty or supremacy are abrogated in the individual members; others, conceding the liberty of the individual members, have thought that there is constituted not one state, but merely an alliance.[1] Here I note that it is not quite

---

[1] Here Leibniz is arguing against a number of French and German writers who, since the time of Bodin, had rigidified federal theory by insisting that all proper political systems were either unitary, or alliances of unitary states – that divided sovereignty, or a federal system in the modern sense, was impossible.

correct to compare the German Empire with the Netherlandish state; for, just as there are certain things in which the bond of our Empire is more strict, so there are others in which the power of our princes seems greater than that of the provinces of the Netherlandish federation, who are granted much less right of war, peace, treaties and ambassadors than are ours.

I know that these thoughts of mine on the nature of the state cannot be reconciled with the opinions of the sharp-witted Englishman Thomas Hobbes. But I also know that no people in civilized Europe is ruled by the laws that he has proposed; wherefore, if we listen to Hobbes, there will be nothing in our land but out-and-out anarchy. He says that by nature men have the right to do whatever seems to them to be useful; that from this their rights extend over all things. But from this, he goes on, arise internecine wars, causing the destruction of individuals, and therefore peace is necessary and this right of all men over all things must be taken away, as must be the individual judgment from which it flows. Each man must transfer his will to the state, i.e. to a monarchy or some assembly of the magnates or the people, or to some natural or civil person, so that each man is understood to will whatever the government or person which represents him wills. Furthermore, this civil person, the government, cannot be anything but unitary, and it is fruitless to divide the rights of supreme power among several persons or *collegia*. For if, for example, one should be given the right to propose laws, another that of imposing tributes, the state would be dissolved in the event of an angry disagreement. For without the power of managing affairs, which is money, nothing can be accomplished, and so it is clear that he who can deny the other the tributes can also deprive him of his remaining rights – which, Hobbes says, is absurd.[1] Even more, it follows from his principles that every monarch (or he who is required to call no assembly of the people) can make arrangements for his successor at will. Nor does Hobbes deny this. And

---

Among these writers, besides Bodin, one would have to number Grotius (*Liber de Antiquitate Reipublicae Batavicae*, 1610) and Pufendorf (*De Jure Naturae et Gentium*), as well as a number of minor figures – Chemnitz, Simmler, etc. In Leibniz' time, the only writer other than himself to see federalism as something more than an alliance (if also something less than a state) was another Hanoverian, Ludolf Hugo, who in his *De Statu Regionum Germaniae*, developed a theory of 'double government' which is the ancestor of modern theories of the federal state. On all of these points see the editor's 'Historical Development of the Theory of Federalism, 16th–19th Centuries' (unpublished doctoral dissertation, Harvard University, 1968), as well as the few paragraphs bearing on this subject in Otto von Gierke's *Johannes Althusius*.

[1] Hobbes, *De Cive* V–VII; *Leviathan*, chs. 13–18.

yet these theories would be exploded in France herself (which some people put forward as an example of an absolute kingdom).

Hobbes' fallacy lies in this, that he thinks things which can entail inconvenience should not be borne at all – which is foreign to the nature of human affairs. I would not deny that, when the supreme power is divided, many dissensions can arise; even wars, if everyone holds stubbornly to his own opinion. But experience has shown that men usually hold to some middle road, so as not to commit everything to hazard by their obstinacy. Prominent examples are Poland and the Netherlands: among the Poles, one territorial representative can dissolve the assembly by his obstinacy; in Holland, when something of great importance is being considered, such as peace, war or treaties, the disagreement of one town upsets everything. And yet, due to the prudence and moderation of those who preside over the whole, most matters are finished according to their wishes. In the German assemblies, too, not everything is transacted by majority vote, but some matters require unanimity, all of which cases would seem anarchy to Hobbes. Some others, who have expressed themselves a bit freely concerning our state, think them monstrous;[1] but if this is true, I would venture to say that the same monsters are being maintained by the Dutch and the Poles and the English, even by the Spanish and the French. They know this who know what the noble orders of the kingdom of France, and those men otherwise selected from the kingdom (*les notables*), once said in public assembly concerning the fundamental laws of the kingdom and the limits of royal power. Nor is it unknown that aid is not obtained from the clergy, which is the third part of the kingdom, by mandates given from the plenitude of power (as they say), but by demands, negotiations, and discussions. Furthermore, half of France consists of provinces called *les pays des États*, like Lesser Brittany, Gallia Narbonensis, the county of Provence, the Dukedom of Burgundy, where the king certainly cannot exact extraordinary tributes with any more right than can the king of England in his realm. Anything further, exceeding custom or law, can have force only if it succeeds in the king's councils. Not even the emperor of Turkey is, in the minds of his subjects, above all laws, as can be seen from the form of the judiciary which condemned the Sultan Ibraim, the father of him who is now in power.[2] The matter was not transacted by an uproar, as in the killing of Osman, but by careful deliberation of those holding the highest

---

[1] The reference is to several works of Pufendorf attacking the Empire as 'monstrous'; they are listed in a note to the *Codex Iuris Gentium* (see p. 176n below).

[2] Mohammed IV.

civilian offices. Following their decision, the chief priest, or mufti, sent a decree commanding the sultan to appear before the Char-Alla, or 'justice of God'. When he refused, he was informed that his subjects had been freed from their oath of fidelity. Although we should not approve this example of the barbarians, who err in whichever direction you might choose. Therefore Hobbesian empires, I think, exist neither among civilized peoples nor among barbarians, and I consider them neither possible nor desirable, unless those who must have supreme power are gifted with angelic virtues. For men will choose to follow their own will, and will consult their own welfare as seems best to them, as long as they are not persuaded of the supreme wisdom and capability of their rulers, which things are necessary for perfect resignation of the will. So that Hobbes' demonstrations have a place only in that state whose king is God, whom alone one can trust in all things.

9. *Mars Christianissimus*
(Most Christian War-God)
(1683)

This effective satire on Louis XIV and his anti-German expansionism, written in Latin and translated into French by Leibniz himself, is beyond doubt his most brilliant and entertaining political work. The constant citation of scripture is probably intended as a parody of Bossuet's style, and the grotesque references to Grotius, Plato and others show what a nice sense of irony Leibniz possessed. More than once Leibniz' genuine rage at French excesses breaks through, and then the irony becomes grim. (The present translation follows Leibniz' own French version, as printed in the Academy Edition; but a few textual variants preserved in the Foucher de Careil edition have been interpolated.)

The majority of men having the habit of regarding their particular interest sooner than the public good, and the present sooner than the future, I am not surprised to see that there are men who see clearly that the salvation of the Church depends solely on the greatness of France, but who [yet] have more regard for the interest of their princes or of their own nation, than for the general good of Christendom, on the pretext of conserving the liberty of their country – which, however, they will not preserve against Ottoman arms, if France does not secure them against slavery. One could, however, pardon to some degree the indiscreet zeal which they show for their country, if they did not allow themselves to speak indignantly of the good intentions of the King [Louis XIV]. As for me, although I am a German I do not fail to be a zealous admirer of French virtue, and, possessing invincible arguments to confound the insolence of these indiscreet persons, I believe myself obligated, in conscience, to bring them to light. I could wish, indeed, that this matter be treated by one of the best writers of France, who would be less exposed to the calumny which a German cannot evade. But I see that it is no longer necessary, even now, to pay attention to the arguments coming from that country, which henceforward will make its rights effective only by arms, knowing well that the fortune or rather the justice of the King will always let him find enough foreign pens.

As early as the year 1672, it was resolved in France that the King would, in the future, no longer need to give reasons to the world for his enterprises, as his ancestors and other potentates had always tried to do by issuing superfluous manifestos. This is why, once it was decided to attack the Dutch, the declaration of war took the place of a manifesto; and the whole reason alleged [for this action] was the will and the good pleasure of the King, namely the ill-satisfaction of His Majesty with the conduct of the Estates-General of the United Provinces. The scandalmongers declared that nothing could be said against men who offered all kinds of satisfaction and wished only to know what the King desired of them; others worried that, the lawyer [who was] the author of the rights of the Queen[1] [of France] having been misled by Isola[2] and by similar authors, it would be found more appropriate to spare themselves a similar confusion. But they all deceived themselves. There was no lack of good reasons in France, and I know that an able man had drawn up a manifesto in which he put his finger on the conduct of the Dutch; but the ministers to whom he presented it found it appropriate to suppress it, believing that any other reasons than those which Cardinal Richelieu called the 'ultimate reasons of kings' would not be seemly for their master. Then the Dutch and their allies strongly pressed the ambassadors plenipotentiary of the King, [who were] sent to Cologne to treat of peace, to communicate to them the claims of the King and the legal principles [raisons de droit] on which he could found them; but the ambassadors rejected this request straight away, as unworthy of the greatness of their master, saying haughtily that they had not come as lawyers, to plead [a case], but as ministers of a great monarch to treat of peace, and to declare his will with regard to what he would or would not allow. The same method succeeded at Nimwegen; there the good Bishop of Gorck was mocked, and was treated simply as a speechifier when he insisted on reasons [for French conduct], and even the Marechal d'Estrades and the Marquis of Croissi did not hesitate to tell him, when the Dutch had already made their peace, that [the Empire] must content itself strictly with whatever the King would allow, and

---

[1] The reference is to A. Bilain, *Traité des Droits de la Reyne Très Chréstienne sur Divers États de la Monarchie d'Espagne* (Paris, 1667).

[2] The reference is to several works of F. de l'Isola: *Bouclier d'État et de Justice* and *Suite du Dialogue sur les Droits de la Reine Très Chréstienne* (both 1667), and *Le Dénouement des Intrigues du Temps* (1672).

receive it as the pure grace of His Majesty. The ambassadors of France who were lately at Frankfurt could not endure that one speak to them of the paragraph in the instrument of the peace of Westphalia which begins: *Teneatur Rex Christianissimus*.[1] I do not know whether their delicate ears found the word *teneatur* rude, or whether the text wounded them a bit: however it may have been, it is certain that they avoided this unfortunate passage no more than the devil makes holy water, and one of them could not stop himself from saying to some person who was talking to him about it: 'Leave me alone about your Peace of Münster; let us have no more of it.' It was not that they were doubtful of the goodness of their cause, or that they were lacking reasons to respond with; it was, rather, that they wanted to remain firm in the resolution made in France, a long time ago, to recognize no longer any judge but the sword – not like an impious person who said: *Dextra mihi deus et telum quod missile libro*;[2] but because they believed, with reason, *quod victrix causa diis placuit*,[3] and that one need not justify victory, which is a decision that the Gods themselves have decreed. But, as this method of settling useless disputes displeases us Germans, [who are] accustomed to *guerres de plume*, I determined to enter the lists, so that what is right will not be betrayed by a silence which some would take, inappropriately, as the admission of a bad cause. I hope to disabuse them in this, and to show incontestably that one could sooner accuse the King of too much moderation than of ambition, since the insolence of his enemies feeds only on the fact that he spares them too much, and that solicitude for Christendom sometimes stops his advances when he is in the best position to press them hard; but one must hope that he will not hold himself back henceforth, and that he will rout these buffoons who wish to make it impossible that the people of Christendom have a leader against the infidels, that heretics be destroyed, and that there be one King, one faith, one law [*un Roi, une foi, une loi*]. Someone will tell me that I defend the King's rights a bit bluntly, and with too much liberty, and that I reveal the mystery too early; but I have reason to believe that it [this work] will not be disapproved in France, for there is no more need to dissemble, and the French have made it clear enough, by their words and by their deeds, that they will no longer be concerned with the judgments of the vulgar (and among the vulgar they comprehend

[1] 'The Most Christian King shall be obliged' – a reference to a passage in a supplement to the Treaty of Westphalia by which Louis XIV renounced Strassburg. See *Theatrum Pacis*, ed. Endter (Nürnberg, 1734), p. 248.

[2] A slightly incomplete citation of Virgil's *Aeneid* x, 773: 'May this arm which is my God, and this javelin which I brandish, favor me.'

[3] Lucanus, *Pharsalia* i, 128: 'The victor's cause pleases the Gods.'

all who are not of their party), since today, unless one has a French soul, one cannot have an *esprit poli* nor be elevated above the common herd. I have [seen] many signs, besides, which make me believe that France will no longer be careful to conceal what she has kept hidden until now. Here are some of them: it was about 15 or 18 years ago that certain suspicious persons, I know not how, got wind of the devices which were used at that time to make Casal fall under the King's sway. His Majesty, having learned of these rumors, which he judged disadvantageous, ordered Sr Gravelle to declare the contrary in Germany, and to assure everyone, on his word as King, that he had no such designs. It was not believed then that it was time for self-revelation on this point.

Perhaps someone will want to say, in order to excuse France, that it is only since then that [the King] has begun to have such designs, and that these scandalmongers were themselves the cause of it, the King having decided that he would be equally exposed to the malignity of their censure, whether he did it or not; so that these gentlemen could have brought about what they feared, like astrologists whose predictions have been the causes of the evils which they predicted. Be that as it may, it is clear in any case that they no longer believe in France that they have any reason to be so scrupulous. Here is another example. The late Elector Palatine sent a person to the King to demand the restitution of several places which the officers of His Majesty had seized. This envoy, having had an audience with the King, insisted strongly on justice and on the good faith of treaties; His Majesty replied to him with much moderation that he claimed nothing except what belonged to him in conscience, and that he had appointed certain persons to examine the matter thoroughly and to confer with the interested parties. This response was suited to those times, for since then, matters have put on a new face, and those are mocked who imagine that the principles of common right would have some force against the assessors of the Chambers of Metz and Brisac, and those are ridiculed who were naive enough to imagine that the ambassadors of France, who were at Frankfurt, would allow them to argue and uphold legal theses; from which one can judge that the French are beginning to overcome that unseemly shame or rustic modesty which they had earlier, and that they [now] act with a liberty worthy of well-born people. This the French ministers, who are to be found here and there, do not try to hide; for the ambassadors who were at Frankfurt, seeing themselves bothered by those who asked why France had never heretofore demanded Strassburg or a number of other presently-occupied places, and why she had not made some mention of her claim when the occasions required it, as at the Treaty of Münster, at the treaty of the execution of Nuremberg, or at least at Nimwegen;

these gentlemen did not blush to answer that earlier these matters had not yet been in a proper state for discussion. It might even be good, perhaps, to consider by what degrees the French have advanced before arriving at the greatness of soul which at present allows them to reveal sincerely the designs which they hid earlier.

The King, no longer having a private tutor after the death of Cardinal Mazarin, did not fail to guide himself sometimes by his maxims and by his advice, as if he had still been living, the more so because M. de Lionne, who had graduated from this school, followed the same principles. Thus the princes of Germany were treated civilly enough, appearances of common right were kept up, and a show was made of preserving the Peace of Westphalia and German liberty. But Lionne having died, M. de Louvois pointed out to the King that the Rhenish alliance had done more harm than good to France, that one no longer needed to worry about the princes of Germany, that there was no money worse used than that which was given to them, that the Empire was a name without power, that it could be vexed with impunity and that France would nonetheless not be lacking in admirers, even in Germany itself. This advice having sufficiently succeeded, M. de Croissi, coming to the ministry after the ruin of M. de Pomponne, ingratiated himself with the King with another new doctrine of his invention, namely that the hobgoblin of the Peace of Westphalia had already set limits to the progress of the King for too long, that it was time to move ahead, and to rise above these scruples; that there was now a new peace of his fabrication, which could be urged as plausibly and more profitably than that of Münster, to which the Germans would be wrong to repair in the future, since they had violated it; that that [the Peace] of Nimwegen, being an act of pure grace of His Majesty, it was for him alone to explain his gift. Now, if France is obligated to M. de Louvois for showing her the weakness of the German princes, if M. de Croissi has relieved the King of the inconvenience of the Peace of Münster, I believe that I shall deserve no less than those gentlemen, by saving the King's Council from all the scruples of conscience which can remain with some of them with respect to the law of nations and to the canons of the Church. I shall show, then, that these things indeed obligate ordinary men, but that there is a certain law, superior to all others, conforming nonetheless to sovereign justice, which releases the King from the obligation to observe them. For St Paul has well observed that the just knows no law,[1] and that he who bears the character of an extraordinary power is exempted, in virtue of his commission, from common human obligations. It is thus for me to show at present that the King has such a character,

[1] I Timothy 1, 9.

and that there is no man today who has received from heaven, even from the antipodes, a greater power in temporal affairs than Louis XIV.

The better to carry out this proof, I must lay here the foundations of a new jurisprudence, in order to destroy at a stroke the objections of two sorts of people, whom I see must contradict me, those of the German jurists and those of the Italian canon lawyers. And I hope to be able to do this all the easier, having on my side, to some extent, the casuists or authors of holy moral doctrine, particularly the Jesuits, who are aware, being as subtle as they are, that they now have much more to hope for from the quarter of the French monarchy, than of the Spanish. I lay down, then, as the fundamental point, that everything belongs to God, and that all things are subject to the eminent right which he has over creatures. From this right of God came that of Moses over the conse-crated vessels whom he borrowed from the Egyptians, and that which the people of Israel exercised over the persons and the goods of the Canaanites.[1] Pope Alexander VI, in his capacity as vicar on earth, claimed [the right] to divide the New World between the Castilians and the Portuguese, although his power did not extend to temporal matters. I shall show, on the contrary, that His Most Christian Majesty who is living today is the true and sole vicar of the world with respect to all temporal matters. To this foundation I add the definition of what is just or unjust, which Plato states and explains very well through the person of a certain Thrasy-machus, whom he makes say roundly: *justum est potentiori utile*.[2] Which agrees very well with what we have said about the right of God over all things, since God is the most powerful of all. The most powerful after God, excepting always the devil, is without doubt His Most Christian Majesty. And there is reported in this connection a *bon mot* of the Emperor Maximilian I, who said one day: 'If I were Jupiter and had to make a will, I would give the kingdom of heaven to my first-born son, and that of France to the second.' If this was true in the time of that Emperor, how much more is it today! For King Louis XIV alone has joined to the crown a large territory, whose length, from the Swiss Alps to the German Sea, includes so many beautiful provinces, that these conquests alone could pass for a considerable kingdom.

To prove this vicarate of His Most Christian Majesty one has no need of intricate arguments, for the greater part of the arguments which Cardinal Bellarmine used to prove the indirect power of the Pope in temporal matters[3] can serve incomparably better to prove the direct power

[1] Deuteronomy 3, 22 and 11. 8 ff.   [2] Plato, *Republic* 1, 338c.
[3] R. Bellarmine, *Tractatus de Potestate Pontificis in Rebus Temporalibus* (Rome, 1610).

of the King. Everything which is prophesied of the Empire of Jesus Christ on earth must be understood [as applying to] the Empire of His Most Christian Majesty. And one must not imagine that it is for nothing that the holy phial came down from heaven, or that the King received the gift of performing miracles, and of curing the sick, inasmuch as Jesus Christ while rising into heaven said that this would be a mark of those whom he would use on earth to extend his kingdom.[1] I know that there are doctors who cast doubt on the miracle which the King performs so often in curing the scrofulous; but one need not trouble himself about the incredulity of those persons, which is so great that the religion of doctors has become proverbial. Some have objected that the Duke d'Épernon, favorite of King Henry III, was inconvenienced by an illness which the King should have cured. But, even if this is true, is it not known that the saints did not wish to cure all of the sick? Moreover, Jesus Christ and the prophets have always had the kings of France in mind, [since they were] destined one day to be the liberators of the Church. And, without speaking of other [Biblical] passages, can anything be more clear than this one of Jesus Christ's when it says: *Lilia agri non nent*?[2] Which signifies, doubtless, that the Kingdom of France must not fall to the distaff side, so that the scepter not be taken away from this warlike nation, and that she never submit either to strangers or to women, since the temporal Schilo or hero whom the people will follow must come from her?[3] And there is no kingdom which I know that can prove [the value of] its fundamental laws so well by means of the holy Scriptures. That the Turks expect their ruin only from France, is something that is known from an ancient prophecy, which a certain Bartholemew Georgiewicz, who was a longtime prisoner of the Turks, brought back from the Levant.[4] There is a prophecy, *de Rege quodam illustrissimi lilii*, in the work of Pareus, in his commentary on the Apocalypse, which confirms the same thing.[5] I know that Grotius, in his work *De Jure Belli ac Pacis*, disapproved of citing prophecies in order to establish [principles of] right thereby.[6] But the jurisprudence of Grotius is far removed from that which we are establish-

---

[1] Mark 16, 15–18.   [2] Matthew 6, 28: 'The lilies of the field do not spin.'

[3] This is an elaborate pun involving the 'lilies of the field' and the *fleur de lis* of the French monarchy, which suggests that the lily-like female members of the French royal family should neither spin nor reap (politically). 'Schilo' is the Hebrew word for 'hero'.

[4] The reference is to B. Georgiewicz, *Epitome de Turcarum Moribus* (1558), particularly ch. VI.

[5] David Pareus (1548–1622), professor of theology at Heidelberg, author of *In Apocalypsin Johannis Commentarius* (Heidelberg, 1622).

[6] Grotius, *De Jure Belli ac Pacis* II, 22, 15.

ing here; besides which he speaks only of prophecies whose interpretation is uncertain, while ours are incontestable. And since even the Messiah proved his right through the prophets,[1] why should his vicar not do it, who must do in a worldly way that which the Messiah did spiritually, and who must establish on earth, happily for the flesh, the kingdom of Jesus Christ, which millennial heretics were waiting for, quite inappropriately, in the form of Jesus Christ in person? God himself confirms every day, by miracles, the right which we attributed to His Most Christian Majesty. Is it not a great enough miracle that a prince who has so many wars on his hands does not lack money? Some absurd people imagine that he possesses that blessed stone which alone can enrich all the kings of the earth; others, seeing that the King succeeds in everything, and that he is informed of everything which happens in enemy countries, associate him with a well-known spirit: but it is not [merely] ridiculous, but impious, to attribute to the devil that which is brought about by a heavenly inspiration. In this matter these persons resemble the Jews, who said that Jesus Christ performed his miracles through the intervention of Beelzebub.[2] What more clear sign of the will of the Gods can one claim than that which we see every day, that is, a perpetual assistance of heaven, which is so great that it seems that men and the times conspire to increase the goodness and the glory of the King? For what is called Fortune is nothing else than a decree of Divine Providence, and it is *contra stimulum calcitrare* to oppose it.[3] Do we not see that the Emperor Leopold is endowed with very great virtues, that all the world admires his zeal and his ardent piety, that there is no prince more assiduous in doing his duty, nor who listens more willingly, or who examines more attentively the petitions and the memoranda which seem to be of so little importance? One sees him constantly in action, now in council, now in his office working on dispatches; in a word, one can say that there is no minister who works more than he: nonetheless, everything goes wrong for him. His Most Christian Majesty, however, who makes his amusement his occupation, who bothers with business only to divert himself, and whose studies go only to prove that he is sufficiently warlike, does not fail to succeed in everything he undertakes. What other inference can we draw, than that heaven has destined this King for great things? For the friends of heaven receive benefits in their sleep;[4] the others can catch nothing, however they run,

[1] Matthew 11. 13, 13. 17 and 23. 34–9.

[2] Matthew 9. 34 and 12. 24.

[3] Acts 26. 14: 'You hurt yourself by kicking at the goad.' (The line comes from St Paul's defense before King Agrippa.)

[4] Psalm 127.2.

and even if they stay up all night or get up very early in the morning.[1]
We lack now only a Jeremiah, who could inform all the powers of the
world that those who oppose the King oppose the heavenly will at the same
time, as those who hoped to defend themselves against Nabuchodonosor,
and relied on the shattered stronghold of Egypt, resemble those princes
who today base their hopes on the House of Austria.

But there is such a Jeremiah, who has just appeared, so that the
Germans have no more excuse. It is a certain village curate in Germany
who has set himself up lately as a prophet, and who proves invincibly by
the Apocalypse that all of the King's enemies will perish.[2] Events have
confirmed his predictions: for the Italians, jealous of the glory of the
King, suffer from the heat of the sun, and from drought; the Dutch,
envious of his happiness, are [being] punished by floods which make them
fear at every moment a final devastation. Ungrateful Sweden has suffered
a horrible cold-wave. The House of Austria is vexed by the rebellions of its
subjects, and the Germans see from one side the Ottoman furor un-
leashed against them, [while] on the other side they are menaced by
Denmark, from which they have received a test [more severe than that
undergone by anyone] since the departure of the children bewitched by
Ham[3] – which ought to make them think of them, in order to prevent
punishment through a prompt penitence, by throwing themselves into
the King's arms. All of the rules of politics cease with respect to this great
prince, and though it seems that he does many things against the order of
prudence, he is seen nonetheless to succeed, because the good Spirit is
with him,[4] and [because] the wisdom of this world is madness in heaven.
The nations set up a clamor, and declaim eagerly against the King and his
anointed;[5] thus it is not to be wondered that the heavenly power, raising
itself against them, scatters them in its anger. Since the King prefers to
humiliate the Dutch by arms, rather than give them the peace that they
were ready to receive from his hands, the wise men of this world expected
only evil from it, above all when they saw England isolated, and Germany
with Spain joined with the Dutch. But God had ordained otherwise. The
danger was assuredly not small and would have been felt even more, if
the Swedish had not saved France by drawing the storm on themselves.
This was written in the book of destiny; and the Swedish, having done it
contrary to their intentions, pushed by a superior power, deserved as

[1] *Ibid.* and I Corinthians 9, 24.
[2] Cf. H. Kromayer, *Commentarius in Apocalypsin Johanneam* (1682).
[3] Apparently a reference to Genesis 10.   [4] I Corinthians 3. 19.
[5] Psalm. 2.1.

little recognition for it, as the King deserved blame for having abandoned them, since they had begun to be tiresome to him, and, in our opinion, useless.

But let us return to the extraordinary actions of the King, which often shock those who believe him to be quite prudent: is there anything apparently more contrary to reason than that which he dared to do last year, when he irritated and scorned both heaven and earth, Europe and Asia, the Pope and the reformed, the Emperor and the Sultan, the kings of Spain, of Sweden and of Poland, the princes of Germany and of Italy, and, in a word, virtually the whole world? It was as if, simultaneously, the Pope had excommunicated him, the people had risen against him, the Turks had seized all the merchants and merchandise of France, the Emperor with the princes of Germany had attacked the frontiers of the kingdom, the Dutch had been helped by the Spanish to retake all the lost territories, [and] the princes of Italy, alarmed by the conquest of Casal, had taken strong resolutions to provide for their liberty. And nonetheless none of these things happened, which one can attribute only to a miracle of the supreme hand, which tied the arms of the ones and shut the eyes of the others, as he did when, following the prayer of the prophet, the Syrian army was struck with blindness.[1]

I believe, then, that I have sufficiently proved, as much by prophecies as by miracles, the extraordinary vocation or mission of the King, for the reformation of the temporal affairs of Christians; [this vocation is] far better established, without doubt, than the mission of those pretended first reformers, who rose up against the Catholic faith.

From which it follows that all kings and princes are obligated in conscience to defer completely to him, to recognize him as arbiter of their quarrels, and to leave to him the direction of the general affairs of Christendom, and that those who oppose him are resisting the will of inevitable destiny. If they are rashly stubborn, and if they scorn the fraternal correction which the King uses in dealing with them, their subjects will be absolved from their oaths of fidelity, *ipso jure*, and will have the right to put themselves, by their own authority, under the jurisdiction of the King. There will be some, perhaps, who fear the renewal of the ill-fated example of the Messinians, whose city was put under the protection of the King with great affection, [but] which was abandoned quite suddenly [*à l'impourvue*], contrary to assurances, and contrary to the honor of the King, with so much haste that not even enough time was given to the most interested parties to secure their lives and property, [thus] leaving them to the Spaniards, who made of them examples of their severity. I grant

[1] II Kings 6. 18.

that nothing is more true than this, and that this affair might discourage the best-intentioned persons; but it must be attributed not to the King, but to the unhappiness of those times, which are now much changed; and one should reflect that every great sect must have its martyrs in the beginning. Above all the Catholics of Germany should recognize their liberator, since it is clear that French arms are destined to [support the] expansion of religion.

Everyone knows that the King made war on Holland only to help the Bishops of Cologne and Münster to pursue the rights of their churches. If, since then, the French have slightly mistreated the dioceses of Cologne and Liege, one must believe that it was done either in spite of the King, or with the consent of the Elector, or at least by *raison de guerre* and for the public good. Is it not known with what warmth the ambassadors of France busied themselves at Nimwegen to secure the free exercise of the Catholic religion in the United Provinces, and how many times they were ready to break the treaties on that account alone? And success has answered their efforts: (that is to say: they never dreamed of it), because they knew that one must first seek the kingdom of heaven, and be assured that the rest will follow.[1] If some still doubt the sincerity and the good intentions of the King, seeing that he has undertaken to torment the House of Austria, which is quite Catholic, they should reflect that the Austrians have become fomentors of heretics, since they think they can support themselves by their assistance; such that one must begin with the ruin of this House, in order to overthrow the foundations of heresy which Charles V laid by his political accommodativeness. I will be told that the King gave aid to Count Teckeli and to other rebels in Hungary, although they were Protestants, [and] even though he saw well enough that Christendom would suffer from it, and that the Turks would derive profit from it. It will be added that Louis XIII did no less for the heretics of Germany, who preserved themselves only through his aid. But I answer that a minor and momentary injury, from which the Catholic and Christian Church suffers, must not be taken into account, when it results in an incomparably greater and more durable good. For the House of Austria being humbled by these devices, and the King becoming arbiter of the affairs of Christendom, it will be easy for him to destroy the heretics and the Turks with one blow and at the same time. He has already shown examples of his power and of his good will at Gigeri and in Candia, without speaking of what he has done elsewhere, and will, doubtless, do further, when he is in a position to give laws to Germany, to Italy and to the rest of Europe, unless there is some other power on foot which can contest his power.

[1] Cf. Matthew 6. 33.

And I doubt not at all that we shall see this happy time arrive before long. The minor Catholic clergy of Germany, badly treated by the Protestants, and abandoned by the House of Austria, is already singing Hosannas as it sees the advance of its liberator. It is true that the bishops, being princes of the Empire, are still wavering a little, and are quite afraid that the ill-named freedoms of the Gallican Church, which may be freedom from the Pope but which are truly slavery with respect to the King, will be introduced in their domains [*chez eux*]; nonetheless the best-intentioned persons, who do not prefer a few temporal rights of their churches to the general good of the Catholic Church, must agree in this matter with the King, following the example of the two good Bishops of Strassburg,[1] whose Catholic zeal was so great that they had no difficulty in sacrificing the temporal sovereignty attached to their church; for charity, which requires that one accept everything in good faith[2] [*prenne tout en bonne part*], forbids us to suspect them of having had other views. The other bishops of Germany can follow their example the more easily because they have reason to believe that no changes will be made during their lifetimes, and that they will be able, despite this [change], to enrich their relatives with the best conscience in the world, since it is not only per-mitted but commanded that one provide for his own; the Apostle saying expressly that those who neglect an occasion for it are worse than the pagans.[3]

As for the German monks, this is another matter; for wanting to be honest and not wanting to deceive anyone, I dare not advise them to attach themselves to France, because the monks of St Benedict and St Bernard, the Carmelites, the Dominicans, and many other orders, which are well enough off in Germany, have been for some time obliged in France to fast or go barefoot, on the pretext of new reforms. As for the secular princes of Germany, it will seem to them a bit hard to be obliged to submit to the authority of the King the nearly royal power which they attribute to themselves; and, as everyone knows that the rich will have difficulty in entering into heaven,[4] so too the powerful find it difficult to accommodate themselves to the Most Christian Kingdom, and to its temporal vicar, who is the King. But they will all come around sooner or later, despite their difficulties. And as rivers all converge finally at the sea, whatever detours they make, in the same way it is inevitably necessary that all the powers, and particularly those of Italy and Germany, be finally engulfed by this fifth monarchy. England, divided within herself, will be desolated, as her

[1] Franz Egon and Wilhelm Egon Fürsten von Fürstenberg.
[2] Cf. I Corinthians 16, 14.
[3] I Timothy 5, 8 (the apostle referred to is St Paul).   [4] Matthew 19. 23.

heresy deserves. The Dutch already feel the approach of their ruin, seeing the shrinking of their commerce, and the definite loss of the Spanish low-countries. So one must hope that this nest of sectarians will soon be destroyed. Denmark and Brandenburg, stirred up against Sweden, Saxony and Brunswick, will devour what is left of the Protestant forces. The Bishops of Rhyn and of Westphalia, and even one day those of Franconia, will no longer resist the Catholic zeal of the King. Austria and Bavaria will no longer be able to resist either, being weakened and frightened by the nearness of the Turks.

One need not worry about the Italians, [who are] ready to receive the yoke, and [who have] degenerated from the virtue of their ancestors. For it is known that the Venetians, for example, moved heaven and earth when the House of Austria undertook I know not what in the territory of Grisons; but now that France has established the seat of her domination in the lovely center of Italy, they dare not say a word. I doubt not at all that this comes from heaven, which takes care to blind them in order to punish them. Surely, when Germany is at the King's beck and call, it will be too late to wake up; for where in the world will they levy [soldiers], having almost no seasoned troops in Italy? Money alone does not suffice to make war, when it is not used in time. I believe that the Italians will be able to make some small effort before capitulating, and that they will fight a little, *non pro aris et focis, sed pro lectulis,*[1] fearful of the horns which the French (with whom they know well that their wives are already secretly conspiring) are preparing for them: this has begun to become obvious since the envoy of France, among other tough conditions which he proposed [in addition] to those of Geneva, added also that it would be permitted in the future that the women of this country enjoy a *liberté française*, and receive the French freely in their homes. Italian women expect their deliverance from them, in order to be emancipated from the yoke of their husbands, no less than the German priests expect theirs in order to be secured against the insults of the Protestants.

Such is the good fortune of France, which helps her to find powerful factions on her side among her very enemies, as is that of the clergy in Germany and that of [the female] sex in Italy. And who would henceforth dare to resist priests and women conspiring at the same time?

---

[1] 'Not for altars and hearths, but for beds.' This is a parody of Lucilius' closing speech in Cicero's *De Natura Deorum* III, xl, 94: 'I have to fight against you on behalf of our altars and hearths, of the temples and shrines of the Gods, and of the city-walls...and my conscience forbids me to abandon their cause so long as I yet can breathe' (trans. H. Rackham, Harvard University Press, Cambridge, Mass., 1951, pp. 380–1).

It seems to me that it would not be out of place here, while writing an apology for the King, to do the same, in passing, for those Germans [called] Gallo-Greeks, my *confrères*, who get on so well with the various Louises of France. Ignorant and vulgar people call us traitors, saying that we sell the fatherland, and strive to put it under the yoke of a foreigner. But I think that the majority of those who reproach us thus, would very much wish to be capable of the same crime. They cry out, then, only from envy, since they haven't the skill or the good luck to bring grist to the mill. I except from this [characterization] some naive people who might be scrupulous about this matter; but, their number not being very considerable, one must laugh at their folly. However, we are not as wrong as some think. The most expert political analysts [*politiques*] all agree that the Commonwealth of Germany is so monstrous and so corrupt,[1] that it needs an absolute master to re-establish good government there. What is German liberty, if not the license of frogs, who croak and jump here and there, and who need a stork [to keep them in order], since this piece of driftwood [the Empire], which made so much noise in falling, is no longer formidable to them?

We should willingly grant, then, that we are working to destroy such a liberty. I know that the majority of my *confrères* do not speak so freely, fearing the name of traitor more than the reality, and trying to color their activities with pretexts drawn from the peace treaties of Westphalia and Nimwegen, from the capitulation of the Emperor, from the Golden Bull, from the executive orders of the circles [of the Empire], from the religious and secular peaces and other laws of the Empire: basing their justifications on the freedom of peace, war and alliances, and on the natural right of self-defense, accusing the Emperor and the Empire of having mistreated, deceived and abandoned some princes to whom these gentlemen belong.

But I, who speak the most sincerely, and who have reasons more valuable than all of theirs – I do not want to imitate them. For I know that these pretexts have nothing solid in them, that the Emperor had the best intentions in the world for the common cause of the allies, and that he made the Peace of Nimwegen only after having been deserted by the Spanish and the Dutch, and when he saw that most of the other allies busied themselves with [the question of] who could best and soonest manage his affairs. I find, then, only one thing to blame in the Emperor (which others perhaps would not blame), which is that he was too stubborn in wanting to maintain the rights of the Empire, not wanting to recognize a power superior to his own, which His Most Christian Majesty

[1] Here Leibniz is referring primarily to several works of Samuel Pufendorf which are listed in a note to the *Codex Iuris Gentium* (below, p. 176n).

received directly from God, as we have just proved. There are some other Gallo-Greeks in Germany who imitate Judas' taking the thirty pieces of silver, because they hope that Germany will not fail to be saved by heavenly mercy; that the money will, however, remain with them, and that they will be in a position one day to laugh at the credulity of the French. But he who laughs last laughs best. Take care, my friends, and consider that one does not laugh at God with impunity, nor at the King, whom God has sent to chastise you. Not long ago I was with some friends in a crowd, where an old man, fired with zeal, declaimed terribly against the Gallo-Greek Germans, whom he called the scourge of the fatherland, the poison of well-born souls, and the disgrace of the human race – whom the French, for all that, fawn over at present, holding them for the best of men. In fine he came little short of consigning them to the devil. Some members of our group, who were there with me, and who had rather tender consciences, were so moved by the good man's words that they trembled at the slightest sound, fearing that some devil would come and seize them from behind. I, who am a little more resolute, did in this situation what St Peter once did, that is, *confirmavi fratres meos*,[1] reproaching them for their want of courage, and showing them how important it is to have a conscience [which is] not doubtful, not scrupulous, but fortified with good reasons. I made them understand that we are working for the cause of the Church, that the name of the fatherland is a bogeyman of idiots, that an *homme de coeur* has the world for his fatherland, or rather that heaven is the common fatherland of Christians[2] and that the particular good of the German nation must give way to the general good of Christendom and to the orders of heaven. I recognize and I consider often enough how miserable the condition of the Germans will be under the French yoke. They already scorn our nation, when it still cuts a figure in the world; what will they not do when it is vanquished and completely contemptible, when they have reason to blame us not only for our naivete, but our cowardice, so unworthy of the past reputation of the nation and of the glory of our ancestors? They will take away our arms, as from men unworthy to carry them; they will abuse the illustrious families, or send them to France; benefices [and] all offices of consequence will be only for Frenchmen, or for the most servile souls that exist among the Germans; elevated minds who seem to preserve some measure of ancient virtue will be afflicted with a thousand evils, until they have accustomed all of them to slavery, and made the nation more fit to be an object of contempt than of fear. These kinds of thoughts are temptations sent by a

[1] Luke 22, 32: 'You in turn must be a strength to your brothers.'
[2] Cf. II Corinthians 5. 1.

demon, which torment me sometimes. For the mind is quick to form such ideas, and it is always difficult to get rid of feelings which seem to be born with us. But I will extricate myself first, and [then] I will make away with these scruples as I raise my soul to heaven.[1] For I reflect that what is taken for misery is true felicity, that good things are brought about through tribulations,[2] and that the Church is never more flourishing than when it appears to be oppressed. You will be even happier with God, O Germans, when the French have made you miserable on earth; you will go more willingly to heaven, leaving without regret this vale of miseries.[3] Go, then, to submit to the yoke which France offers you, and hasten to merit heaven by your promptness, your obedience, patience and other Christian virtues, by putting His Most Christian Majesty as soon as possible in a position to fight the Turks and the heretics. If this costs you your liberty, you will console yourselves by thinking that it is for the growth of the kingdom of Jesus Christ that you suffer so great a loss.[4]

But I take up the thread of my discourse, and I am certain that those who have well understood the reasons adduced above will, if they are of good faith, remain in agreement that His Most Christian Majesty has received from God a full power to do far more than we have seen him do until now; for one must grant that he uses it with great moderation, in view of his right to carry out whatever occurs to him, provided that it serve his greatness. For he is vicar-general of the earth, meant to exercise sovereignly the whole temporal jurisdiction and power, since God has declared him liberator of Christians and protector of the Church against the heretics and against the barbarians. That the Pope [should have] honor[ed] a king of Poland (though the most martial and intrepid in the world) with that title, is only a piece of Italian flattery, and, to speak plainly, a mockery of our King, who is in fact the sole vicar of the world, and the Pope his church-warden. His mission is heroic, ordinary laws do not obligate him at all, and his greatness is the sole measure of his justice, since everything that serves to augment it serves the glory and the well-being of the Church. Thus he can fail only by too much moderation, and everything which he does with the intention of aggrandizing himself will always be just. I should think that the Rev. Father de la Chaise, s.j., regular confessor of the King, whose knowledge and prudence are generally recognized, would be nearly of the same opinion; for being a man of conscience, how could he approve a number of things which are done in the King's name, and satisfy all of the scrupulous, if he were not devoted to such a general remedy?

[1] Luke 1. 46.   [2] Cf., *inter alia*, II Corinthians 4. 17 and II Timothy 3. 12.
[3] Cf. I Corinthians 15, 19.   [4] Cf. Romans 8. 17–1 .

There are some who flatter themselves that they can defend France's enterprises with reasons drawn from ordinary right; but they deceive themselves greatly, and when they engage in argumentation, one soon sees them cornered. As a result, as I have shown above, the wisest among the French avoid all disputes about right, and speak only as politicians, exaggerating, with great reason, the goodness and prudence of their monarch, who knows so well how to exploit his advantages. For some know nothing of, and others do not wish to say that they know anything of, the absolute right which heaven has given to their King. They will make use of it secretly, for all that, when the time comes. Witness this French minister who,[1] reasoning about the peace which was concluded a little later at the Pyrenees, strongly advised the King to sign all the renunciations which could be demanded of the [Spanish] Infanta, his betrothed, and to approve them as authoritatively as could be desired, even with oaths: and [who also advised] that he should never fail to have a free hand when the King of Spain came to die; for there is no good Frenchman (he said) who would wish to advise the King to neglect the interests of his crown, for which he is responsible to God and to posterity. There precisely is an outline of the jurisprudence and of the morality such as we have just established, that is, that the greatness of the King and of the French crown is above all other rights and oaths, of whatever character they may be.

But since this is so, it would be wrong to conceal so great a truth, which needs to be preached to be believed. And it is the more necessary to proclaim it, as it is impossible to defend the enterprises of France with principles [*raisons*] of ordinary right, as I have already remarked. And to make it more widely known, I shall have no difficulty in presenting here a part of what the enemies of France have a habit of complaining about so that it will be better recognized that there would be no way of excusing the actions of this crown, if the King did not have the privilege of doing what seems good to him, in his capacity as temporal vicar of God.

I shall begin with what happened in the times of Louis XIII. Cardinal Richelieu, in order to ease the conscience of this scrupulous prince, took steps to insure that several French doctors [of law] approved the alliances which he undertook with the heretics. A masked author called Alexander Patricius Armanus, who opposed this in a work called *Mars Gallicus*,[2] was held to have been the famous Jansen, Bishop of Ypres. All the minor

---

[1] Cardinal Mazarin.
[2] Alexander Patricius Armanus, pseudonym for Cornelius Jansenius, author of *Mars Gallicus, seu De Justitia Armorum et Foederum Regis Galliae* (2nd ed., 1639).

K

French writers have run aground on this reef, and disinterested persons have judged that not one of them had satisfactorily answered its arguments. Indeed, when France declared war against the House of Austria, nothing obliged her to go to that extremity. For the Imperial forces, even though they had been victorious at Nordlingen, were not lacking in a disposition towards peace, after having banished all doubt about their military capacity [*après avoir eprouvé l'incertitude du sort des armes*]; and if France had been willing to be a mediator rather than a party [to further conflict], it would have been easy for her to obtain a solid and equitable peace: the majority of German princes were not much adverse to it. But this was not the aim of France: she sought to fish in troubled waters, to overthrow the already shaky House of Austria, and to ruin Germany, which she saw as the only obstacle to her greatness, by herself. But she did not care to recognize, Catholic as she claimed to be, that the Emperor had undertaken the war only to preserve his domains, and afterwards (the occasion seeming favorable) to oblige the Protestants to give up what they had occupied in violation of the express provisions of the Settlement of Passau. In any case, since it was for France alone, and still is for France alone to give peace or war to Europe, the most zealous persons blamed on her all the blood of Christendom spilled from that time to our own: 'It is France alone', they say, 'who set Europe in flames.' It is believed that the French fomented dissensions in England, and that they are not altogether innocent of the infamous parricide which was the result of them.[1]

The rebellions in Portugal, in Catalonia, in Naples, in Hungary, are their work, and they make no secret of it. What efforts have they not made to upset the peace which was made at Munster, between the Spanish and the Dutch! What shall we say of the peace sworn to at the Pyrenees, and of the Queen's renunciation, which was an essential point of the said peace?

Certainly, if there is a way to trust in assurances in human negotiations, if the public pledge of kings has some effect, if religion and conscience are not simply names invented to fool the simple-minded, this peace ought to have been solid and sure; but since it has been broken and trampled underfoot on the first favorable occasion, one must grant (they say) that he who would henceforth trust the word of France is in fact simple-minded, and worthy of being deceived; this is why the Dutch, the Spanish, the Emperor, and the rest of the allies who treated peace at Nimwegen are being at present, or will soon be, punished for their credulity.

For if they had believed that the French would undertake far more against the Empire and the low-countries in time of peace than in the middle of war, they would have been blind; or rather, they would have

[1] The reference is to the execution of Charles I (1649).

preferred to fight together than to perish separately. If we return to the beginnings of the last war, is there anything more violent than the way in which the late Duke of Lorraine was deprived of his estates? His whole crime was that he did not want to be at the mercy of some French governor or *intendant*, and that he sought to establish his security by the most innocent defensive alliances in the world. The war against the Dutch was so far removed from any appearance of reason (I speak in the guise of the enemies of France) that not even a single pretext for it could be found. Nonetheless, everything violent that France has done since that time, in Germany, in the low-countries, and elsewhere, has been excusable only because it was a necessary consequence of that war. It is on this basis that the French armies have marched across Germany (in order to keep at a distance the assistance which might come to the Dutch or divert France); that they have taken Trier, surprised and dismantled the ten towns of Alsace in a way which did not adhere very closely to good faith, and carried out all kinds of hostilities in the Rhenish Palatinate, all of it on the basis of the slightest suspicions, which *raison de guerre* alone (but the most unjust war ever undertaken) authorized. They have had the insolence to declare to the Emperor that he must be the first to withdraw his troops from the lands of the Empire, and that the King would do the same, when the Emperor had given his word (and several other princes would have stood as guarantors) that he would make no more sorties out of his hereditary lands, that is to say that the King of France had more right in the Empire than the Emperor himself. Everyone is supposed to keep quiet and trust the word of the French ministers, who preach everywhere that the King sought nothing in the war except the chastisement of (I know not what) insolence of the Dutch: as if the same desire would not yet bring him to humiliate others in their turn, and as if he had the right to act like a school-master who, switch in hand, treated the others like little boys. But everyone saw that his aim went farther than simple bravado; that he would assure himself of the posts on the lower Rhine, putting strong garrisons there; that the crime of the Dutch was to have blocked the complete occupation of the low-countries; in fine that the King's ambition was a little 'interested', and looked as much to profit as to glory. As for the '*dépendences*' [parts of the Empire claimed by France], and the *dépendences* of the *dépendences ad infinitum*, which surpass the principal [France herself]: it must be true (they say) that whoever lets himself be dazzled by these kinds of reasons is truly simple-minded; that there is nothing so unreasonable as this Chamber of Justice, established by the King himself, which always rules in favor of the King, and which claims that those who do not submit to its decrees are deprived of their rights;

that it is the ultimate insolence to try to make its will pass for a general law, to prescribe for the Empire a fatal period of a few days or weeks, during which it must declare itself on the cession of the eighth part of Germany; and if the Empire is late, by however little, all the evils which happen will be imputed to it, and the King will wash his hands of the whole affair.[1] On one side they want to force the Spanish to accept precisely the arbitrator that France names, and on the other they refuse to allow the Empire to enter into arbitration or into a mediation devised by both sides. They maintain that the taking of Strassburg was the most violent and the most Ottoman political act that a Christian prince has ever undertaken, and that it is the height of impudence to try to excuse it; that this *coup* was made in peacetime without any shadow of a pretext, against freshly given pledges which guaranteed that everything would remain in the condition that it had since the departure of the King's ambassadors for Frankfurt; that all judicious people have judged that, after this, it would be useless to rely on the rules of right and on the laws of honor; that conscience, good faith, and the law of nations are cruel terms and vain shadows, since they no longer look for even a pretext for violence. For in earlier times even those who carefully examined the minutest points of the laws of France took care not to think of Strassburg, for fear of being taken for visionaries or for sophists surprised *en flagrant délit*, since the words of the Peace of Münster are too clear, and leave so little room for chicanery that it seems that the ministers who conceived them [the pretexts] have, in a prophetic spirit, pre-viewed and anticipated all the escapes which an impudent sophist could think of; but, if they have been clever enough to keep their mouths shut in front of those who might still have some trace of shame, they have not had enough to join hands with those who haughtily trample reason underfoot. For it has done them no good to have declared in very clear terms that no part of Alsace except what the Empire held would be ceded to France; to have named the places ceded by their names and nicknames; and to have quite expressly excepted the very principalities and estates of the Empire which France has already taken in, that is the Bishopric and city of Strassburg, the princes of Petite-Pierre, the Counts of Hanau, and the free nobility of Alsace.

Some French lawyers,[2] seeing themselves pressed from the side of the Peace of Westphalia, have retired into another line of defense, and, finding nothing in our times which favors them, look for imaginary rights from the time of Dagobert and Charlemagne. I am astonished that they

[1] Psalm 26. 6.

[2] See, *inter alia*, A. Aubery, *Des Justes Prétensions* (Paris, 1668).

do not also demand of the great Seigneur [Sultan] the conquests which the Gauls made earlier in Greece and in Galatia, and that they do not prosecute the present-day Romans for the money which their ancestors had promised the Gauls for saving their capital, [and] whose payment Camillus had interrupted. Indeed, the serious authors among them are ashamed of these ridiculous impertinences for, if they were allowed, it would be useless to cite henceforth the peace treaties of Münster and of Nimwegen, and to contest some place or land with an Emperor, king or prince who ought to be destroyed or despoiled altogether as a simple usurper, since all of Germany with the low-countries and nearly all of Italy would be enveloped in the general claim of Charlemagne's Empire, if it had to be revived today. There are nonetheless some people who suspect that His Most Christian Majesty intends these vast and vague claims, since he offers to the Empire, in case it leaves and cedes to him what he has taken recently, the willingness to renounce all his other rights – which, however, he does not explain at all; in which he acts wisely, for one always has a better opinion of unknown things, and often secrets which are made public are exposed to derision.

I have wished to represent naively what is said against the claims of the King, so that everyone sees that there is no means of saving them except by the expedient which I have used, which exempts the King from the necessity of answering to principles of right, whatever force they may have. But, since the vulgar know nothing of this beautiful invention, one should not be surprised if those who have been freshly despoiled torment themselves and move heaven and earth with tragic words, if they show us fields inundated with Christian blood to satisfy the ambition of a nation [which is the] sole disturber of the public peace, if they make us see the thousands immolated by iron, by hunger and by miseries, only so that they have some cause to write on the gates of Paris the name of Louis the Great in letters of gold. 'It is only for France', they say, 'to make Europe peaceable and happy. What greater crime can one conceive than to be responsible for all the evils of Christendom, for so much innocent blood spilled, for outrageous actions, for the curses of the miserable, for the moans of the dying, and lastly for the tears of widows and of orphans which rise to pierce heaven,[1] and which will move God sooner or later to vengeance; this great God, whose judgments are so terrible that the faces of the *tartuffes*[2] and the words of the sophists will not deceive one who does

---

[1] Cf. Rousseau's *L'État de Guerre* (*c.* 1753–5, Vaughan I, pp. 293 ff.), which closely parallels Leibniz on these points.
[2] The reference is to Molière's play, *Tartuffe*. In French the word has come to mean a secretly licentious hypocrite who affects piety.

not distinguish between a king and a peasant, except to augment punishments in proportion to the greatness of the sinners and to the nature and consequences of their crimes?' In this fine field the enemies of France push their declamation as far as the eye can see; but they surpass even themselves, now that the Turk is going to fall upon Christendom: 'Two hundred thousand Christians thrust by the sword into the barbarians' graveyard, or perhaps taken away to a slavery worse than death, in a condition fatal to souls: this (they say) cries out for vengeance against those who have stirred up and helped the rebels in Hungary with money, arms and advice, although they saw in advance the dreadful evils which this conduct would draw down upon those Christian people exposed to this danger. And finally, they say, let it not be imagined that the authors of these beautiful schemes repent of them, [for] one sees, now that the peril has reached its highest degree, now that Vienna has been on the point of surrendering, now that the Church drowns itself in tears and grovels in the ashes to get some relief from God, one sees, I say, these madmen pushing the King to disperse, by using his allies, the German forces necessary to repulse the common enemy, and, what is more, to openly attack the House of Austria at the same time that it is overpowered by the weight of the Ottoman power, to the great astonishment of all Christendom, [and] all of it without any appearance of reason, on frivolous pretexts of some small *dépendences*, whose legal proof they do not even dare to undertake: as a consequence of which, doubtless, either Vienna will perish or the Emperor will be forced into a shameful peace, pernicious to Christendom as well, which will make this prince henceforward contemptible to the whole world; or, finally, [German] hatred [of France] will be rendered immortal, in case the Turks should happily be repulsed, since the Emperor must judge that he will not be able to save himself from the traps France has set for him, except by an immortal and eternal war, which can end only with the complete enfeeblement of one or the other party, which will make it unable either to undertake affronts or to feel them – a thing which one can achieve only after making rivers of blood run. But if it had pleased the King (they say) in a time so perilous for Christianity, to show the greatness of his soul by sacrificing to the public good several inches of land in the low-countries, and by behaving toward the Germans in a way which did not force a nation until now considered generous to make a desperate move to save its honor and its salvation; if it had pleased the King to agree to the just requests of the Emperor, who wanted to end simultaneously the quarrels which France might have with the Empire and with the low-countries (which are a part of it), without wanting to separate, by a suspect craftiness, or by an insupportable imperiousness, allies so united by blood, by right and by interest, in order to ruin each in its turn; in short if it had pleased him to act in such a way, after the Peace of Nimwegen, that one could reasonably have hoped for some quiet; if, I say, His Most Christian Majesty had wanted to grant these things to the prayers of the Holy Father and the tears of all Europe prostrate at his feet, he could have tranquilly kept the greatest part of what he had taken, lain the foundations of a solid peace in Europe, whose author and arbiter he would have been; [he could have] won all hearts, and drawn public acclaim on himself, and, finally, undertaken expeditions against the barbarians infinitely more glorious and perhaps more important than anything he could do in Europe. But France having held to a course quite opposed to these good counsels, she forces the others to desperate resolutions and acts in such a way that it will be henceforth an impardonable folly to trust her word and to hope for a good peace,[1] inasmuch as neither the sworn renunciation [of Spain] nor the promise which the King had given to change nothing after the departure of his ambassadors for Frankfurt has been able to guarantee the Peace of the Pyrenees; all of that did not stop the seizure of Strassburg, and the order which that prince gave last year to raise the blockade of Luxembourg, in view of the forces with which the Turks were menacing Christianity, has been found illusory, since at present when the Turk has passed from threats to actions in a quite terrible way, even this does not stop the French officers from choosing this very time of general consternation, while Germany trembles and the rest of Europe is in a state of astonishment, to carry out their master's business, to finish off the poor low-countries, and to set off a new war light-heartedly – an action which one could not undertake to excuse without an extreme impudence or simple-mindedness. There are some who hope that France will not do [these things] with impunity, and that the vengeance of heaven will swiftly follow so black an action; that the public hatred, the disabusing of well-meaning men (who until now have been able to retain some measure of good opinion about French conduct), and an infamy which will pass on to posterity, can take the place of a sufficiently great punishment; that among the French themselves, people whose conscience is still not extinguished by a long practice of crimes, will tremble at the sight of the magnitude of this impiety; that awareness of the badness of a cause is not always without effect, even among soldiers and the people, whom the slightest reversal of fortune can cut down, or

---

[1] Cf. Kant's *Eternal Peace*, 1st section, 6th preliminary article: 'No state at war with another shall permit such acts of warfare as must make mutual confidence impossible in time of future peace...' (trans. C. J. Friedrich, *The Philosophy of Kant*, Modern Library, New York, 1949, p. 434).

stir up into dangerous schemes, which are hatched in the souls of many malcontents, [and] which a long series of successes has covered rather than extinguished.

'People delude themselves, then, that France will soon repent of her conduct, and that the evils will fall on their author's heads. For', they say, 'she must do one of these two things, namely: either seize by the hair [*prendre aux cheveux*] a wonderful occasion to exercise her generosity, by giving to the Empire and to Spain a tolerable peace, or again, trampling underfoot all respect and all shame, must fall on Germany with all her forces to oblige it to choose between Mohamed IV and Louis XIV. Now that France, not wanting to have any regard for piety, and not daring to make a public profession of complete impiety, is losing this favorable conjuncture, by the prudence of [following] the middle course, which Machiavelli observes always to have destroyed great schemes,[1] they hope that, when the Turk shall be repulsed, France will be able to repent either of her piety (such as it is) or of her perfect impiety.'

There, then, is a portion of what is said publicly against France; for the veneration which one owes to great princes has made me suppress those expressions [which are] the most biting and the most *outré*, [and] which run throughout books and conversations.

Which cannot satisfy those who seek a defense for France in common right. But our principles will extract them from their embarrassment, and will give them a means of turning confusion against these rash censurers who undertake to criticize the actions of the best and greatest of kings, of whose saintly intentions they have no knowledge. For if they could look into the interior of his soul, or if they heard him talk with his confessor, I think that they would rein in their slanderous language. This great prince has foreseen everything: he knows the evils which he does or which he permits, [and] he himself trembles when he envisages the loss of so many thousands of souls. But what do you want? How can he resist the vocation from on high which obligates him? He sees that all other ways of curing the ills of Christendom, except those that he undertakes by iron and fire, would be only a palliative; gangrene cannot be cured except by means which involve cruelty. One must cut to the root of our miseries. *Habet aliquid ex iniquo omne magnum exemplum quod utilitate publica repensatur.*[2]

---

[1] Machiavelli, *Discourses* I, xxvii.

[2] A slightly incomplete and inexact citation of Tacitus' *Annales* xiv, 44. The original Latin reads: 'Habet aliquid ex iniquo omne magnum exemplum, quod contra singulos utilitate publica rependitur', and is translated by Jackson thus: 'All great examples carry with them something of injustice – injustice compensated, as against individual suffering, by the advantage of the community.'

Jesus Christ himself said that he had come to bring the sword, and not peace, in order thereby to establish a true peace.[1] Since, then, not only the light of an inward vocation (which could suffice for pretended reformers), but also outward signs of an extraordinary mission (namely miracles and the perpetual assistance of heaven), assure him of the justice of his cause, and even oblige him to forge ahead, it is essential that he follow God, who summons him to the general restoration of the affairs of a corrupted Christendom, that he seek his grandeur as necessary to the execution of so great a plan, that he ruin the Austrians who are opposed to it, since, as long as this House subsists, the union of Christians under one leader and the conquest of heretics are impracticable.

There will be some who will imagine that His Most Christian Majesty would do better to begin his beautiful designs by the routing of the Turks than by the affliction of the poor Christians: but these people do not reflect at all that it is the Germans and the Flemish who live on the frontiers of France, and not the Turks; that one must pass from one's neighbors to people far away, and move in these great matters by solid degrees, rather than by vain and perilous leaps. But, without looking for political reasons, here is one of conscience: which is that the King wishes to follow the example of Jesus Christ himself, who began with the Jews, and then ordered the Apostles to turn *ad gentes*;[2] and the King, in imitation of this, will create for himself, by the reduction of the Christians, a sure passage to go one day to the infidels.

Leibniz omits the words, 'contra singulos' ('as against individual suffering'), which makes the passage simpler. And Leibniz' last word, 'repensatur', is incorrect. Cf. Tacitus, *The Annals* (trans. John Jackson, Harvard University Press, Cambridge, Mass., 1937), p. 178.

[1] Matthew 10, 34 and John 14. 27.
[2] Matthew 28, 19 and Mark 16. 15.

10. Manifesto for the Defense of the Rights of Charles III
(1703)

Leibniz wrote the *Manifesto* during the War of the Spanish Succession to defend the rights of the House of Hapsburg to the throne of Spain, after the grandson of Louis XIV had brought Spain into the Bourbon orbit by being named King of Spain in the will of the last Hapsburg king, Charles II. In the *Manifesto*, Leibniz demonstrated his legal ability in a long proof of the illegality of the will of Charles II, to which he added an extremely effective, if somewhat exaggerated, account of French manners and morals, designed to prove that Spain would be ruined by the atheism and libertinism of France. This last section shows that Leibniz was a rather able (if early) sociologist, and that he perceived in 1703 some of the flaws in French society which much later writers (such as de Tocqueville) saw as the cause of the Revolution. And he anticipated Montesquieu in his dislike of the over-centralization of France since the time of Richelieu, and in his fear that the nobility had been made useless. (The present translation follows the version printed in vol. III of Foucher de Careil's edition of Leibniz; since the work is somewhat repetitious some passages, merely reenforcing arguments which are already clear, have been cut.)

Charles III, King of Spain and Archduke of Austria, appearing in person in Spain to take possession of the entire monarchy, in the condition in which it belonged to Charles II, his predecessor; the statement [of the rights] of His Catholic Majesty is based first on the incontestable right which the Emperor, his father, and the King of the Romans, his elder brother, left to him in a proper form; and in the second place on the public good and the safety of the great and of the people – whom conscience and their highest interest ought to bring to range themselves on the side of His Majesty. This Manifesto will make both points as clear as daylight, in the most succinct possible way.

As for the question of rights, it is well known that the Emperor Leopold is the son of Ferdinand III, Emperor of the Romans, and of Marie-Anne, Infanta of Spain, daughter of Philip III, and sister of Philip IV, monarchs of Spain; and that he was the sole heir of the rights of the Infanta, his mother, because of the premature death of his elder brother Ferdinand IV, King of the Romans. Now, the posterity of the Infanta

Marie-Anne, reduced to the Emperor alone and to his two sons or to their descendants, alone succeeds to all the rights of the Spanish monarchy after the death of the last king, Charles II, son of Philip IV. For, though it is true that Philip III gave his elder daughter, Anne of Austria, to Louis XIII, King of France, who had by her Louis XIV and the late Duke of Orléans; and that Philip IV had two daughters, of whom the eldest, Maria Theresa, was given to Louis XIV, King of France, and the second, Marguerite Theresa, to Leopold, Emperor of the Romans, whose daughter, Maria Antonia, born of this marriage, married Maximilian, Elector of Bavaria:

Nonetheless, the rights of all these persons, who could have been obstacles to the son of the Emperor Leopold – namely the rights of Anne and of Maria Theresa, Queens of France, and of Maria Antonia, Electress of Bavaria have been extinguished and annulled by their renunciations, [which were] approved by their spouses before these marriages...; such that there are no other descendants than those of the two Queens of France, Anne and Maria Theresa, [and they are] excluded by renunciations [which are] the most solemn that human prudence can devise – sworn on the Evangelists, confirmed by the oaths of their spouses and by the most authoritative public treaties. That of the Pyrenees [1659], which was a treaty of peace between the two crowns [of France and Spain], which brought peace to Europe by ending a great and long war, serves particularly as a fundamental law on both sides. Now, without the renunciation [of Spain by the Infanta at the time of her marriage to Louis XIV], the marriage would not have taken place; thus it must continue in force, unless those who oppose it declare haughtily that they make treaties only to deceive, that oaths serve them only as traps, and that justice and religion pass, among them, only for chimeras pure and simple.

However, strange to tell (and this is a very bad example to set for Christendom), the armies of France invaded the Spanish Netherlands after the death of Philip IV, on the frivolous pretext of a right of devolution, established [by the civil law] between [private] individuals in these provinces, according to which the daughter of the first marriage is preferred in certain cases to the son born of the second; one saw French writers, supplied with public authority to establish pretended rights of their Queen, go so far as to put in doubt the validity of the renunciation by this princess. But their sophisms were destroyed by opposing writings on the part of the Emperor and of Spain, in a way which earned the approbation of the disinterested part of Europe, which condemned highly the manifest and insupportable injustice of the conduct of France. And it was from this time that the designs of this crown, tending to the establishment of universal monarchy and to the oppression of public liberty, were recognized, and that the most interested powers saw themselves forced to take measures to block it as early as possible.

These [French] writers looked for quibbles drawn quite inappropriately from the civil law, and they alleged primarily that the renunciations of the daughters, which gave up their rights inherited from their fathers, were odious and limited in a number of ways: as if everyone did not know that civil laws affecting individuals cannot be prejudicial to the law of nations, and to public law, which regulate the succession in kingdoms and the observation of treaties between crowns, and that the aim of these civil laws, on this point, was only to stop daughters from ruining themselves by their accommodativeness. A king, on the contrary, cannot provide better for his daughter, than by securing for her a marriage with another great king; and the safety of the state, which ordains the blocking of a transfer of a monarchy to a nation which one has good reason to fear, is infinitely preferable to the interests of a single person, whose happiness is already taken care of, and who, as a result, renounces quite voluntarily and most reasonably and efficaciously, that which one cannot grant her together with this marriage...

Some passionate partisans of the Bourbon party, little versed in law, have alleged some other reasons [which are] of little importance against the force of the renunciation. And since one cannot act to the detriment of others' rights, they imagine that the renunciation of a father or of a mother cannot destroy the right which could belong to the children: and that, as a result, that which Queen Maria Theresa and the King, her spouse, promised, cannot do harm to the Dauphin and to his children. But, besides the fact that the Most Christian King, at least, cannot support the claims of the Dauphin and his line, bound as he is by his oath: one must know that it is true that one cannot derogate from a right acquired from another, and that even a father cannot in the slightest diminish that [right] of his children [who are] already born; but as for that of future children, all jurisprudence (with respect to dispositions which can be made to their disadvantage, by the consent of other interested parties, and with the confirmation of the ruler, if necessary) counts it as non-existent, and [considers] as nonentities those who are without attributes, and, as a result, as not yet having a single acquired right. Without this it would be impossible to make laws, pacts, alienations or stable transactions, since those who are not yet born cannot consent, and would always be ready to oppose what has been done. And this would happen above all between princes and republics; for one can never bind posterity, and as a result treaties, cessions and exchanges between the powers would be only personal, and would always be in danger of being overturned. This would deprive men of the means of ending wars by some durable convention, and would, as a consequence, be absolutely contrary to natural law, to the Divine law, and to the law of nations.

This is why the French court, seeing that the whole world was horrified by these maxims, which tended to violate the most express oaths, and to overturn everything which is most sacred among men, bethought itself of another expedient, and undertook to recognize the renunciation as good and valid, in order to save (if possible) the appearance of good faith. But this was [done] after having forged a piece of chicanery which seemed suited to elude the effect of it, and to fool those who are dazzled by words.

It was with this in view that the partisans of France at the court of Madrid drew up a will in the name of the late king, when he was near his end, in which, in article XVII, they made him interpret the Treaty of the Pyrenees and the contract of marriage with Queen Maria Theresa, together with the renunciation which is inserted therein, in a manner contrary to everything that had always been understood; as if the aim of this renunciation was nothing but the stopping of the union of the two crowns on one head – a thing which could be avoided (they said) by calling the Duke of Anjou, second son of the Dauphin, to the crown of Spain, on the condition that if the Duke of Burgundy[1] should die without leaving successors in France, the Duke of Anjou would be obliged to choose, and that in case he should prefer the crown of France, the Duke of Berry, his younger brother, would become king of Spain on the same terms, which would also apply to their successors. And the Most Christian King, accepting this pretended will, wanted to avail himself of this interpretation...

It is not at all necessary to decide here whether the will in which this strange interpretation was placed in advance, should be attributed to the late King, and whether the will is valid. It is known that the King, even a few weeks before his death, as always previously, had committed himself to the Emperor in the strongest and most positive way, to preserve the succession for him and his posterity, recognizing that this would be entirely in conformity with law. It is known, too, that this prince had always been constant in his sentiments, despite all the solicitations to the contrary, believing that he was bound to it [an Austrian succession] in conscience, and that he could not depart from it without doing to the Emperor and to his [heirs] the greatest wrong in the world, and without

---

[1] That is, the Dauphin, eldest son of Louis XIV.

plunging Spain and the whole monarchy into the greatest misfortunes...
Thus it is not credible that the late King, in the last moment of his life,
would depart from what he had always wanted for such strong reasons,
supposing that he was of sound mind [*que son esprit ait été dans son assiette*],
and that no one used evil arts to oblige him to sign a will [which was]
contrary to his constant and perpetual will. One would need proofs as
clear as daylight to be persuaded that everything went as it should in so
strange an action.

The civil laws have followed natural reason, in requiring that wills be
accompanied by a good number of irreproachable witnesses, and other
solemnities suited to exclude fraud. If this must be observed in the will of
a [private] individual, for how much greater reason must one pay attention to it when it is a question of the successor of a king and of one of the
greatest monarchies of the world, and when there are so many reasons for
suspicion! It was essential to omit nothing of what could remove suspicions and doubts. It was essential *not* to shut in the King, nor to forbid
the presence of the Queen, of the ambassador of the Emperor, and of the
great, as against the Bourbon party. It was essential that so great and
extraordinary an action be almost public. It was essential that the King
order, of his own volition, that such a will be drawn up, and not that
one bring him one already drawn up, and that one try to force him to sign
it.

It was essential that one not abuse the name of God and the rights of
conscience, and that one not feign a popular sedition in order to give false
terrors to a displaced and dying prince, who had already been overpowered and whom one threatened cruelly with eternal damnation and
with the violence (at hand, but imaginary) of a brutal mob, in order to force
him to sign whatever was wanted – without speaking of other considerations which make this will insupportable.

But even if it had been made by King Charles II by his own choice,
and in the most incontestable way in the world, it would be useless to
change the fundamental law of the state and of the Peace of the Pyrenees
by an interpretation contrary to the text, to reason and to the whole of
jurisprudence, to the prejudice of commitments [already] made and of
rights acquired by another.

All the world agrees that it is not in the power of a king to dispose of his
kingdoms by will, whether he does it directly, or whether he claims to do
it as an interpreter of laws or pacts, if this interpretation cannot be maintained otherwise; and the French upheld this truth themselves, when they
did not yet hope that a will of a king of Spain could be favorable to them.
It is now a question of examining this interpretation in itself, to find out

whether it is true that a Bourbon prince, the descendant of Queen Maria Theresa, can inherit Spain notwithstanding the renunciation of this princess, provided that he is not at the same time heir presumptive of the crown of France; and whether this exception can be maintained on the pretext that the motive of the renunciation is nothing else than the stopping of the union of the two crowns under one king, and thus ceases in her person.

To overturn this exception from cellar to attic [*de fond en comble*] and show that there has never been a fraud more insupportable and less capable of excusing the violation of the most solemn treaties and oaths, it is more than sufficient to show: 1. That the jurisconsults have for a long time generally condemned this 'exception based on a motive which ceases'. 2. That France has made a very bad use of it. 3. That one ought to have spoken quite differently, in the marriage-contract, if this exception had been in conformity with the sentiments of the contractors. 4. That the motive itself, which is claimed to have ceased, does not cease in this case. 5. That the act of renunciation itself shows this. 6. That it appears that they must have had other motives [as well]. 7. That the act itself shows signs of this. 8. That this is said expressly. 9. That still another motive is particularized, even in formal terms, which applies here, among those which are understood. 10. That, finally, if all the motives noted really ceased, the 'exception based on a motive which ceases' is rejected in formal terms in the act itself. These points will be verified in order.

1. The 'exception based on a motive which ceases', which is brought up in the pretended will, is so little applicable here, that there is no true jurisconsult who would dare to reason as they have, for fear of prostituting himself. One needs only to have what is called a *jurisprudence cérébrine*, that is, the kind that ill-instructed persons think up in their heads for frivolous reasons, in order to confound the *condition* with the *cause* expressed in some will. True jurisconsults have provided for this, for a long time, by rejecting this exception in such a case. Gaius, the ancient Roman jurisconsult, in the seventeenth law of ownership in the *Digest*,[1] which treats conditions and designations, observes that if the testator says, 'I give my land to Titius, because he looked after my affairs', this legacy is legal, even if the reason should be found false. But if the reason had been given conditionally, that is, if the testator had said, 'I give him my land, if it is found that he looked after my affairs', nothing would be owing to him if this were not true. This distinction is quite judicious. There is a great difference between 'if' and 'because': the declaration

---

[1] *Corpus Iuris Civilis: Digesta* xxxv, 1, 17 (edited by T. Mommsen, Weidmann, Berlin, 1877; also summarized in the *Institutes*).

modified by an 'if' is in suspense; but the declaration for which one wants to *give* the reason is pure and absolute, and can subsist even if this reason should not exist... [1]

II. In contracts as well... one cannot interpret motives as one likes, to the prejudice of another. Otherwise it would be easy to overturn all conventions, following the new method which France wanted to use in order to depart from the last treaty which she made with the late King of England [William III] and the Estates-General [of the Netherlands] concerning the Spanish succession – in which case she wanted to use the same frivolous exception based on a motive which ceases, by citing whatever motive seemed good to her, and then making it pass for 'ceased' whenever it seemed good to her. For she claimed that the sole motive for the treaty had been to stop the war, which was not at all [true], since one must pay attention not only to peace, but also to justice: and if, to maintain peace, one wanted to suffer everything, the most evil [persons] would prevail everywhere...

III. Although this alone is more than sufficient, nonetheless there are still many other things to say, which absolutely destroy this fraud. It is clear above all that, if the intention of those who took part in the renunciation had been simply to stop the unification of the two monarchies in the person of a single monarch, and to limit the disposition to this single case, they could and would have spoken as one ordinarily explains his intentions in situations of so great an importance, to obviate doubts and prevent difficulties: that is to say, they would have explained clearly that in case King Louis XIV had two male children by Queen Maria Theresa, the second could succeed [to the throne] of Spain, or, that if he had only one male together with some daughters, the eldest of the daughters could succeed there, etc. Instead of this it is said, on the contrary, what has already been observed. Can one believe that so clever a negotiator as Cardinal Mazarin, and the whole Ministry of France (which has dreamed from that time of means to elude this renunciation, as the letters of the Cardinal and the speeches published immediately after the marriage made known) would have neglected to have had distinctly marked a provision of this consequence in favor of the House of Bourbon, if they had seen any way of doing it, if they had known that this would be the sense of the act, and if they had dared to make the slightest mention of it? One would,

---

[1] In this passage, which is somewhat unclear, Leibniz appears to mean that a motive cannot 'cease' in law unless it was stated conditionally – that is, stated in terms of 'if', rather than 'because'. The clause in question in the Peace of the Pyrenees was not stated conditionally; hence Leibniz' argument that its motive cannot cease.

in fact, have had to lose his common sense to persuade himself of this, and that alone would suffice to prove certainly that the interpretation which has been forged, a bit late, is ridiculous and insupportable... If the court of France overlooked or failed to explain so manifest a meaning, if it was the true one, those who took part in the business were the stupidest of men; but if they dared not lay it on the table, seeing well that it would be rejected at once, and that it was contrary to the nature of the act, which could not get by with this declaration (as is the evident truth), they were dreaming of malice and of fraud, supposing that they had held to this sense *in petto*,[1] and claimed to use it at the right time and place...

IV. What is more, the exception based on a motive which ceases does not apply, since this motive of stopping the union of the two crowns, which is alleged as the sole cause of the renunciation, has not ceased at all. It is true that at present they abstain from uniting these crowns, but they are putting themselves at present in a position to be able to unite them one day, when the occasion presents itself. And while they promise to refrain from doing this in the future as well, there is no assurance [that they will not]: for, besides the fact that these distinctions and reservations are perilous and should be treated cautiously in so great an affair, reasons for suspicion could not be greater than in this case, since one will have no other guarantee against what is feared, than the word and the good faith of the Bourbons – among whom an open profession is made, in speeches and in arguments, and still more in facts and in actions, of not being the slave of one's word...

V. Thus evident necessity and the safety of Spain (in order that she not be reduced one day to a province) demand that she not be exposed [to such a possibility], given so many reasons for apprehension, which leap at one's eyes. And the most certain means of obviating this fatal conjunction is that which the act of renunciation itself has suggested: that is, 'to prevent henceforth' (these are the formal terms) 'the occasions of such a conjunction', and thus to cut the thread of the succession of French princes in Spain, in order to bring to an end the hopes of the French and the fears of the Spanish...[2]

The renunciation, pure and absolute, of the late Queen Maria Theresa, for herself and for her posterity subsisting in full force, there is no more room to doubt that the Emperor alone, and his line, has the right to the Spanish succession in preference to all others, and that His Imperial

---

[1] 'Within the breast', i.e. secretly.
[2] Sections VI to X are omitted here because they deal with minor points mentioned elsewhere in the *Manifesto*.

Majesty, as well as the King of the Romans, having ceded their rights to the Archduke, second son of the Emperor, now Charles III, King of Spain, His Catholic Majesty should be universally recognized as the true and sole successor and monarch of all the provinces of the Spanish monarchy. One can even say that France has recognized that the Emperor's line has the advantage in point of law since, in renewing her [proposed] treaty of a pretended partition [of Spain into Hapsburg and Bourbon parts], she had consented that the Archduke should have the body of the Spanish monarchy, from which she wanted to detach only the states of Italy, which were to have been divided between the Dauphin and the Duke of Lorraine, without speaking of some other changes of less importance.

This is why the partisans of the Bourbons, defeated in point of the right of succession, now have recourse to a pretended legitimate possession, as if the peoples of the Spanish monarchy had voluntarily received the Duke of Anjou to be their king. But one should not attribute to these people, without manifest proof, having had the intention to commit a flagrant injustice and to derogate from the right of the legitimate successor. It is one of the greatest principles of justice that, except in a case of extreme and indispensable necessity, which knows no law, one cannot deprive anyone of what belongs to him, unless he is guilty [of a crime]. Now, what can one blame on the Emperor, who, in conformity to a great principle of legality, rejected the most advantageous offers of France and of other powers who had made the treaty of partition – the aim of His Imperial Majesty being only to do nothing which was not conformable to law, and about which the king and people of Spain could complain with an appearance of justice? The late King, moreover, was firmly resolved to keep his word to His Imperial Majesty, and what was done, allegedly by him, in the will, should be counted for nothing, as has been sufficiently shown. Besides, everyone knows that even if it happens that *force majeure* obliges subjects and a whole country to do homage to a conquering usurper, or to abjure their master, as often happens in war, when a place is taken by the enemy, the true lord always retains his right whole and unscathed, until he renounces it by the treaty of peace, or otherwise.[1] Now, if this force or necessity does not in the slightest destroy the right of a legitimate ruler, how much less is it destroyed in this case, where such necessity does not exist! For the Most Christian King did not take care to make himself master of the Spanish monarchy assured of the help of the

---

[1] Leibniz develops this point at greater length, with particular reference to the rights of the Holy Roman Emperor, in his *Observations on the Abbé de St Pierre's Project for Perpetual Peace* (1715), for which see pp. 181ff. below.

rest of Europe; besides which the fiefs and lands of the Roman Church and of the Empire cannot be given to him who has no right to them, without the consent of the lord of the fief...

There was not, then, the shadow of a necessity which could bring the kingdoms [Castille and Aragon] and provinces of the monarchy of Spain to give themselves to a Bourbon prince, contrary to the incontestable right of the Emperor. But, in addition, it is not true that the 'voluntary' reception of the Duke of Anjou as ruler or king, which the partisans of the Bourbons attribute to the people, is authenticated. The will of nations does not express itself through magistrates or regents, but through the assemblies of the estates of kingdoms and provinces. It was necessary, then, that those who had turned themselves into regents assemble what is called the *cortes*, or the estates, both in Castille and in Aragon, before making the slightest decision concerning the succession. For it is well known that a king does not have the right to give away his kingdom by testament, even if that which is attributed to Charles II had been formally correct... It is quite evident that, if these required formalities had been observed, and if the will of the estates and the people had been followed, ...all fear of foreign arms, as well as all bad practices within, would have ended, [and] the right of the House of Austria, which would have preserved everything in its old and entire condition, would have prevailed without difficulty. But, to the great astonishment of everyone, those who held the helm of government did nothing of the kind, in order to have [a sense of] the true opinion of the people and of interested parties: quite the contrary, some persons in the [pro-French] cabal at the Spanish court had themselves named as regents in the pretended will attributed to the late king; they proclaimed the Duke of Anjou; nobody dared to oppose this, intimidated by the fear of French actions, and by fear of being mistreated. Self-preservation, the love of tranquility, and the terror of an already triumphant party, had the same effect in the provinces of Spain; and foreign governments followed the torrent, and were won over. However, these irregularities and acts of violence cannot at all give rights to somebody, nor take them away from somebody else, nor pass for the will of the people.

One need only attend the proof to assure oneself that if the Bourbons, if they dare, give liberty to the countries of the monarchy, and let them choose voluntarily and with free will a king to govern them, that if they bring to an end the terror of arms, and if newly arrived Frenchmen leave Madrid and all of Spain, but above all the low-countries and Milan, King Charles III and his allies will do as much, and will pull back their troops, and we will see on which side the choice will fall.

At present, the right of the House of Austria [to the Kingdom of Spain], inherited by King Charles III, being fully established, it is not necessary to prove at great length the second point in this case, which is that conscience and consideration for the public good and the safety of the [Spanish] monarchy ought to bring the great and the people to range themselves at the side of their true and legitimate king. For as to conscience the right of the prince being clear according to what was just shown [in section I of the *Manifesto*], one cannot claim ignorance as an excuse, and the Bourbons, refusing all judgment or arbitration, and basing themselves only on arms and usurpations, condemn themselves, and recognize the right of the King, as they had already done, in effect, by their pretended division [of the Spanish empire into Bourbon and Hapsburg parts]... And as this is a question not only of the rights of the King, but of the safety of the monarchy, which is on the brink of being irremediably precipitated into an abyss of misfortunes, the conscience of those who are in a position to contribute, in all kinds of ways, to the redressing of matters, are changed with it; and they will be responsible before God and before men for the horrible evils which they will have caused or which they could stop. For those who might have flattered themselves, at the beginning of this revolution, against all manner of reasons, that the monarchy would remain in peace, and that one could receive a prince of Bourbon, the grandson of the Most Christian King, without receiving the despotic yoke of French domination, will have been disabused of these frivolous hopes by the event and by the undertakings of the French, who already govern them switch in hand.

Now, that the safety of the Spanish monarchy and nation has never been in greater danger since the invasion of the Saracens, is the most obvious thing in the world. One cannot, for all that, dispense with saying something about it – without, [however], covering so vast a field – to show that one must expect great misfortunes from a Bourbon king, and that one has nothing to fear from an Austrian king. One must consider that the misfortunes which can happen through the will of a Bourbon king, or even despite him, as a result of circumstances, through his volitions and his desires, based either on his inclination or his interest, will be quite contrary to the well-being of the state and the genius of the people. A king can have inclinations [which are] separate from his interests, and the one can be as dangerous as the other. Now the inclinations of the Bourbons are known, if they follow past tendencies; at least, one must suppose that they conform to the manners of their nation. For even if they do not follow them altogether, they will always be inclined to tolerate them; will not the interest of such a king be to give his confidence to those of his nation

whom he considers most devoted and attached to his person and most fit
to serve him in his plans?

The manners of the French are absolutely alien to the manners or
customs of Spain. There is in France a great freedom, particularly in
respect to sex, and it is to be feared that they will bring this with them to
the prejudice of good morals. What caused the Sicilian Vespers is well
known; but one would not want to linger over so odious a matter; there is
moreover an infinite opposition between the usages of Spain and those of
France, and there are books written expressly on this subject. On the one
hand everyone is grave, serious and steady; everyone is for the exact
observation of laws and customs; everyone is content to conform himself
to them, and wants others to conform themselves; for those matters which
the law has not regulated, the wisdom of the nation has provided, and has
introduced customs which take the place of laws. In conversation and in
social intercourse, just as no one wants to inconvenience others, no one
wants to be inconvenienced by them, and even the youth partake of the
gravity of the nation. But on the other hand, that is, on the French side, it
is quite the contrary. Everyone allows himself no repose, and leaves none
to others; the grave and the serious pass for ridiculous, and measure or
reason for pedantic; caprice, for something gallant, and inconstancy in
one's interactions with other people, for cleverness: everyone meddles
[with others' affairs] in [private] houses, and pursues people to their very
homes, and picks shameful fights. Youth above all glories in its folly and
in its disorders, which go quite far today, as if this were a sign of wit; it
respects neither sex, nor age, nor merit.

Can one conceive that, the court and the provinces once full of such
people, who will be both in favor and in office, the Spanish nation can
accommodate itself to them without finally corrupting itself through so
many bad examples? Please God that this never happen! Some will say
that these [fears] are trifles, but [the truth of the matter] is no less than
that [which has been described]; for, besides the fact that piety, virtue and
reason are above everything else, the pleasantness of life consists in large
measure in not being inconvenienced at home by dangerous intruders; it is
incomparably harder to be troubled, laughed at, affronted and mistreated
in one's domestic life, in one's person, in what is one's own, and to drag
through a life full of sorrow caused by the contempt and the insolence of
those with whom one must live, and whom one is obliged to put up with
despite himself and despite even fear, than to be put under the yoke of a
conqueror, or to be oppressed by a tyrant who affects one only in
general or in the purse.

The question of religion, again, cannot be of little importance, particularly in a highly Catholic country. Everyone knows that in France people are only half-Catholic; please God that they were sufficiently Christian! The authority of the Pope, even in ecclesiastical matters, is considered there only when they want to flatter him, in order to have him in their thrall, to oppress him one day with the others. They caused a thousand affronts to a saintly Pontiff [Innocent XI], because he was devoted to justice, and did not approve the ambitious schemes of France. Thus they attacked openly the authority of the Holy See, and persecuted those who defended it as heretics. They suppressed the liberties of the churches by [using] the ill-established claims of regal rights, in violation of the express doctrine of the General Council of Lyon; and exemplary bishops, who were not the slaves of the court, to the prejudice of their conscience, were treated with the last degree of inhumanity. In addition there was formed a long time ago a large faction in the church of France, which leaned toward entirely overthrowing the authority of the Pope, and reforming several dogmas of the Catholic, Apostolic and Roman Church as abuses. This party is now triumphing among the secular clergy of France, and one will see the effects of it one day, if God permits that the House of Bourbon gain the peaceable possession of the two monarchies, and that as a result the Pope, with Rome, be at its discretion.

The ambition of France has also kept the Mohammedans in Europe, whom the Emperor was on the verge of chasing out. Let it not be said that this crown was fearful of the growth of the House of Austria, for she had only to take part in the spoils; Greece together with Thrace (to say nothing of Asia) awaited her and were assured to her. But she preferred to save herself for the unjust invasion of the monarchy of Spain; and even now she is making efforts to push the Ottoman Porte to attack Christendom anew. It is this crown which, by its greediness, has caused a horrible letting of Christian blood for nearly thirty years, by constantly attacking others; and almost all the evils that Europe has suffered during that time ought to be imputed to her. Those are the merits which the House of Bourbon can put forward to win so great a prize as that of the monarchy of Spain, and to take it away from the Emperor, always so faithful to his God and to his allies.

But the worst thing of all is that atheism walks today in France with its head up, that pretended great wits are in fashion there, and that piety is turned to ridicule. This venom spreads with the French spirit, and wherever this genius puts its foot and makes itself superior, it brings it with it. To submit to French domination is to open the door to dissoluteness and to libertinage; one can be sure as well that piety cannot reign where justice is trampled underfoot, as France has done to it so many times, and with so much haughtiness; and if the insolent spirit of the French, as soon as they are the masters, must oblige honorable people not to allow them to get the upper hand in their country, their feelings and their impious actions must frighten men of good will and good prelates, as much as all those [members] of the clergy who are zealous for the house of God. One must have a sufficiently good opinion of the Bourbon princes to believe that evils happen and will happen despite them, and that they do not favor profligacy or impiety: but bad habit, once minds have got the taste of it, is stronger than ordinances, and we see it now in France itself, where, under a king [who is] devout, austere and absolute, disorder and irreligion have surpassed anything that has ever been seen in the Christian world. God permit that one not need to guard himself against this French evil, and that the greatness of this nation [Spain], which always believes, if it is not thwarted, not be a new scourge against religion! Spain will feel the effects of it, the Churches above all; and the Spanish will be most culpable if they submit to this dangerous nation, and thereby put it in a position to master the rest of Europe.

The interest, as well as the inclination of a Bourbon and French king, will be to make himself absolute in order to be able to exercise despotic power. Everyone knows that this form of government is established in France, that it is exalted there by flatterers, and that a grandson of a king of France cannot fail to be imbued with these maxims. There the liberties of the great and of the people have been reduced; the good pleasure of the king takes the place of everything else; even the princes of royal blood are without the slightest authority; the great are only title-holders and are ruining themselves more and more, while persons of little importance are elevated to serve as instruments for oppressing the others. In the *pays d'États* the Estates are assembled only for form's sake, and these assemblies serve only to execute the orders of the Court, without any regard for their grievances. The nobility is impoverished to the last degree, vexed by quarreling and investigations, obliged to use itself up in service to the king and to sacrifice its welfare and its blood to the ambition of a conqueror, while it nourishes only hopes for chimerical riches and for advancements which are given only in very small numbers. Those who occupy civil positions, particularly lucrative ones, having once enriched themselves at the expense of the community because they were given free rein, are now squeezed like sponges by re-examinations of their accounts and their affairs, by the venality of offices, by the creation of new burdens, and by great sums which are demanded of them without any reason, and which they are obliged to pay to save themselves from harassment. The people are trampled upon without mercy and reduced to bread and water by tithes, taxes, imposts, head-taxes, [by being required to supply] winter-quarters and passage for war-makers, by monopolies, by changes in [the value of] money which take suddenly from everyone a good part of his goods, and by a thousand other inventions; and all of that is only to serve the insatiability of a court which cares not at all about the subjects which it already has, and which seeks only to augment the number of miserable people by extending its estates.[1] Now, all the peoples of the monarchy of Spain being on the point of suffering the same fate, will not the true Spaniards who love their country and the honor of their nation be moved by this?

One has only to imagine everything that the turbulent and wrangling spirit of the French is capable of undertaking in Spain to enrich the king, and to increase his power at the expense of his subjects. France is swarming with advice-givers, with professional partisans hungry for the gold and silver of the Indies and for the riches of Spain, which they already devour with their eyes. The king will make himself master of the commerce of America, and will dispose of the mines of Peru at his pleasure, letting in French entrepreneurs; individuals will have only what it is necessary to leave them to continue the operations which it is not appropriate for the prince to undertake. In Spain one will see farmers of the kind one sees in France, and businessmen who will bleed the people white, in order to make them (they will say) more industrious and [to make them] work harder; but they will not benefit at all from their work, whose profit will be only for the Court and for foreigners...

The great and the nobles will not be exempted from vexations; on the contrary, those whose power gives (however little) umbrage will soon be trampled on: they will be swallowed up in the search for alienated crown lands, and they will be obliged to renounce [their estates] on several pretexts. They will be given employments of a flattering distinction, but which are sumptuous and designed to ruin them; gentlemen will be involved in luxury and in law-suits; they will be obliged to appear at court, at the *arrière ban*,[2] and in the armies, under pain of being scorned or even maltreated. Lucrative and confidential jobs will be either for foreigners, or for the *petits compagnons*[3] of the country, [who are] pliant and good for doing or suffering anything, without worrying about the

---

[1] Leibniz had made many of the same points thirty years earlier in a fragment called *Mala Franciae* (*c.* 1672), Acad. Ed. IV, I, pp. 516–17, in which he urged that the king and certain ministers were enriching themselves, while the nobility and the people were being 'consumed by a slow fire'.

[2] That is, at the assembly of the 'rear-vassals'.

[3] Today one would probably translate this expression as 'collaborators'.

honor and the well-being of the fatherland. Churchmen will not be better treated in the slightest, and the example of France will serve as a rule. The king, assisted by that of France, will force the Pope into whatever concordat he wants; the court will seize the income of almost all the benefices and will give away pensions from it; it will introduce regal rights in all their rigor; secular judges will overrule ecclesiastical sentences under the pretext of [reforming] abuses; they will clip the wings of the prelates they believe too rich, and will demand so many 'free gifts', bit by bit, that the condition of the clergy will not be better than that of the laity, whom they will be obliged to help in supporting misery.

As for public affairs, it can easily happen that the Duke of Anjou, in order to be supported by his grandfather or by his father, will be obliged to sacrifice to France, or to the interest of the Bourbons, a part of the estates or of the rights of the monarchy...One should not doubt at all that the French plan to keep the monarchy of Spain in the House of Bourbon, contrary to the clauses of the will, and to the prejudice of the heirs, if they are once the masters of it; that they will not fail to unite this monarchy to the crown of France if the occasion arises, and to reduce Spain to a province; that a Bourbon king will not want to govern her less despotically one day, than he does at present, when they still have a revolution to fear (which they will no longer fear when they shall have taken root); that confidence, the principal or most lucrative jobs, commerce (particularly that with America), the commanding of troops, the strongest places, and the keys of state, will be for the French or for those who will be dependent on them, and devoted to the court; that one will govern on the model of France, that one will pull down the great, that one will oppress the small without any regard for rights and privileges, and that one will impoverish both [groups] by an infinity of imposts, extortion and vexations, in order to put the king in a position to contribute much to the universal monarchy of the Bourbons...

There are some people who say that all these fears relate to an uncertain future, and that one need not torment himself with ideas about a possible future. But the evil, in great part, is already present and on the point of coming to maturity and fulfillment; they [the Spanish] are already halfway in chains, and, if they do not wake up fairly soon, they will no longer be in any condition to be liberated from slavery, either by their own efforts or by those of their friends. But, even if all of the evil was reserved for the future, does not everyone know that all of human prudence has only the future as its object? For one must take precautions, if possible, against great evils which can come about easily...

It is precisely this fatal nonchalance, by which men are only too attached to the present, which has caused the majority of bad counsels whose fatal results we now see. It is what has brought about the [moral] looseness of some, who neglect the fatherland, and think only of living comfortably for the rest of their days (though they deceive themselves in this, the evils being only too close), and the corruption of others, who try to profit from the present [misfortunes], and even to contribute to the misfortune of the country for their own advantage. These principles are unworthy of men who make a profession of wisdom, honor and probity; and one must have renounced feelings of honesty and of conscience to support them.

There are some characters of this stamp, that is, won over to the Bourbons or mired in an effeminate flabbiness, who flatter themselves, or throw dust in the eyes of others, in trying to weaken the greatest and justest fears, when they maintain that the two branches of the House of Bourbon will readily fight with each other; thus (they say), the affairs of Europe will return to the condition they were in before the death of the late king. But, besides the fact that the Duke of Anjou, even if he wanted to, could not detach his interests from [those of] the king of France..., the true interest of the two branches of Bourbon is to remain united. They will be in a better position to aid each other than those [branches] of the House of Austria, because of the contiguity of their states. The Duke of Anjou, under his grandfather or under his father, will be the absolute monarch of the whole monarchy and will put himself in a position to use all of its great capacities for common designs, of which France will always be the soul and the prime mover...

But, by receiving the legitimate king, these fears cease. The princes of the House of Austria will govern mildly and according to the laws; and, if they should want to oppress the liberty and the privileges of the people, they would not be in a position to do it, not being able to hope for help from their German branch, which is far away, and having France to fear next to them. Thus Spain and Europe will remain in their original condition; there will be no other problem than the necessity of driving the French out of the positions they have occupied under the pretext of helping us. Since we have almost all of Europe on our side, which is as interested as we are, we are assured of success, with the assistance of God, protector of justice and revenger of evil actions.

To conclude, let us imagine Spain, and the provinces under her rule, under the yoke of the French, [with] morals corrupted, religion and piety scorned, honest men insulted, the people reduced to ammunition-bags, the great diminished and threadbare, foreigners masters of the power and the riches of the country, the king governing *à l'Ottomanne*, his favorites, officers, soldiers and other ministers of his power exercising harshly that which Samuel foretold for the people of Israel[1] – dishonoring families, seizing whatever they find to their liking, and not answering complaints except by laughing or by new affronts, from which there is no hope of deliverance, since the French will doubtless not fail to take precautions against vespers similar to those of Sicily, and since the rest of Europe will be, in large measure, in the same [state] of oppression, and far from any ability to give aid to those who will be oppressed. Besides which the other nations will hate and have contempt for that [nation] which they consider to have been the cause of common misfortunes because of its imprudence and lack of courage, when they see her applauding those greedy *misérables*, who formerly came to her for work and bread.

Those who are not touched by the picture of these horrible and inevitable misfortunes are worthy of still greater evils, and do not deserve to bear the glorious name of 'Spaniard'.

The Gonsalvos, the Ximenes, the Toledos, the Pizarros, and all the other Spaniards of old, the founders of a great monarchy, rulers of so many nations – if they returned to the world, would they admit as being of their blood those whom they see ready to submit to the yoke of their enemies, through an unworthy cowardice, if they were in a position to save themselves from it, and if Europe lent them a hand? But one must believe that there were only a few of this number [of cowards], and that the very ones who received a French prince, seeing how much they had been deceived, will be the most desirous of remedying the error which they made; that conscience, duty, honor, the safety of the fatherland, and the happiness or misery of each particular man will make a lively impression on a people which was never before accused of being base-hearted; and that this entire generous nation, rendering justice to its legitimate king and to itself, will show the whole world that it has not degenerated from the valor of its ancestors.

[1] I Samuel 10.

11. Codex Iuris Gentium (Praefatio)
(1693)

In 1693 Leibniz published a large collection of medieval documents supporting
the position of the Empire against the claims of the French. To this collection he
attached a preface, about half of which is translated below. In it Leibniz showed
that he was moving a little away from his earlier view that the Republic of
Christendom could be restored, and toward a more modern position which
accepted the existence of independent national states. But the most important
part of the preface is that containing an excellent statement of his general
theory of justice as the charity of the wise, which he attempts to relate to international principles. There are also a great many observations about the psychology of rulers which show that Leibniz could, when he liked, be fairly 'realistic'.
(The present translation, from Latin, follows the text to be found in vol. IV of
the Dutens edition. The parts of the text which have been translated are those
which contain the main theoretical propositions; what has been cut are mainly
historical examples, most of them now rather obscure.)

1. Although the scope of this work is clear from the title, with the attached
preface, and particularly from the index of documents, it seemed to me
nonetheless that it would be useful to prefix a somewhat more ample
introduction, in order to speak of the proper use of public acts, and to
show by examples what sort of thing can be expected from our collection,
indicating at the same time the sources of the true law of nature and of
nations. It is true that Lysander was accustomed to say that children
play with nuts, and old men with oaths;[1] and today, in truth, we would
not be wrong in many cases to say that rulers play cards in private life
and with treaties in public affairs. That one break treaties through
thoughtlessness or cupidity is something which is justly condemned:

---

[1] Lysander, a Spartan statesman and general, was noted, in Mathieu's words, for
his 'ambition and lack of scruples'. The present saying is to be found in
Plutarch's *Lysander* VIII.

sometimes, however, it is not wrong even for good men to do it, when one has good reason to suspect the good faith of others, and when a *cautio damni infecti* cannot be counted on.[1] From which the subtle author of the *Elementa de Cive*[2] drew the conclusion that between different states and peoples there is a perpetual war; a conclusion, indeed, which is not altogether absurd, provided it refers not to a right to do harm, but to take proper precautions. Thus it is that peace with a powerful enemy can be nothing else than a breathing-space of two gladiators, and sometimes does not even have the character of a truce. This much was shown recently by the almost ridiculous fact that a truce was established a little after a peace treaty,[3] in contrast to what ought to happen; it is not difficult to judge what sort of peace it must be which needed a truce. Neither is it doubtful that the imposition of unfair conditions stimulates the shame of the vanquished and, on the other hand, increases the appetite of the victor. For that reason a fashionable joker in Holland, after he had attached to the façade of his house, according to the local custom, a sign which read 'perpetual peace', had placed under this fine slogan a picture of a cemetery – since there death does bring about peace. And Aitzema, famous for his knowledge of these things, bore witness to this sentiment even in his epitaph:

> *Qui pacem quaeris libertatemque, viator*
> *Aut nusquam aut isto sub tumulo invenies.*[4]

This, therefore, is the state of human society, and it often happens that, because of the geographical or historical situation, a prince must fight continuously, and almost constantly treat of peace and alliances. For about two or three centuries the French and the English had no other dealings with each other, until the English, losing the Continent, disappeared from the scene, leaving their place to the Spanish. We see that the same thing happened afterwards between Emperor Charles V and King Francis I of France, from whom we have so many treaties as not to be able to believe that they had any time left to fight; and on the other hand we have reports of so many armed conflicts that they seem never to

[1] I.e. when a 'security against injuries' which are threatening or impending cannot be said to have been guaranteed by a prospective enemy.
[2] Hobbes, *De Cive* I, chs. 11–13.
[3] Leibniz refers to the Truce of Ratisbon (1683), which the Holy Roman Empire was obliged to make with France, despite the fact that the two powers were at peace following the Peace of Nimwegen (1678), following France's seizure of Strassburg and other German territories in 1681.
[4] Saying attributed to Leo Van Aitzema (*d*. 1669): 'O passerby who seeks peace and liberty, you will find it either in this tomb, or nowhere.' Cited in Acad. Ed. I, I, p. 127.

have made peace. A person distinguished in these studies told me one day the saying of a certain recent ambassador about a great prince [who was] always negotiating; a witty saying, indeed, although it cannot all be rendered in Latin: it is to be hoped – he said – that this prince live sumptuously, *car il traite toujours*.[1] An expedient of French policy today is precisely this: as soon as one inflicts an injury, talk at once of peace. Thus one receives the advantages of war, and at the same time seeks praise for [being] a peaceable spirit.*

II. Some will perhaps be surprised that an editor of acts and treaties should discourse in his preface on the weakness of paper chains; and will retort that esteem for public acts must diminish if it is recognized that sovereigns have secret intentions quite different than those which are declared. But it is my plan to say clearly how things really are, and to determine the true value of the harvest; there are in fact two separate questions (each of which has its own importance): what has been done, and in what spirit it has been done. Besides, from what is obvious one divines what is hidden, and phenomena are observed in order to discover the reasons for that which appears. I say therefore willingly that there are two kinds of history, public, and secret, or (to use Procopius' word) anecdotal;[2] just as there are two causes of war which Grotius recognizes, which he calls *justificae* and *suasoriae*[3] – although, in my judgment, the *suasoriae* can be divided in their turn into [wars of] utility and of sentiment; for the best advice does not always prevail, [and] more often a king acts as

---

* Cf. the comparable argument in Leibniz' *Remarks on a French Manifesto* (1688), F de C III, p. 86: 'I find that it is the essence of French politics to weigh down its neighbors with so great a number of injuries that, reproaches not being able to increase in proportion to the injustices, she is rid all at once of the complaints which she would have drawn on herself had she done only the hundredth part of the same evils. Can an assassin who has cut the throats of a hundred passers-by with his own hand, and done other horrible things, be condemned more and punished more, in proportion, if he has already redoubled the number of his cruelties? It is only God who forgets nothing and who finds the just measure; but, among men, the extremest evils almost efface the memory of the first ones, and one gets used to them... The invasion of the Spanish low-countries, in violation of an express renunciation under oath; war carried into Holland...; the Peace of Nimwegen overthrown as soon as made: these are actions which no longer seem as black as they are, since they have been surpassed by others far more atrocious. The true secret of embellishing quite ugly things, is to put them next to others still more incomparably unsightly....'.

1 'For he is always negotiating.'

2 'Anecdotal', in Procopius' history of Justinian and Theodora, means 'unpublished' or 'secret'.

3 Grotius, *De Jure Belli ac Pacis II*, I, i.

a man than as a king, and things of great importance are decided by small causes. There are thus two rules for [writing] history, but which cannot be equally observed in [writing] the one and the other kind of history: the rule of public history is to say nothing which is false, [whereas the rule] of secret history, on the other hand, is to omit nothing which is true; the first [kind of] history thus appears incomplete. But this is called for by the nature of things: and just as in legal controversies the parties and their lawyers use many arguments before the judges which do not appear in their written acts and are not put into the records – since both the attractions of women and the splendor of gold often have more force than the laws and testimonies – thus also many things remain secret in the acts of the powerful and in the causes of treaties, especially because often facts which pass unobserved have a greater effect than is thought. Thus sometimes a remark which is maliciously reported or invented strikes the soul of a prince or of his minister, and leaves its sting; from which issue hidden impulses of hatred and revenge, masked by colors sought for their appearance. And not rarely great revolutions are brought about by noble souls, simply to refute something which they take as contemptuous of them.

Often, too, a night [on which] the prince has slept badly, after which he has made rash decisions, because of an unsuitable mental and physical condition, is soon paid for by many thousands of unfortunates with their blood. Often the abuse of power by a woman is that which pushes a husband or a lover to act; more often the inclinations of ministers are communicated to their sovereigns. And it must be admitted that, just as in the theater it would be unsuitable for stage machinery to be seen, so too history would sometimes lose part of its beauty, if one always observed its real causes; and it appears that heroes have acted on the basis of childish inclinations, or because of a passion for women, or even because of servile greed. In truth, we are reading about the deeds of men, not of Gods; and it is sufficient for their glory and the records of posterity that there remain many actions carried out with wisdom, courage and circum-spection. Bad examples are best ignored from time to time. Thus one must not trust lightly those who recount unworthy things perpetrated underhandedly by princes – things which could have been known only by a few people, and which are not willingly commended to posterity [even] by those who actually knew them. But, nevertheless, while one believes flatterers very little, one is only too ready to lend his ear to those who write satires. There are historians who habitually represent men as worse than they are in reality;[1] and nonetheless the malignity of men and their

[1] Cf Leibniz' *Réflections sur l'Art de Connaître les Hommes* (1708): 'It is true that

hidden envy of the powerful confers authority on these writers, who recount the inventions of their brain, as if they themselves had been present. To this one can add national feelings, [which are] hostile to each other. Thus I note that in general the French believe in many fables about Charles V and about the Ferdinands and the Philips which, I know not by what means, have crept into history through [excessive] freedom in composition. The Germans and the Spanish, in their turn, willingly believe in all the fables contemptuous of Louis XIII, and in [those] about the ministers Richelieu and Mazarin which almost exceed the possibilities of human malice: yet the former was neither so feeble, nor the last two capable of so much in either direction [good or evil]. History is, then, quite unfaithful, unless one relies on the testimony of great men or on the text of public acts.

III. Collections of public acts are thus the most trustworthy part of history, and they transmit to posterity, as do coins and inscriptions, the certainty of facts. The invention of printing, then, has made things such that one can put more trust in paper than in stone or metals. How many treaties and decrees of antiquity, indeed, though consigned to bronze plaques or stones, must be accounted lost? How few have been conserved in the *Arundeliani*[1] or on other marble fragments? But simple paper, once printing was invented, is protected by the easiness with which it is multiplied. Collections of treaties of alliance, of peace, of concessions are thus the elements which underpin and support the whole edifice of history. For, after one has fought a great deal in vain, and a great deal of blood has been spilled, and one has used up the skill of diplomats, the fruits of war are to be seen in peace; and how much each one has gained appears not so much from battles and sieges as from the text of the treaty of peace. Thus when one must stop the game, the counting of the playing-pieces tells how much each one has gained or lost, which, until that moment, had remained in suspense...

IV. From this it can be understood that the collection of documents is of use to those who deal with public affairs no less than the scholar, in understanding the most important events of the past. In truth, those who hold the affairs of state in their hands will find in these monuments models to examine, and the means by which to recognize their own ability with

perfect virtue is rare, but extreme wickedness is no less so. Machiavelli has already remarked on this...' (In *Lettres de Leibniz*, ed. A. Foucher de Careil, Librairie Philosophique de Ladrange, Paris, 1854, p. 133.)

[1] Inscribed Greek marbles which became widely known after Lord Arundel commissioned Selden to publish Latin translations of the inscriptions (*Marmora Arundelliana*, 1699).

M

pleasure, or to fruitfully increase it; will find the formulae which are suitable to international law and to the public usage; and, what counts most, will be able to draw therefrom examples and authoritative precedents, with which they can equip themselves for future negotiations, and defend their opinions in debate. Nothing else will be found more often in the reports of ambassadors, than that which refers to past acts. I know that such reports were considered as treasures and consulted as oracles by ministers of kings; and publication takes away none of their usefulness, though men usually measure value by rarity. Private persons, then, whom curiosity has impelled to consider these matters, will, when they have understood the importance of such collections, have the impression of having been led into an archive, as if they were set down in the midst of [state] business. I say this not because I think that our undertaking has so much value, but because I hope that others will be induced to complete it more fully, as a great service to the public. And in documents appears not only the diversity of the world of men, in which Mars and Venus serve as benefactors of nations, and empires are enlarged by victories and marriages; but also it is possible to observe the beginnings of great events at their own sources. It is pleasant, then, to be admitted to solemn events, to observe ceremonies, to know the changes in things, in rules, in customs and in legal norms, over several centuries; and to wonder at the changes of human genius and of languages amidst the very simplicity of our old people and their *naïvetés*.

v. This work, then, to condense its usefulness into the briefest space, will serve the art of politics, that of history, that of erudition in general, but above all [will help one] to understand the law of nations. We already spoke of political artifices: these are concealed under the forms of treaties but, with the aid of historical exegeses and of shrewd authors, we are coming, for the most part, into the light. Thus it happens that historians and collections of documents increase and reflect each other's light. Those who undertake to treat some public question and to examine the right of princes, discover how uncertain history is if it does not rest on documents; to the point that in those authors who take hearsay as their basis, rather than documents, the scene of events is completely falsified...

xi. But it will be useful to say something more about the use of this work for international law and about [the relation of] natural law to that of nations: indeed the title *Codex Iuris Gentium* was adopted precisely because it had this objective. The doctrine of law, taken from nature's strict confines, presents an immense field for human study. But the notions of law and of justice, even after having been treated by so many illustrious authors, have not been made sufficiently clear. Right is a kind of moral possibility, and obligation a moral necessity. By moral I mean that which is equivalent to 'natural' for a good man: for as a Roman juris-consult has well said, we ought to believe that we are incapable of doing things which are contrary to good morals.[1] A good man is one who loves everybody, in so far as reason permits. Justice, then, which is the virtue regulates that affection which the Greeks call φιλανθρωπία [philanthropy], will be most conveniently defined, if I am not in error, as the charity of the wise man, that is, charity which follows the dictates of wisdom. So that assertion which is attributed to Carneades, that justice is supreme folly,[2] because it commands us to consider the interests of others while we neglect our own, is born of ignorance of the definition of justice.

Charity is a universal benevolence, and benevolence the habit of loving or of willing the good. Love then signifies rejoicing in the happiness of another, or, what is the same thing, converting the happiness of another into one's own. With this is resolved a difficult question, of great moment in theology as well: in what way disinterested love is possible, independent of hope, of fear, and of regard for any question of utility.[3] In truth, the happiness of those whose happiness pleases us turns into our own happi-ness, since things which please us are desired for their own sake. And since the contemplation of the beautiful is pleasant in itself, and a paint-ing of Raphael affects a sensitive person who understands it, although it brings him no [material] gain, so that he keeps it in his [mind's] eye, as the image of a thing which is loved; when the beautiful thing is itself capable of happiness, this affection passes over into pure love. But the divine love excels all other loves, because God can be loved with the greatest result [*Deus cum maximo successu amari potest*], since nothing is happier than God, and nothing more beautiful or more worthy of happiness can be conceived. And since he possesses supreme power and supreme wisdom, his happiness does not simply become ours (if we are wise: that is, if we love him), but even creates ours. But since wisdom ought to guide charity, it will be necessary to define it [wisdom]. I believe that we can best render the concept that men have of it, if we say that wisdom is nothing but the science of happiness itself. Once again we return to the concept of happiness, which this is not the place to explain.

XII. Now from this source flows natural right [*ius naturae*], of which there are three degrees: strict right [*ius strictum*] in commutative justice;

---

[1] Taken from Book XVI of Papinian's *Quaestiones*, as cited in the *Digest* XXVIII, 7, 15.

[2] Taken from the *Epitome* of the *Divinae Institutiones* of Lactantius, ch. I.

[3] Leibniz often referred to this argument at the time of the dispute (1697) between Fénelon and Bossuet over the nature of disinterested love.

equity (or, in the narrower sense of the term, charity) in distributive justice; and, finally, piety (or probity) in universal justice: hence come the most general and commonly accepted principles of right – to injure no one, to give to each his due, and to live honestly (or rather piously); as I once suggested, as a youth in my little book *De Methodo Iuris [Nova Methodus*, sections 71–5].[1] The precept of mere or strict right is that no one is to be injured, so that he will not be given a motive for a legal action within the state, nor outside the state a right of war. From this arises the justice which philosophers call commutative,[2] and the right which Grotius calls a legal claim *[facultas]*.[3] The higher degree I call equity or, if you prefer, charity (that is, in the narrower sense), and this I extend beyond the rigor of strict right to [include] those obligations which give to those whom they affect no ground for [legal] action in compelling us to fulfill them, such as gratitude and alms-giving – to which, as Grotius says, we have a moral claim *[aptitudo]*, not a legal claim *[facultas]*.[4] And as [the principle of] the lowest degree of right is to harm no one, so [that of] the middle degree is to do good to everybody; but only so far as befits each one or as much as he deserves; for it is impossible to favor everyone. It is, then, here that distributive justice belongs, and the precept of the law which commands us to give to each his due. And it is here that the political laws of a state belong, which assure the happiness of its subjects and make it possible that those who had a merely moral claim acquire a legal claim; that is, that they become able to demand what it is equitable for others to perform. In the lowest degree of right, one does not take account of differences among men, except those which arise from each particular case, and all men are considered equal; but now on the higher level merits are weighed, and thus privileges, rewards and punishment have their place. This difference between the two degrees of right was nicely suggested by Xenophon,[5] in his example of the boy Cyrus, who was chosen to judge between two boys, the stronger of whom had forcibly exchanged garments with the other because he found that the other's coat fitted him and his own fitted the other better. Cyrus pronounced in favor of the robber; but he was admonished by his teacher that in this case it was not a question of deciding whom the coat fitted better, but only to whom it belonged, and that the other manner of judging might

---

[1] *Nova Methodus Discendae Docendaeque Iurisprudentiae*, one of Leibniz' earliest works, takes up these questions in sections 71–5 (in Dutens IV, iii, pp. 211–14).
[2] Cf. Aristotle, *Nicomachean Ethics* (1130*b*).
[3] Grotius, *De Jure Belli ac Pacis* I, I, 4.   [4] *Ibid.*
[5] Xenophon, *Cyropaedia* I, 3, 17; mentioned by Grotius in *De Jure Belli ac Pacis* I, I, 8.

more properly be used only when he himself had coats to distribute. Equity itself demands strict right, or the equality of men, in our dealings, except when an important consideration of a greater good makes us depart from it. What is called respect of persons, however, has its place, not in exchanging goods with others, but in distributing our own or the public goods.

XIII. The highest degree of right I have called probity, or rather piety. What I have said thus far can be interpreted as limited to the relations within mortal life. Simple or strict right is born of the principle of the conservation of peace; equity or charity strives for something higher— [namely] that while each benefits others as much as he can, he may increase his own happiness in that of the other. And, to say it in a word, strict right avoids misery, while the higher right tends toward happiness, but only such as is possible in this life. But that we ought to hold this life itself and everything that makes it desirable inferior to the great advantage of others, and that we should bear the greatest pains for the sake of those near us: all this is [merely] taught with noble words by philosophers,[1] rather than proved by solid demonstration. For the dignity and glory, and our mind's sense of joy on account of virtue, to which they appeal under the name of honor [*honestas*], are certainly goods of thought or of the mind and are, indeed, great ones, but not such as to prevail with all [men], nor to overcome all the bitterness of evils, since not all men are equally moved by the imagination; especially those who have not become accustomed to the thought of virtue or to the appreciation of the goods of the mind, whether through a liberal education or a noble way of living, or the discipline of life or of a sect. In order really to establish by a universal demonstration that everything honorable is useful and everything base is damned, one must assume the immortality of the soul, and God as ruler of the universe. In this way we can think of all men as living in the most perfect state, under a monarch who can neither be deceived in his wisdom nor eluded in his power; and who is also so worthy of love that it is happiness [itself] to serve such a master. Thus whoever expends his soul in the service of Christ will regain it.[2] The divine providence and power cause all right to become fact [*omne ius in factum transeat*], and

---

[1] Latta's edition of the *Monadology* quotes a passage from Leibniz' *Iuris et Aequi Elementa* which enlarges on this point: 'If you had listened very attentively to Cicero declaiming on behalf of rectitude as against pleasure, you would have heard him magnificently perorate about the beauty of virtue, the deformity of base things, about a conscience at peace with itself in the depth of a rejoicing soul, about the good of an untarnished reputation, about an immortal name and the exultation of glory' (Latta, p. 292n.; original in Mollat, p. 30).

[2] Matthew 10. 39.

[assure that] no one is injured except by himself, that no good action goes unrewarded, and no sin unpunished. Because, as we are divinely taught by Christ, all our hairs are numbered,[1] and not even a drink of water is given to the thirsty in vain;[2] nothing is neglected in the state of the universe. It is on this ground that justice is called universal, and includes all the other virtues; for duties that do not seem to concern others, as, for example, not to abuse our own bodies or our own property, though they are beyond [the power of] human laws, are still prohibited by natural law, that is, by the eternal laws of the divine monarchy, since we owe ourselves and everything we have to God. Now, if it is of interest to the state, of how much more interest is it to the universe that no one use badly what is his? So it is from this that the highest precept of the law receives its force, which commands us to live honorably (that is, piously). It is in this sense that learned men have rightly held, among things to be desired, that the law of nature and of the nations [*ius naturae et gentium*] should follow the teachings of Christianity, that is, τὰ ἀνώτρα, the sublime things, the divine things of the wise, according to the teaching of Christ. Thus I think that I have interpreted the three precepts of the [Roman] law, or the three degrees of justice, in the most fitting way, and have indicated the sources of the natural law.

XIV. Besides the eternal right [or law] of rational nature, flowing from the divine source, there is also held to be voluntary right, derived from custom or made by a superior. And in the state the civil law [*ius civile*] indeed receives its force from him who has the supreme power; outside of the state, or among those who participate in the supreme power (of whom there may be more than one, even in the same state), is the sphere of the voluntary law of nations, originating in the tacit consent of peoples. It is not necessary that this be the agreement of all peoples or for all times; for there have been many cases in which one thing was considered right in India and another in Europe, and even among us it has changed with the passage of centuries, as this very work will show...

XV. But Christians have yet another common tie, the divine positive law contained in the sacred Scriptures. To these can be added the sacred canons accepted in the whole Church and, later, in the West, the pontifical legislation, to which kings and peoples submit themselves. And in general before the schism of the last century, it seems to have been accepted for a long time (and not without reason) that a kind of common republic of Christian nations must be thought of, the heads of which were the Pope in sacred matters, and the Emperor in temporal matters,

---

[1] Luke 12. 7.　　　　　　　　　　　　　　　　[2] Matthew 10. 42.

who preserved as much of the power of the ancient Roman emperors as was necessary for the common good of Christendom, saving [without prejudicing] the rights of kings and the liberty of princes...

XVI. ...We have thought that our *Codex* should concern itself with some things which refer to the Pope and to the [ecumenical] Councils. The jurisdiction of these two appeared so nearly universal, that even those who rejected the judgment of the Pope appealed nonetheless to the Council. And it is necessary to recognize that sometimes the solicitude that the Roman pontiffs had for the canons and for Christian doctrine proved useful; because they, influencing kings either by the authority which they had, or through fear of ecclesiastical censure, were the obstacles to many evils...But since even the best of human institutions are subject to corruption, it happened that the pontiffs overreached themselves, and abused their power...These arbitrary undertakings of the clergy made things such that, in the end those who claimed too much lost also that which it would have been just and opportune for Christians that they had kept...

XX. ...The basis then of international law [*iuris fecialis inter gentes*] is the same natural law whose principles I made clear a little earlier. On it are founded the institutions of international law, which changes according to time and place...He possesses a personality in international law who represents the public liberty, such that he is not subject to the tutelage or the power of anyone else, but has in himself the power of war and of alliances; although he may perhaps be limited by the bonds of obligation toward a superior and owe him homage, fidelity and obedience.[1] If his authority, then, is sufficiently extensive, it is agreed to call him a potentate, and he will be called a sovereign or a sovereign power; from which arises the law called *souveraineté* in French and *suprematus* in Latin and which, nevertheless, does not exclude the existence in the state of a superior any more than in the Church primacy excludes the existence of a prior. Those are counted among sovereign powers, then, and are held to possess sovereignty, who can count on sufficient freedom and power to exercise some influence in international affairs, with armies or by treaties ...In free states a juridical person is considered by analogy to a natural one, inasmuch as he possesses a will. If the latter is not adequately provided by the constitutional laws for arriving at a definite will for the state, the form of the latter is somewhat irregular, as was rightly taught

---

[1] Leibniz' view of sovereignty is fundamentally the same in the *Codex* as it had been in the *Caesarinus Fürstenerius* (1677); in both he held that sovereignty involved, not *absolute* independence and internal supremacy, but a relatively high *degree* of those attributes.

by the most learned Monzambano [Pufendorf],[1] by whom this matter was abundantly illustrated...

XXII. But it is well to break off at this point, if it is not desirable that the preface become a book...

12. On the Works of the Abbé de St Pierre
(1957)

These three pieces, two of them written in the year before Leibniz' death, show both his continued interest in his own desire for a resuscitation of the Republic of Christendom, and a new sense of rather sad amusement about the possibility of such a scheme's being effected. In his letter to the Abbé de St Pierre himself, he is cordial and even flattering; in his *Observations* on the *Project* he is more critical, and faults the Abbé's defective knowledge of German history, recommending (again) a reformed Papacy and Empire as the foundations of European peace. And in his letter to Grimarest (1712), he is in a playful (but serious) mood, suggesting that his own 'romances' are as good as St Pierre's. (The letter to St Pierre and the *Observations* are contained in vol. 4 of Foucher de Careil's edition; the letter to Grimarest, only part of which is reproduced here, is to be found in vol. v of Dutens' edition.)

LETTER TO THE ABBÉ DE ST PIERRE   (February 1715)

I consider myself highly honored by the receipt of your project, and by the request which you make of my opinion about a matter which interests the whole human race, and which is not entirely outside my range of

---

[1] Leibniz may be referring to any one of three works by Pufendorf which treated political 'irregularity'. In Book VII, chapter 5, of his *De jure Naturae et Gentium*, Pufendorf asserts that 'the essentials of a perfect and regular state require that in it there be such a union as makes everything...appear to come as it were, from one soul'. In his once-famous *De Statu Imperii Germanici*, he discussed the irregularity of the structure of the Empire, calling it 'deformed' and 'monstrous' because of its lack of a central power. And in section 22 of his *Disquisitio de Republica Irregulari*, he made much the same point, observing that in Germany 'the civil bond had so degenerated and relaxed that it hardly had more force than the alliance of an [international] system'. Which of these works Leibniz had in mind is not clear.

interests, since I have since my youth applied myself to law, and particularly to that of nations. The packet from M. Varignon arrived at Hanover long before I returned to my house; and after my return I was quite busy. But I finally made an effort to pull myself together, and to read your excellent work with care. I found there [much that is] solid and agreeable; and, after having understood your system, I took a particular pleasure in the variety of objections, and in your clear and straightforward manner of answering them. Men lack only the will to deliver themselves from an infinity of evils. If five or six persons wanted to, they could end the great schism in the West, and put the Church in good order. A sovereign who really wants to can preserve his state from the plague. The House of Brunswick has not succeeded badly in this, thank God; the plague, in my time, has stopped at its frontiers. A sovereign could also safeguard his state against famine. But, to bring about the end of wars, it would be necessary that another Henry IV,[1] together with some great princes of his time, favor your project. The evil is that it is difficult to suggest it to great princes. An individual person dares not throw off all restraint; and I am even afraid that the minor sovereigns would not dare to propose it to the greater. A minister could, perhaps, do it at the point of death, particularly if family interests did not oblige him to continue his policies to the tomb and beyond. However, it is always good to tell the public about [such things]; someone may be moved by them, when one least expects it.

Semper tibi pendeat hamus
Quo minime retis gurgite piscis erit. (Ovid)[2]

There is no minister now who would wish to suggest to the Emperor that he renounce the succession [to the throne] of Spain and the Indies. The maritime powers and so many others are all at sea over it[*y ont perdu leur latin*]. It is most often adversities which keep men from being happy. The hope of making the Spanish monarchy pass into [the hands of] the House of France has been the cause of fifty years of war; and it is to be feared that the hope of taking it away again will disturb Europe for fifty years more. To help the Emperor run the Turks out of Europe would

---

[1] Leibniz refers to the *Great Design of Henry IV*, written by the king's minister Sully between 1611 and 1635, which contains what purports to be Henry's scheme for a peace-keeping federal union of Europe. A good analysis of the *Great Design* is to be found in F. H. Hinsley's *Power and the Pursuit of Peace* (Cambridge University Press, 1964, pp. 24 ff.).

[2] Inexact quotation of Ovid's *Ars Amatoria* III, 425–6: 'Ever let your hook be hanging; where you least believe it, there will be a fish in the stream' (Mogley's trans., Loeb Classical Library, p. 149).

perhaps be the way to manage this evil. But such a scheme would still present great difficulties.

Since you are preparing, Sir, a more ample third edition, it would perhaps be good that your work be even further embellished with examples and with history. The arguments will not become any better, but this ornamentation will give them an ingress. This was the fashion in the time of M. La Mothe le Vayer.[1] Today French writers, on the pretext of avoiding pedantry, have too much lost the habit of using marks of erudition in their works; they are not less vigorous on this account, but they are drier. A certain middle ground would be well in a work like yours. But if this would hold you up too much, you needn't consider it. My remarks, however, may afford some occasion for it. I wish you, Sir, as long a life as is needed to enjoy the fruits of your labors, and I am with zeal, Sir, your

G.W.L.

OBSERVATIONS ON THE ABBÉ DE ST PIERRE'S 'PROJECT FOR PERPETUAL PEACE' (1715)

The project for perpetual peace in Europe, which M. l'Abbé de St Pierre did me the honor of sending to me, has reached me only quite lately, because of a long absence; and afterwards a multitude of matters kept me from reading it sooner. Finally, I read it with attention, and I am persuaded that such a project is, on the whole, feasible, and that its execution would be one of the most useful things in the world. Although my approbation is not of any weight, I have, nonetheless, judged that gratitude obliged me not to conceal it, and to add some remarks for the pleasure of an author of such merit, who must have much reputation and resoluteness, to have dared and been able to successfully oppose a host of prejudices and the outbursts of the scoffers.

When I was quite young, I became acquainted with a book entitled *Nouveau Cynée*,[2] whose unknown author advised sovereigns to govern their states in peace, and to let their disputes be judged by an established tribunal; but I no longer know how to find this book, and I no longer recall any details of it. Everyone knows that Cyneas was a confidant of the king Pyrrhus, who advised him to rest [content with what he had] at

---

[1] François de La Mothe le Vayer (1588–1672), French writer, known particularly for his *Considérations sur l'Eloquence Française*.

[2] *Le Nouveau Cynée* (1623), by Emeric de Crucé, advocated a European federal system as a means of bringing about peace; for an analysis see Hinsley, *Power*, pp. 20 ff.

once, because that would also have been his goal, as he confessed to him, if he had conquered Sicily, Calabria, Rome and Carthage.[1]

The late Landgraf Ernst of Hesse-Rheinfels,[2] who commanded armies with distinction in the great German war [Thirty Years' War], applied himself to religious controversies and to *belles connaissances*, after the Peace of Westphalia. He then abandoned the Protestants, got into a colloquy between Father Valerian Magni,[3] Capucin, and Dr Haberkorn,[4] celebrated theologian of the Augsburg Confession, and ventured, in his leisure, which was distinguished by the trips he made *incognito*, to write several works in German, in French and in Italian, which he had printed and gave to his friends. The most important was in the German language, [and was] entitled *le Catholique Discret*, in which he argued freely, and often most judiciously, about theological controversies. But, as this book contained some delicate points, he communicated it to very few people, and he made an abridgement of it which appeared in the stalls of libraries. There was, in this work, a project similar to that of M. l'Abbé de St Pierre; but it is not in the abridgement.

The tribunal of the society of sovereigns was to have been set up at Lucerne. While I had the honor of knowing this prince for only a little while before his death, he let me in on his late thoughts, and he gave me a copy of this work, which is quite rare.

But I grant that the authority of Henry IV [of France] is worth more than all the others. And, while one can suspect him of having the overthrow of the House of Austria more in view than the establishment of a society of sovereigns,[5] one sees in any case that he thought this project possible; and it is certain that if the powerful sovereigns proposed it, the

---

[1] Probably suggested to Leibniz by Boileau's *Épitre* I, lines 61–90. In the key lines, 87–8, Boileau says:

> Le conseil était sage et facile à gouter,
> Pyrrhus vivait heureux s'il eut pu l'écouter.

(ed. C. Boudhors, Société les Belles Lettres, Paris, 1939).

[2] Ernst von Hesse-Rheinfels (1629–93), a convert to Catholicism who attempted to defend it on purely rational grounds in his *Catholique Discret*, was one of Leibniz' most important correspondents. Their letters are collected in Rommel's *Ungedruckter Briefwechsel über Religiose und Politische Gegenstände* (Frankfurt, 1847).

[3] Valeriano Magni (1587–1661) was sent to Germany as a missionary by Pope Urban VIII.

[4] Peter Haberkorn (1604–76), is described by Mathieu as a 'strenuous defender of Lutheran orthodoxy'.

[5] This anticipates Rousseau's similar conclusion in his *Jugement sur la Paix Perpetuelle*, in Rousseau: *Political Writings*, ed. Vaughan (Blackwell, Oxford, 1962), vol. I, pp. 394–5.

others would accept it gladly. But I don't know whether the lesser would dare to propose it to the greater princes.

There was a time when the Popes had half-formed something rather like this, by the authority of religion and of the universal Church. Pope Gregory IV, together with the bishops of Italy, and of western and eastern France, made himself judge of the differences between Louis *le debonnaire* and his children. Nicholas I claimed, under cover of law, [the right] to judge with a synod and to depose Lothar, king of the Ostrogoths; and Charles the Bald, the uncle of this prince, supported the Pope's claims in order to further his own interests. Gregory VII haughtily pretended to a similar right, perhaps a greater one, over the Emperor Henry IV; and Urban II, his successor after Victor III, exercised that [the right] of actual director of the temporal affairs of the universal Church, though indirectly, by outfitting overseas expeditions against the infidels. One can see that the Popes passed for the spiritual heads, and the emperors or kings of the Romans for the temporal heads, as our Golden Bull says, of the universal Church or of Christian society, of which the emperors were to be the born generals. It was like a *droit des gens* among Latin Christians for several centuries, and the jurisconsults reasoned on this basis; one sees some examples of this in my *Codex Iuris Gentium* [1693], and some reflections about it in my preface.

The kings of France were treated more gently than the others, because the Popes had greater need of them. At the Council of Constance [1414–18] it was suggested that a bit more form be given to this society [to help] in treating the affairs of nations. And since there was no Pope at that time, the Emperor Sigismund was made the director of the society of Christendom. Measures were also taken to hold such councils often. But the Popes, who should have used them to exercise and extend their authority, not having the qualities of a Nicholas I or a Gregory VII, opposed this, fearful of being themselves submitted to censure. And this was the beginning of their decline. Also one saw, a little after this, some very bad Popes, who had difficulty in maintaining the authority of their ancestors. The rise of two rival houses followed with the re-establishment of letters. Finally, the great Reformation in the West changed the state of things extremely, and created a schism, by which the greater part of peoples whose language was originally Teutonic was detached from the peoples whose language was originally Latin.

However, I believe that if there had been Popes with a great reputation for wisdom and virtue, who had wanted to follow the measures taken at Constance, they could have remedied the abuses, prevented the rupture, and sustained or even advanced Christian society.

Still, one can say even now that the Emperor has some right of direction in Christian society, and it is this which his office gives him – in addition to precedence [over mere kings]. Thus I do not believe that it would be just or appropriate to destroy with one stroke the rights of the Roman Empire, which has lasted for so many centuries. Charles VI has just as much right as [had] Charles V to go and receive the Imperial crown at Rome, and to make himself recognized as King of Lombardy and Emperor of the Romans in those places; he has not lost a single one of the rights which Charles V had before; he is not even beyond possessing them. The jurisconsults know that one does not lose his rights, nor even the possession of them, when the occasion to exercise them does not present itself; and that one is not obliged to demonstrate them either, until those who exercise these rights wish to do away with them. So, since M. l'Abbé de St Pierre has given us two plans for the Christian society, one in which the Emperor with the Empire make up one member; and one in which the Empire is destroyed, and in which the Emperor would have a voice only as an hereditary sovereign [in Austria], and in which the electors would each have one vote, I must be for the former plan. And justice itself would prefer this plan, following the very principle of M. l'Abbé de St Pierre, that the Christian society must leave things in their present state. And since the Duchy of Savoy and the Principality of Piedmont enhance the Empire quite as much as any principality in Germany, I do not see how one could justly detach them, and make of them a separate member in the Christian society, with a vote distinct from the Empire's. It is not necessary to discuss other similar points at present; for example, it is certain that the Duchy of Courland and the Republic of Danzig are dependencies of Poland, and could not be cut off following the rules of justice, unless Poland consents to it.

I find that M. l'Abbé de St Pierre is right to consider the Empire as a model for the Christian society; but there is this difference, that in the [society] which would conform to his project, the complaints against the sovereign would not be allowed;[1] instead of which, in the Empire, subjects can plead against their princes, or against their magistrates. There

---

[1] This seems to anticipate St Simon's criticism of the Abbé's *Project* in his *De la Réorganisation de la Société Européenne* (1814), in ch. 3 of which St Simon observes that the effect of St. Pierre's plan would be 'to perpetuate in Europe the order of things existing at the moment at which it had been established'. This, said St Simon, would 'favor the abuse of power by making the power of sovereigns more formidable to the people', by 'depriving the latter of every resource against tyranny.' The Abbé's scheme, he concluded, 'could be nothing else than a reciprocal guarantee between princes to maintain arbitrary power'. St Simon, of course, goes farther than Leibniz in his criticisms.

are also some other very important differences: for example, in the tribunal of the Imperial *Kammer*, the assessors or judges are not dependent on the instructions of princes, or of the states which have appointed them: they have only to follow the movements of their conscience; instead of which, according to the project, the deputies to the Christian Senate will follow the instructions of their principals; also, they will be removable at their good pleasure; but the assessors of the Imperial *Kammer* no longer obey the electors, princes or circles who named them. It is quite otherwise in the Imperial and in the Circular diets, where the deputies depend entirely on the orders of their principals; instead of which, in the House of Commons in the English Parliament, the members do not depend on the shires and burgs which named them, not being subject to revocation [of their appointments], and having to follow only the movements of their conscience, like the assessors of the Imperial *Kammer*. The defect of the union of the Empire is not, as M. l'Abbé de St Pierre seems to take it, that the Emperor has too much power, but that the Emperor, as Emperor, does not have enough. For the Empire has almost no revenues which are not alienated or neglected, and the resolutions of the Diets, as well as the decisions of the [Imperial] tribunals, are executed with great difficulty, since they go against the powerful.

It seems that he conceives the German union as having begun with some treaty; but this cannot be reconciled with history. Under the Carolingian kings of Germany, there was already a large number of counts and of hereditary petty *seigneurs*; but there were still almost no hereditary dukes who governed entire provinces. These governors commanded the armies and were chosen according to merit, but among the greatest nobles. However, the kings were not at all absolute; all important matters were regulated in Diets, almost as things are done today in Poland. But bit by bit a number of counties and *seigneuries* was acquired by a single noble, by inheritance and by royal favors, particularly when he was allied with the royal family. Now, that of Charlemagne being extinct in Germany, those who succeeded to the royalty were obliged to favor these last-mentioned dukes, their equals; thus little by little the duchies and the great marquisates became quasi-hereditary, and a great part of the petty nobility was submitted to the vassalage of the great, such that it was obliged to carry its banners under theirs. The Emperors did not fail to retain supreme authority for several centuries. The vassals of the great princes were not only the sub-vassals of the Emperor; but, when he [the Emperor] came to the provinces, he had there all the authority which he exercised in the Diet, where the minor nobility had the right to speak as much as the great. And also the rulers of other provinces who had come with the Emperor, to pay court to him, intervened [in provincial affairs], like those [rulers] of the province [itself]. The bishops, above all, and the royal abbeys had a great deal of credit, as the depositories of religion and, to some degree, of the laws. For the other nobles, being military men, rarely had a passable knowledge of letters. Things went along in this way until the Great Interregnum, that is to say until the Empire passed out of the family of the Swabian Emperors. Then necessity obliged some nobles and cities to make alliances in order to maintain public peace. I published one of them in my *Codex Iuris Gentium Diplomaticus*; but there was never a general one [alliance]. This was also the time that the cities began to take part in government. However, each [regional ruler] made himself almost absolute in the territory which he held of the Empire, and divided it among his children, which had not been permitted at all formerly. Rudolf of Hapsburg did not fail to re-establish, in some fashion, the authority of a leader; but the Empire did not remain in his family. There were feeble rulers, frequent changes of family, disorders, neglect, which mired the Empire in the danger of total dissolution, until it reverted to the House of Austria, and until the government took under Frederick III, under Maximilian I and under Charles V, by means of Diets and pacifications, the form which has remained to it, to which those who made the Peace of Westphalia have added the final touches.

If, in France, the Capetian family had been extinguished, and if the crown had passed from family to family, and if the other great families had been preserved, France would apparently be today a body similar to the German body, although it would never have had a single treaty of union which formed it, just as there has never been one [such treaty] in Germany.

LETTER II TO GRIMAREST: PASSAGES CONCERNING THE ABBÉ DE ST PIERRE'S 'PROJECT FOR PERPETUAL PEACE' (JUNE 1712)

I have seen something of the project of M. de St Pierre, for maintaining a perpetual peace in Europe. I am reminded of a device in a cemetery, with the words: *Pax perpetua*; for the dead do not fight any longer: but the living are of another humor; and the most powerful do not respect tribunals at all. It would be necessary that all these gentlemen contribute a *caution bourgeoise*, or deposit in the bank of the tribunal, a king of France, for example, a hundred million *écus*, and a king of Great Britain in proportion, so that the sentences of the tribunal could be executed on their money, in case they proved refractory. I do not know whether M.

l'Abbé de St Pierre will have [read] a book entitled *Nouveau Cynée*,[1] published more than thirty years ago, whose author, who does not reveal his name, gives to princes the advice which Cyneas gave to Pyrrhus, [that is] to prefer their repose and their comfort to their ambition, and proposes at the same time such a common tribunal. I recall that a wise prince of earlier times, whom I knew [Landgraf Ernst von Hesse-Rheinfels],[2] wrote a discourse like this one, and wished that Lucerne, in Switzerland, might be the seat of the tribunal. As for me, I would be for establishing it at Rome itself, and for making the Pope its president, just as before he played the part of judge, in effect, between Christian princes. But it would be necessary at the same time that ecclesiastics resume their old authority, and that an interdiction and an excommunication make kings and kingdoms tremble, as in the time of Nicholas I or Gregory VII. Here is a project which will succeed as easily as that of M. l'Abbé de St Pierre: but since it is permitted to write romances, why should we find bad the fiction which would recall the age of gold to us?

[1] See p. 178, n. 2.   [2] See p. 179, n. 2.

13. Excerpts from Letters to Landgraf Ernst of Hesse-Rheinfels, Bossuet and Thomas Burnett

The following excerpts from seven letters written by Leibniz between 1683 and 1712 give some sense of the range of his political interests. To Landgraf Ernst he speaks mainly of the idea of a 'right of resistance' to rulers, concluding that ordinarily such resistance is unjustifiable, and almost always unwise; to Bossuet he suggests means of re-uniting the 'Republic of Christendom' under a re-formed (and tolerant) Catholic Church; for Thomas Burnett he provides his fullest account of constitutional government and of natural élites, and makes characteristic remarks about the public duties of great scientists (like Newton) and about French aggression and possible means of containing it. (The letters to Landgraf Ernst are to be found in Rommel's *Leibniz und Landgraf Ernst von Hesse-Rheinfels*; those to Bossuet are in vols. I and II of Foucher de Careil's edition; and those to Burnett are contained in vol. III of Gerhardt's edition.)

EXCERPTS FROM TWO LETTERS TO LANDGRAF ERNST OF HESSE-
RHEINFELS CONCERNING ABSOLUTE POWER AND RESISTANCE
(1683–91)

1. The question whether it is good to have hereditary and absolute princes can be taken in several senses – one, whether the people are obliged to obey them, and two, whether a prince can in good conscience claim such a right, and exercise it, if it is transmitted to him by his ancestors. The third [point is] whether, according to the first or the second [sense], it is being asked only what form of government would be the best, and the most in conformity to the spirit of Christianity. As for the first, I believe that Your Highness agrees with others that the people are obligated to obey or to suffer, and that one cannot rebel without crime, which seems to conform to the spirit of Christianity, as well as to true politics; for ordinarily rebellions are more dangerous than bad government. It is true that there can be exceptions to the general rule. Grotius

agrees that if a tyrant acts manifestly for the destruction of the state, one could oppose him;[1] but it would still be necessary to act with moderation. ...As for the conscience of princes themselves, one could say that it is not power, but the bad use of power, which is worthy of blame, though this would not be sufficient. For though a prince be virtuous, he cannot answer for his successor, and one could say that he is wrong to establish or to keep a right which is so subject to corruption in hands other than his own, and which can become pernicious. Marcus Aurelius was blamed for nothing, except for leaving the Empire to a son [Commodus] who was unworthy of it. It is true that a prince can put into good order the education of future princes, but there is no reason to count on this; such that I would come out against absolute power, if in our times we had seen tyrants comparable to those monsters of Emperors that Rome saw in other times. But today there is no prince so bad that it would not be better to live under him than in a democracy. This is why everything comes down to the much-agitated question, which of the forms of government is best. It is to be hoped that the most powerful be always the most wise, or that the most wise be the most powerful; but human wisdom is quite limited, and often the greatest minds make the greatest mistakes. Wisdom, moreover, is not always easy to recognize; there are false wise-men, as there are false brave ones. People have a veneration for high birth which they do not have for virtue, so that I believe that elective kingdoms would be quite subject to trouble, as has been recognized; for even in these very kingdoms, one is obliged to hold to the [hereditary] succession in so far as one can. One sees too that it is not always good that princes have their hands tied, for this makes them incapable of providing for the needs of the state quickly enough. If the King of England were as absolute in his kingdom as the King of France is in his, I believe that he would early oppose the advances of France, and Europe would not be in the condition in which she finds herself. The peoples of the north, having recognized by experience how little it had helped them to keep their kings under the tutelage of senators, and to have fifty kings instead of one, have found it appropriate to release them from this yoke. But, on the other hand, Your Highness remarks very judiciously that absolute princes are too prompt in undertaking wars, and that it would be better for the keeping of the general peace that all people be governed by princes whose power was bound by Estates; this I am obliged to admit. For when a bellicose people or great kingdom has an absolute prince, the neighboring states, governed by less absolute princes, are in great danger and are obliged to give the same power to their

---

[1] Grotius, *De Jure Belli ac Pacis.*

princes to protect themselves against [foreign] enterprises. Good princes, however, whatever power they have, remember always that in the eyes of God they are never proprietors, nor even usufructuaries, of their countries, but simple administrators of goods belonging to God; that they are not leading beasts, but souls that God has redeemed by that which was most precious to him; that he will ask them for a rigorous accounting, and that an unjust war is almost the greatest of crimes which can be committed.

II. As for the question, whether subjects can resist the sovereign power, and in what cases, I am strongly of the opinion of Grotius, and I believe that as a rule resistance is forbidden to them. For ordinarily the evil of rebellion is greater than that which one claims to remedy. I am not entirely of the sentiment of Bellarmine,[1] if he believes that the Christians of the early Church were entitled to drive out pagan magistrates; all of ancient Christendom was of another opinion, and I am astonished that this Cardinal dared to maintain the contrary. The best [thing] is to be on the side of passive obedience, which means that subjects are not obliged, indeed, to act and to obey magistrates who command injustices of them, but also that they are obliged to suffer injustices, in so far as they can, which are done to them. This is also the true and sole means of setting just limits to ecclesiastical and secular power; the Church has the right to make use of spiritual arms, to keep sin in check, to excommunicate impenitent people, to forbid to Christians that which it is bad to do; but she cannot authorize undertakings by subjects against their lords on pretext of heresy, impiety or tyranny. When, however, the sovereign power is divided, it is another matter; for I reason *in thesi*, and not *in hypothesi*, and I am not of the opinion of Thomas Hobbes, who overstated things, and who thought that sovereign power was indivisible; I also remain in agreement with Grotius, that one can resist a tyrant in some circumstances, when he is a monster who seems to have vowed public ruin.[2] It is a little as if one imagined that all subjects, and particularly princes of the blood, were in one ship with their king, and that the king had the evil design of wanting to blow them up; I believe, certainly, that one would have the right to stop him, even by killing him, if it were impossible to do it otherwise. But one must spare him, if it can be done. One must treat a man of this kind almost like a wild man...However, I hold that it is a greater perfection to be able to suffer without resistance,[3]

---

[1] R. Bellarmine, *Apologia* IV, and *Pro Juramente Fidelitatis*.
[2] Grotius, *De Jure Belli ac Pacis*.
[3] But cf. Leibniz' *Monadology*, props. 49–50, in which suffering is identified

and it is this that one must advise as much as one can – men being only too much given to violence.

EXCERPTS FROM TWO LETTERS TO BOSSUET CONCERNING THE
RE-UNIFICATION OF CHRISTENDOM
(1692–9)

1. Monseigneur,

I do not want to delay a moment in responding to your letter, [which is] so full of goodness, in as much as it reached me the day after I thought of an important example which can serve in the matter of the reunion [of the Catholics and Protestants]. You have all the reason in the world to say that one must not take as easy that which, at bottom, is not such at all. I grant that the thing is difficult because of its nature and of circumstances, and I never contemplated easiness in so great a matter. But it is a question of establishing, above all, that which is possible or permissible. Now, all that which has been done, and of which there are examples approved by the Church, is possible; and it seems that the Protestant party is so considerable that one must do everything that can be done for them. The Calixtins of Bohemia were much less [considerable]; nevertheless you see, by the executorial letter of the Council of Basel, which I attach here, that in taking them back [the Church] suspended a notorious decree of the Council of Constance, with respect to them; namely, that which decided that the use of the two species [of communion] is not commanded of all the faithful. The Calixtins did not recognize the authority of the Council of Constance at all and, not agreeing in the slightest with this decision, Pope Eugene and the Council of Basel passed over this matter and did not demand that they submit to it, but left the matter to a new future decision by the Church. They laid down only this condition, that the re-united Calixtins had to believe in what is called 'concomitance', or the entire presence of Jesus Christ in each of the species, and to allow, as a result, that communion with [only] one species is complete and valid, so to speak, without being obligated to believe that it is lawful. These concordats between the deputies of the Council and those of the Calixtin estates of Bohemia and Moravia were ratified by the Council of Basel. Pope Eugene made his joy known in a letter written to the Bohemians; later Leo X, a long time afterwards, declared that he approved of them,

with imperfection. Here the difference between the metaphysical and the Christian meaning of 'suffering' causes Leibniz some difficulty.

and Ferdinand promised to protect them. This, however, involved only a handful of people: a single Ziska[1] could have made them formidable; a single Procopius could have preserved them by his valor: [but, in fact,] not a [single] prince or sovereign state, not a bishop or archbishop took part in it. Now, [however,] it is virtually the whole north which is opposed to the south of Europe; it is the greater part of the Germanic peoples opposed to the Latins; for Europe can be divided into four principal languages: Greek, Latin, German, and Slavonic. The Greeks, the Latins, and the Germans are three great parties in the Church, [while] the Slavonic is divided among the others; for the French, Italians, Spanish [and] Portuguese are Latins and Roman [Catholics], the English, Scottish, Danish [and] Swedish are Germans and Protestants, [while] the Poles, Bohemians and Russians or Muscovites are Slavic – and the Muscovites, with the peoples of the same language who were subject to the Ottomans, and a good part of those who are subject to Poland, follow the Greek rite.

Judge, Monseigneur, whether the greater part of the German-speaking people does not deserve at least as much accommodativeness as was shown toward the Bohemians. I beg you to consider this example well, and to tell me your feelings about it. Would it not be better, for Rome and for the common good, to regain so many nations, though one would have to remain in a state of disagreement on some points for some time – since it is true that these differences would be still less considerable than some of those which are tolerated within the Roman Church, such as, for example, the point concerning the necessity of the love of God, and the point of probabilism, to say nothing of the great difference between Rome and France? If, however, the matter were treated as it should be, I believe that the Protestants would one day be able to explain their views concerning dogma much more favorably than seems [likely] at first, above all if they saw signs of a true zeal for effective reform of recognized abuses, particularly with respect to worship. And, in fact, I am persuaded, in general, that there is more difficulty [to be resolved] in practices than in doctrines.

II. You will recall, Monseigneur, that it was agreed that it would be necessary to join three means in order to arrive at a peaceable reunion. The first is the means of *exposition* concerning certain controversies, by showing that, when people understand each other well, there may be agreement. These controversies are verbal at bottom, though they are quite often taken as real and have caused a good deal of noise and evil... The second means is that of *deference*, when one party gives way to the

[1] J. Ziska (*c.* 1380–1424), general of the Hussite army in Bohemia, defeated Emperor Sigismund in 1420.

other and grants it something in certain matters. If these are dogmas, this can be brought about only by good proofs; but it is not our plan to enter into this at present. If they are practices, people can and must sometimes give way to each other, in bringing about what seems to be best for enlightenment [*édification*] and peace. We believe that our doctors [of theology] can give way on some dogmas [which are] received among them, and [that] yours [can] as well; but it turns out that these dogmas are not universally established or received among either group. And we are also of the opinion that one must, as soon as possible, return to the hierarchy and government of the body of the visible Church, recognizing the leadership of its head, and conform so far as is reasonable to the enlightened practices which obtain on your [the Catholic] side: as we hold that, on your side, one must apply himself strongly to abolish certain abusive practices which are only too well publicly established in some places, particularly with respect to the worship of images – which is disapproved even on your side by wise persons, and sometimes even by regulations. And the occasion of reunion with the Protestants can be useful to authorized and well-intentioned persons of your party (among whom I number a Pope who is zealous, as he ought to be) in realizing that which the courtiers at Rome once eluded by their stratagems at the Council of Trent, that is, the purging of the Church of several abuses – to which the liberty not to allow them, which will be left to our side, will contribute a great deal, and will seem the less extraordinary because the Greeks, the Maronites and other easterners [who were] reconciled with the Roman Church have kept their rites, and because the Council of Florence approved it.

The third means is that of *abstraction* or *suspension*, or leaving out of account [*en faisant abstraction de*] certain points on which one cannot agree, or on which one could not agree so soon, by setting them aside, either forever, when they are of little importance, or until the decision of a future ecumenical Council. And this means must come to the aid of the two others, in certain permitted cases, to shorten their length. For we agree that it is necessary to lay down, as the foundation of the whole negotiation, the great maxim that each, on his side, must make the most extreme effort which is possible without injuring his conscience, by showing the greatest obligingness for the others that he can have without offending God: in order to forward the great work of reunion in so far as he can, [and] to obviate such great evils as those which the schism has brought about, that is, the loss of so many thousands of souls and the spilling of so much Christian blood, not to speak of other miseries which this schism has caused and will be able to cause still if it is not stopped.

Thus everyone can be re-united under a single hierarchy even before all the dogmas ordinarily insisted upon by your side are agreed on, or all the abuses disapproved by our side are redressed: provided that everyone takes certain essential steps which can be agreed on at the beginning of the reunion.

EXCERPTS FROM THREE LETTERS TO THOMAS BURNETT
(1699–1712)

1. Mr Hakeman told me of having had the honor of speaking with Mr Newton, who showed him his work on colors, but told him that he did not want to publish it so soon; I beg you, Sir, if you are in London and he is as well, to undertake an embassy to him on my behalf and for the public good. You know, Sir, my principles, which are to prefer the public good to all other considerations, even to glory and money; I doubt not at all that a person of Mr Newton's strength shares my feeling. The more staunch one is, the more one has this disposition, which is the great principle of an honorable man, and even of justice and of true piety; for to contribute to the public good and to the glory of God is the same thing. It seems that the goal of the whole human race should be principally the knowledge and the development of the marvels of God, and that it is for this that God has given it the empire of this globe. And, Mr Newton being one of those men of the world who can contribute most to this, it would be almost criminal of him to let himself be diverted by impedi-ments which are not absolutely insurmountable. The greater his talent, the greater his obligation. For in my opinion an Archimedes, a Galileo, a Kepler, a Descartes, a Huygens, a Newton are more important with respect to the great goal of the human race than great military men [*capitaines*], and they are at least on a par with those esteemed legislators whose aim has been to lead men to what is truly good and solid. The end of politics, after virtue, is the maintenance of abundance, so that men will be in a better position to work in common concert for those solid [objects of] knowledge which cause the sovereign author to be admired and loved. Many can contribute to this by experiences which furnish materials, but those who can profit from them, like Mr Newton, to advance the great building of science, and who can interpret its interior, are, so to speak, [members] of the privy council of God, and all the others work only for them. Thus when one has such persons, who are rarer than people think, one must profit from them as much as possible...

I have still not had the leisure to read the entire book entitled *Two Treatises of Government*, against the principles of Mr Filmer. I did notice, however, a great justice and solidity in the reasoning. There are, never-theless, some passages, perhaps, which demand a more ample discussion, as among others what is said of the State of Nature, and of the equality of rights of men. This equality would be certain, if all men had the same [natural] advantages, but this not being so at all, it seems that Aristotle is more correct here than Mr Hobbes. If several men found themselves in a single ship on the open sea, it would not be in the least conformable either to reason or nature, that those who understand nothing of sea-going claim to be pilots; such that, following natural reason, government belongs to the wisest. But the imperfection of human nature causes people not to want to listen to reason, which has forced the most wise to use force and cunning to establish some tolerable order, in which providence itself takes a hand. But when a [certain] order has been established, one should not overturn it without extreme necessity and without being sure of succeeding in it *pro salute publica*, in a way which does not cause worse evils.

Since the [English] Parliament has decided the question concerning a standing army by [drawing] a distinction, keeping part of the troops while disbanding the others, it is no longer necessary that individuals take a hand in judging the matter. If God preserves the King of Spain[1] for a long time, there will be no immediate danger. The general question of politics, whether a standing army is contrary to liberty and leads to an absolute monarchy, should not be treated, like metaphysical questions, by precise statements. The great republics of Rome and of Carthage had continuously several armies on foot; it was not this, but the corruption of morals which ruined Roman liberty. And in our times the republic of the United Provinces of the Low-Countries has kept its [liberty] during an almost continual war of eighty years. It must be granted, however, that an army of mercenaries under an hereditary leader, who has more-over a great deal of power in the state, can be a great instrument of ambition to overturn the laws. But one must consider as well how dan-gerous it is to be disarmed next to a neighbor [France] whose power is great and which is continually armed, above all when there are certain fatal situations, such as is, for example, the revolution which everyone fears in the monarchy of Spain. Thus one must weigh maturely from which side the danger is more pressing. If there were not a king as heroic and as far removed from arbitrary power as the present one [William III], and if there were not externally a danger as imminent as that of the revolution in Spain, one could say that Parliament has still kept too many troops. But if the external danger increased, everyone would say that

[1] Charles II.

there are not enough: one must also believe that then Parliament would put everything in order quickly, and one must hope that it will be able to do it in time. It should also be considered that external danger is a great preservative [of liberty] within, keeping the chief of state from thinking of making himself absolute, since domestic disorder could be fatal to him. Such that I maintain that the English nation has never had more to fear from without, and less from within, than under the present king – except that one must at present fear becoming the slave of passions in this corruption of morals which is beginning to rule over all of Europe, more than being submitted to arbitrary power. In a word: one must fear presently that which can come from libertinage more than what can go against liberty.

II. The end of political science with regard to the doctrine of forms of commonwealths [*républiques*], must be to make the empire of reason flourish. The end of monarchy is to make a hero of eminent wisdom and virtue reign (such as your present king). The end of aristocracy is to give the government to the most wise and the most expert. The end of democracy, or polity, is to make the people themselves agree to what is good for them. And if one could have all [three] at once: a great hero, very wise senators, and very reasonable citizens, that would constitute a mixture of the three forms.[1] Arbitrary power is what is directly opposed to the empire of reason. But one must realize that this arbitrary power is found not only in kings, but also in assemblies, when cabals and animosities prevail over reason, which happens in judicial tribunals as well as in public deliberations. The remedy of a plurality of votes, given either publicly or secretly, in balloting, is not sufficient to curb these abuses. Elections serve after a fashion against cabals, and make it easy to assure oneself of votes by bad means; but they have this inconvenience – that each [voter] can follow his [own] whim and his wicked designs, without the shame of being discovered, and without being obliged to present reasons for them. Thus one must think in this world of laws which can serve to restrain not only kings, but also the deputies of the people, and judges.

Your Harrington, in his *Oceana*, had as his aim the recommendation of a kind of republic which was among the best. I have still not seen his book, but the extracts from it which I have seen make me doubt that he had sufficiently penetrated to the heart of this important matter. I find only that he was right to recommend the government of the United Provinces, [on whose side] people align themselves with reason in important matters of state. (This is so, among other [reasons], because

[1] Cf. Aristotle, *Politics* IV, 9; Cicero, *De Republica* I, xlv.

they do not follow [the principle of] the plurality of voices blindly there, but mix it with what is called 'friendly coming to terms' [*composition amiable*].) It is a manner of dealing [with men] in which someone tries to lead another to his end by force of persuasion [only]. But as this means is very uncertain, and is good for nothing with stubborn and malevolent people, someone could invent certain quite practical and quite efficacious laws to curb the abuses which ignorance, passion and malice bring forth.

It is not enough to stop the court from buying votes in order to exercise its arbitrary power; one must see as well that the arbitrary power of those who undertake to oppose good counsels without reason be restrained; otherwise it is quite certain that liberty [which has] degenerated into license will disappear and will relapse into arbitrary power, be it of a foreigner or of a native: for it is also sure that the absolute power of kings is more durable than the license of individuals, and [that] nothing is more certain to bring about tyranny than this anarchy. Particularly at present these [moral] faults are dangerous in matters of state, because of the transcendent power of the house of Bourbon, in view of which one cannot act with impunity...And what I say to you, Sir, about the danger to which liberty is exposed by license, comes only from my reflections and from the affection which I have for true liberty, which is one of the greatest jewels of human nature, but after reason; liberty, as I have told you on other occasions, being only the power of following reason – a definition which serves even in theology.

III. Those who say that France is sufficiently overthrown are [either] quite ignorant or quite malicious. We already see France [in a] superior [position], since England retired [from the Continent], and when the house of Bourbon has become the peaceable possessor of Spain and of the Indies, as it is of France, it will be, humanly speaking, irresistible; and if it has England on its side, it will engulf England and the rest [of the states of Europe]. It is ridiculous to base our security on what the Bourbons will fight about among themselves; if they are wise, they will not do this, and they will be the arbiters of Europe. Must we base our safety on the supposition of the stupidity of someone else? It is not sufficient that the crowns of France and Spain be on two different heads; it is dangerous enough that there are two heads whose true interest is to be on good terms with each other, and that one is thus at their discretion. Everything which they have conceded to England is precarious and negligible. Please God that they never place their creature in England, as it will be easy for them to do after the peace; and it seems that they and their partisans are waiting only to see the Dutch disarmed, to strike their blow.

Humanly speaking, and if God does not give help *ex machina*, England and Holland, religion and liberty are lost – if peace is made with the Dutch as France proposes. This leaps to the eye, and one must be extremely blind or malicious not to recognize it. Since the peace between England and France has still not been made, or at least made public, one must hope that the Queen [Anne] and the ministers of the nations will not precipitate it, and will provide better for the security of Europe, as much as for the Protestant succession in Great Britain.

14. Judgment of the Works of the Earl of Shaftesbury
(1712)

This late piece contains a number of disconnected but characteristic observations on charity, honor, virtue, the doctrines of Aristotle and Hobbes, and other subjects which have a bearing on Leibniz' politics. Only those few passages having such a bearing are included here. (The original text is to be found in vol. v of Dutens' edition.)

I. The *Letter on Enthusiasm* contains a thousand beautiful thoughts: and I believe that raillery is a good protection against this vice; but I do not find it at all suitable for curing people of it. On the contrary, the contempt which is enveloped in raillery will be taken by them as affliction and persecution. I have remarked that when one rails at errors and absurdities in religious matters, one irritates infinitely the people who are favorably inclined toward it [religion], and that this is the true way to pass for an atheist in their minds. I don't know, either, whether the use of ridicule is a good touchstone, for the best and most important things can be turned to ridicule; and it is not always certain that truth will have those who laugh on its side, being most often hidden from vulgar eyes. I have already said that all raillery contains a little contempt; and it is not just that one try to make contemptible that which does not deserve it. But it is good that one always be in a good humor, and that joy, rather than irritation, appear in our conversation and in our writings [*ouvrages*].

II. The *Essay on Free Manners, on Spirit, and on Good Humor* seems to have the same purpose of bringing the men of our times to humanize themselves, and to make things more cheerful [*égayer les matières*]; and this work is marvellously suited, by its arguments and by its example, for this purpose. What is said there, but ironically, on behalf of those who claim that men are wolves to each other, and against those who believe in their natural goodness, is nicely turned. But one can say that ordinarily men are neither very bad, nor very good; and Machiavelli has well observed that the two extremes are equally rare,[1] with the result that great actions are [rare] also.

The Iroquois and the Hurons, uncivilized [*sauvages*] neighbors of New France and of New England, have upset the too-universal political maxims of Aristotle and Hobbes. They have shown, by their surprising conduct, that entire peoples can be without magistrates and without quarrels, and that as a result men are neither taken far enough by their natural goodness nor forced by their wickedness to provide themselves with a government and to renounce their liberty. But the roughness of these savages shows that it is not so much necessity as the inclination to advance to a better [condition], and to arrive at felicity through mutual assistance, which is the foundation of societies and of states. But it must be granted that security is the most essential point in this.

I find it well said, on p. 98, that true virtue must be disinterested, that is to say, as I interpret it, that one must come to find pleasure in the exercise of virtue, and disgust in that of vice, and that this should be the aim of education.

The remark is also good, on p. 99, that individual friendship is little recommended by our religion, which directs us toward charity, that is to say, toward a general benevolence. One can also say that a tested friendship is very rare; and that it must be the result of a great and fine passion, or of great virtue, which is found in two persons at the same time. It is true that true friends who are very virtuous would be capable of going far.

Our illustrious author refutes with reason, on p. 109, those who believe that there is no obligation at all in the state of nature, and outside of government; for, obligations by pacts having to form the right of government itself, according to the author of these principles, it is manifest that the obligation is anterior to the government which it must form.

It is a common saying that interest governs the world; but there is reason to say, [as does the author] on p. 115, that it is rather the passions that do so. The Duke de Rohan begins his book on politics[2] with this

---

[1] The reference is probably to Machiavelli's *Discourses* I, 27.
[2] The reference is to *De l'Intérêt des Princes et États de la Chrétienté* (1638), by Henri, Duc de Rohan.

sentence: that princes command peoples, and that interest commands princes. It would be desirable that this were true; for in that case one would listen to reason better. But reason demands also that, besides mercenary interests, we be concerned with our satisfaction: it commands us to strive for felicity, which is nothing else than a state of enduring joy; and whatever tends in this direction is our true interest.

With regard to those who refer everything to themselves, of whom he speaks [on] p. 118, and who seem [to be] opposed to those who love their friends, parents, fatherland, state, and even men in general, I believe that, if we understand these things one can reconcile them, provided that the ones and the others listen to reason. Our [own] good is no doubt the basis of our motives, but quite often we find not only our utility but even our pleasure in the good of another; and in this last case there is precisely what ought to be called disinterested love, as I have already done earlier, in explaining the principles of justice, in the preface to the *Codex Iuris Gentium*. Thus the felicity of another often becomes part of our own. And it will be found that virtue, that is to say, the habit of acting reasonably, is that which brings about an enduring pleasure – the most that one can promise himself.

I highly approve what is said on pp. 123 ff., to make it clear that true honor [*honnêteté*] does not depend essentially on the opinion of others. It is true that this word has degenerated a little today, as well as the sentiments; and when one says 'an honorable man', one means a man who has the ability to make himself esteemed, who makes a good appearance – a 'speciously proper outside' [*speciosum pelle decora*].[1]

I would not dare to be lukewarm toward him who defies men to subject true generosity or true courage to ridicule. Men have enough of a disposition to turn the better into the worse; and satires are listened to with too much favor.

It is well-observed, [on] pp. 130 ff., that he who is a truly honorable man will not even be capable of considering a bad action. M. Bayle said something approaching this which I have strongly approved, [in my] *Theodicy*, section 318, having observed [in] section 75, that those who said of Cato that it was impossible for him to fail to do his duty meant only to praise him further. The less one is tempted by vice, perhaps, the more one is strengthened in virtue. But it is a quite important question, which of these two is better – to be irresolute, or to be confirmed in vice. Our illustrious author seems to agree with this passage in Horace, Book ii, Satire 7, verses 18 ff:

> *Quanto constantior idem*

[1] Horace, *Epistolae* I, 16, 15.

In vitiis, tanto levius miser, ac prior illo
Qui iam contento, jam laxo fune laborat.[1]

One suffers less, in fact, when one has made his resolution, than when one is in a [state of] embarrassing irresolution; and the authors of the philosophical sin have gone still further, because those who sin with less remorse are, according to them, more innocent. But Aristotle is for the half-wicked [*demi-méchants*], whom he calls incontinent; and one can say that their malady is more curable. The completely vicious are like those who have gangrene, who do not feel their illness.

The unsatisfying reasoning of some modern philosophers makes [Shaftesbury] say, [on] p. 132, that things being what they are today, honor and good morals do not appear to gain much from philosophy and from profound speculations; and that it is necessary to adhere to common-sense. He adds that ordinarily men's first judgments on this matter are better than their later reflections and thoughts. That may be, when one reasons according to the principles of Mr Hobbes, and perhaps even of Mr Locke; but I would be quite sorry if this were true according to the true philosophy, which I flatter myself I have outlined in my *Theodicy*.

IV. I come to the second volume, or treatise, entitled *An Inquiry concerning Virtue and Merit*. It is completely systematic and contains very sound opinions on the nature of virtue and of felicity, showing that the affections which nature has given us bring us, not only to seek our own good, but also to achieve that of our relations and even of society; and that one is happy when he acts according to his natural affections. It seems to me that I could reconcile this quite easily with my [own] language and opinions. In fact, our natural affections produce our contentment: and the more natural one is, the more he is led to find his pleasure in the good of others, which is the foundation of universal benevolence, of charity, of justice. For, as I have explained in the preface to my *Codex*, cited above, justice is at bottom nothing else than charity conformed to wisdom. It is only reluctantly, and for a greater good, that justice sometimes obliges [us] to do evil. Wisdom ordains that this benevolence have its degrees: and as the air, though it extends all around our globe, to a great height, has more body and density near us than has that which is in the high regions of our atmosphere, one can say as well that the charity which bears upon those who most nearly touch us, must have more intensity and more force.

[1] Loemker (*Leibniz: Philosophical Papers and Letters*, vol. II, p. 1202), translates Horace's lines:
'The more content he is in his vices, the less miserable;
Better than the man who struggles, with his rope now taut, now loose'.

Critical Bibliography

PRINCIPAL EDITIONS OF LEIBNIZ' WORKS

G. W. Leibniz, *Sämtliche Schriften und Briefe*, edition of the German (formerly Prussian) Academy of Sciences at Berlin, pub. Berlin, Darmstadt, Leipzig, 1923– . (This critical edition, when completed, will have published all of Leibniz' writings in more than forty volumes; thus far only about a dozen have appeared. All variants of texts are included in extremely extended scholarly notes; general readers may prefer to read more straightforward editions, such as Foucher de Careil's or Klopp's (see below).)

Dutens, Louis, *Gothofredi Guillelmi Leibnitii...Opera Omnia*, Geneva, 1768 (6 vols.). (The first relatively complete edition of Leibniz' works; vol. IV, containing juridical writings, and vol. VI, containing commentaries on St Pierre, Shaftesbury, etc., are still useful. And vol. I contains Fontenelle's fine 'Éloge de Leibniz'.)

Foucher de Careil, A., *Œuvres de Leibniz*, Paris, 1859–75 (republished by Olms Verlag, Hildesheim and New York, 1969), (7 vols.). (An extremely useful, if not always perfectly accurate, edition of many of Leibniz' most important political writings. Vols. I and II contain the papers dealing with the re-unification of Christendom; vols. III and IV those dealing with French expansion and Imperial defense; vol. V those having to do with Leibniz' efforts to get Louis XIV to undertake an expedition against Egypt; vol. VI a miscellany; and vol. VII those papers dealing with the founding of academies, as well as the correspondence with Peter the Great.)

Gerhardt, C. I., *Die Philosophischen Schriften von G. W. Leibniz*, Berlin, 1875–90 (7 vols.). (Still the best relatively complete edition of the philosophical works; vol. III contains a number of important political letters.)

Gerhardt, C. I., *Die Mathematische Schriften von G. W. Leibniz*, Berlin and Halle, 1849–55 (7 vols.). (Contains a few pieces which have a bearing on Leibniz' political thought.)

Grua, Gaston, *G. W. Leibniz, Textes Inédits*, Paris, 1948 (2 vols.) (Vol. II, particularly, contains important 'new' pieces, including the brief *Felicity* and a number of juridical writings.)

Guhrauer, G. E., *Leibniz's Deutsche Schriften*, Berlin, 1838 (2 vols.). (Contains Leibniz' most important pieces on German defense against France, German academies of arts and sciences, etc.)

Klopp, Onno, *Die Werke von Leibniz*, Hanover, 1864–84 (10 vols.). (The best edition of the historical and political writings, containing, in addition to some of the pieces in the Foucher de Careil edition, a number of memoranda and letters dealing with the interests of the House of Hanover, the British succession, etc.)

Mollat, G., *Rechtsphilosophisches aus Leibnizens Ungedruckten Schriften*, Leipzig,

1885. (Contains the 'Meditation on the Common Concept of Justice' and other important writings on natural and positive law.)

Rommel, C. von, *Leibniz und Landgraf Ernst von Hessen-Rheinfels* Frankfurt, 1847. (An exchange of letters between Leibniz and the Landgraf dealing with every aspect of politics, theoretical and practical, over a period of more than twenty years.)

ENGLISH EDITIONS CONTAINING IMPORTANT POLITICAL PIECES

Duncan, G. M. (trans.), *The Philosophical Works of Leibniz*, 2nd. ed., New Haven, 1908. (Contains a few pieces which have a marginal bearing on Leibniz' political thought.)

Latta, Robert (trans.), *The Monadology and other Philosophical Writings*, Oxford, 1898. (Contains an English translation of parts of the *Codex Iuris Gentium*, as well as appended passages from some of the works on natural law found in Mollat's edition; very useful for those who know no Latin. The introduction also is good.)

Loemker, Leroy, *Leibniz: Philosophical Papers and Letters*, Chicago, 1956 (republished at Dordrecht, 1969) (2 vols.). (The most comprehensive edition of Leibniz' works in English, it includes a half-dozen pieces which are essential to any study of Leibniz' political thought. The introduction is extremely useful.)

GENERAL COMMENTARIES ON LEIBNIZ WHICH TREAT HIS POLITICAL THEORY

Carr, H. W., *Leibniz*, London, 1929. (Full of remarks and anecdotes, scattered throughout the work, which have a bearing on Leibniz' politics.)

Cassirer, Ernst, *Leibniz' System in seinen Wissenschaftlichen Grundlagen*, Marburg, 1902. (A magnificent work whose commentary on Leibniz' political philosophy is, however, the weakest part of the book – due, in large part, to Cassirer's effort to treat Leibniz as a forerunner of Kant, which is accurate only in a very limited way.)

Dewey, John, *Leibniz' New Essays concerning the Human Understanding: A Critical Exposition*, Chicago, 1902. (In a few brief pages at the end of his book, Dewey says illuminating things about the relation of Leibniz' ethics to his theology.)

Peursen, C. A. van, *Leibniz* (trans. H. Hoskins), London, 1969. (In ch. 4 van Peursen treats the problem of the relation of justice to freedom, evil, imperfection, etc.; he, however, is apparently content with the distinctions Leibniz draws.)

Rescher, Nicholas, *The Philosophy of Leibniz*, Pittsburgh, 1967. (Devotes a chapter to Leibniz' ethical and political thought; like van Peursen, Rescher appears to be satisfied with some of the distinctions which are criticized in the introduction to this edition. But Rescher's view is backed by plausible evidence and should be studied as an alternative to the present treatment.)

Russell, Bertrand, *A Critical Exposition of the Philosophy of Leibniz*, Cambridge, 1900. (One of the few great commentaries on Leibniz, though it is very harsh indeed in its assessment of his ethical and political philosophy. Russell sometimes imputes unworthy motives to Leibniz, and accuses him of altering his views for the edification of various crowned heads; and this is probably quite unjust.)

SECONDARY SOURCES: BOOKS, MONOGRAPHS, JOURNAL ARTICLES

Aceti, G., 'Indagini sulla Concezione Leibniziana della Felicita', *Rivista di Filosofia Neo-Scolastica* XLIX, 1957, pp. 99–145. (An historical review of the development of the concept of felicity in Leibniz' writings, beginning with the early juridical works and ending with some of the late writings included in this volume; useful but rather uncritical.)

Barber, W. H., *Leibniz in France: from Arnauld to Voltaire*, Oxford, 1953. (Covers a huge range of topics, from Leibniz' actual contacts with French intellectuals to Voltaire's satirizing of him a half-century after his death.)

Baruzi, Jean, 'Du "Discours de Metaphysique" a la Theodicée', *Revue Philosophique* CXXXVI, 1946, pp. 391–409; and (particularly) *Leibniz et l'Organisation Religieuse de la Terre*, Paris, 1913. (Extremely useful in relating Leibniz' religious ideas to his ethical and political thought, and particularly in clarifying his concept of charity.)

Basch, Victor, *Les Doctrines Politiques des Philosophes Classiques d'Allemagne*, Paris, 1927, ch. 3. (Deals mainly with topical political pieces such as Leibniz' *Securitas Publica* and the various anti-French polemics; little emphasis on political philosophy.)

Bobbio, Norberto, 'Leibniz e Pufendorf', *Rivista di Filosofia* XXXVIII, 1947, pp. 118–29. (Mostly a commentary on Leibniz' critique of Pufendorf's *De Officio Hominis*.)

Cairns, Huntington, *Legal Philosophy from Plato to Hegel*, Baltimore, 1949, pp. 295 ff. (An account of Leibniz' legal thought which paraphrases the originals almost literally; good summaries of such early works as the *Nova Methodus*.)

Cassirer, Ernst, 'Leibniz', in the *Encyclopedia of the Social Sciences*, New York, 1933, pp. 400–2. (Argues mainly that Leibniz was the forerunner of modern theories of the 'rights of man' – which is true only in a highly qualified, non-political sense.)

Fontenelle, Bernard le Bovier de, 'Éloge de Leibniz', in *Gothofredi Guillelmi Leibnitii...Opera Omnia*, ed. L. Dutens, Geneva, 1768, vol. I. (Delivered by Fontenelle in the Academie Française shortly after Leibniz' death, this was the first public appreciation of his talents by an equal; it enlarges on a number of Leibniz' more interesting practical political activities, and gives a good idea of the staggering scope of his interests.)

Friedrich, C. J., 'Philosophical Reflections of Leibniz on Law, Politics and the State', *Natural Law Forum* (Notre Dame Law School) XI, 1966, pp. 79–91. (Probably the best short account in English of Leibniz' political thought, though it confessedly avoids philosophical problems.)

Gierke, Otto von, *Johannes Althusius und die Entwicklung der Naturrechtlichen Staatstheorien*, Breslau, 1880 (trans. B. Freyd as *The Development of Political Theory*, New York, 1939), and *Das Deutsche Genossenschaftsrecht*, Berlin, 1868 (trans. E. Barker as *Natural Law and the Theory of Society*, Oxford, 1934, pp. 137, 146 (*inter alia*). (Both contain a few passages on Leibniz, some of whose force is weakened by the late nineteenth-century German obsession with the theory of the state's 'personality' – on which point see Rupert Emerson, *State and Sovereignty in Modern Germany*, New Haven, 1928.

Grua, Gaston, *Jurisprudence Universelle et Theodicée selon Leibniz*, Paris, 1953, and *La Justice Humaine selon Leibniz*, Paris, 1956. (The most comprehensive effort to treat every facet of Leibniz' political, ethical and religious thought, with a great deal of attention devoted to philosophers and theologians who influenced Leibniz; these are essential books.)

Hegel, G. W. F., *Lectures on the Philosophy of History* (trans. E. S. Haldane and F. H. Simson), London, 1896, vol. III, part III, section 2, pp. 325–48. (Hegel slights Leibniz, but some of his acid remarks on Leibnizian optimism are diverting.)

Hermann, Karl, *Das Staatsdenken bei Leibniz*, Bonn, 1958. (Probably the best and most comprehensive short and modern treatment of Leibniz' political thought; it does on a small scale much of what Grua does on a larger one.)

Hertz, F., 'G. W. Leibniz as a Political Thinker', in *Festschrift Heinrich Benedikt*, ed. H. Hantsch and A. Novotny, Vienna, 1957. (An adequate short account of several practical topics in Leibniz' political theory; philosophical issues are not treated.)

Jalabert, J., 'La Psychologie de Leibniz: Ses Caractères Principaux', *Revue Philosophique* CXXVI, 1946, pp. 453–72. (Contains observations on Leibniz' theory of pleasure as a feeling of perfection which have some bearing on his ethical and political thought.)

Janet, Paul, *Histoire de la Science Politique*, Paris, 1872, vol. II. (Janet brings out with particular strength the modernity of Leibniz' emphasis on welfare as the chief responsibility of rulers.)

Klibansky, Raymond, *Leibniz' Unknown Correspondence with English Scholars and Men of Letters*, London, 1941. (Throws light on Leibniz' effort to secure the throne of Great Britain for the Electors of Hanover and to arrest the expansionism of Louis XIV; it includes an interesting letter on this last point to Addison (1708).)

Leoni, Bruno, 'Probabilità e Diritto nel Pensiero di Leibniz', *Rivista di Filosofia* XXXVIII, 1947, pp. 65–95. (Draws useful parallels between Leibniz' logical and juridical works.)

Mathieu, Vittorio, *Scritti Politici e di Diritto Naturale di Gottfried Wilhelm Leibniz*, Turin, 1951. (Contains a good introduction to some of Leibniz' political writings, and an extremely useful and detailed bibliography.)

Meyer, R. W., *Leibniz und die Europäische Ordnungskrise*, Hamburg, 1948 (trans. J. P. Stern as *Leibnitz and the Seventeenth Century Revolution*, Chicago, 1952. (A good account of Leibniz' involvement in the social and scientific issues of his day; it draws a number of parallels between some of Leibniz' philosophical doctrines and some of his political ideas – some of them illuminating, others not very plausible.)

Mollat, G., 'Zur Würdigung Leibnizens', *Zeitschrift der Savigny-Stiftung* 7, 1887, pp. 71 ff. (A surprisingly thin piece by the editor of the important collection of writings on law and justice noted in the first section of this bibliography.)

Pfleiderer, E., *G. W. Leibniz als Patriot, Staatsmann und Bildungsträger*, Leipzig, 1870. (Makes Leibniz more German than he was by emphasizing occasional and patriotic pieces; attention devoted to Leibniz as educator and founder of academies.)

Ritter, 'Paul, *Leibniz's Ägyptischer Plan*, Darmstadt, 1930, and 'Leibniz als Politiker', *Deutsche Monatsschrift für Christliche Politik und Kultur* 1, 1920, pp. 420 ff. (An exhaustive treatment of Leibniz' best-known political piece, the *Consilium Aegyptiacum*.)

Ruck, Erwin, *Die Leibniz'sche Staatsidee*, Tübingen, 1909. (Worth reading, but disfigured by the controversy over the state's 'personality' which also lessens the value of the works of Gierke (cited above); cf. Gierke's review of this book in the *Deutsche Literaturzeitung* 31, 1910, pp. 564–9.)

Schrecker, Paul, 'Leibniz: ses Idées sur l'Organisation des Relations Internationales', *Proceedings of the British Academy* XXIII, 1937, pp. 193–229, and 'Leibniz's Principles of International Justice', *Journal of the History of Ideas* 7, 1946, pp. 484–98. (The English article is a re-worked and shortened version of the French one; both draw extremely interesting correlations between Leibniz' juridical theories and some of his logical and metaphysical principles.)

Solari, Gioele, 'Metafisica e Diritto in Leibniz', *Rivista di Filosofia* XXXVIII, 1947, pp. 35–64. (An admirable effort to link up Leibniz' metaphysics with his ethics and politics; it contains persuasive criticisms of Janet (see above) and others on Leibniz' theory of welfare.)

Ward, A. W., *Leibniz as a Politician*, Manchester, 1911. (A competent but very brief account of Leibniz' practical political activities, including diplomacy; all philosophical problems are avoided.)

Zimmerman, Robert, *Das Rechtsprinzip bei Leibnitz*, Vienna, 1852. (Still one of the better commentaries on Leibniz' juridical writings; it treats, e.g., the much-neglected *Nova Methodus*, and attempts to relate human to divine justice.)

Index

Alexander the Great, 34, 91, 100, 101, 102
Althusius, J., 30, 77, 79n.
Aquinas, St Thomas, 5, 16, 72n.
Aristotle, 5, 20, 21, 22, 30, 45, 60, 63, 69, 75n., 78n., 79n., 85n., 99n., 114, 172n., 192, 193n., 196, 198
Arnauld, 7, 15

Barbeyrac, 64
Bayle, P., 197
Bellarmine, Cardinal, 112–13, 126, 187
Bentham, 25
Bierling, letter to, 21n.
Bismarck, 25n.
Bodin, 27, 117n.
Boileau, 179n.
Bosses, des, vii, 13n., 31
Bossuet, 1, 8, 19, 30, 31, 34, 45n., 171n.; letters to, 188–91
Britain, Leibniz's efforts to gain throne of for House of Hanover, 31, 37–8, 192ff.
Burke, 22n., 79n.
Burnett, T., 22, 23, 24; letters to, 191–95

Caesar, 58, 95, 96, 99, 102
Calvinism, 16
Cassirer, E., 19n.
charity (see also justice), 3ff., 6, 17ff., 31, 54, 57, 59–61, 83, 171ff., 198
Christ, 3, 11, 13, 81
Christian doctrine, 3–5, 14, 57, 67
Cicero, 58n., 59, 60n., 68n., 133, 193n.
Clarke, S., 13n., 39
Claudius, 47
compossibility, Leibniz' doctrine of, 9
Conciliar movement, 180–1
constitutionalism, 193
Corpus Iuris Civilis, 151
Crucé, E., 178, 184n.

democracy, 23–4, 186
Democritus, 13

Descartes, 2, 8, 45, 65, 71, 109n., 191

education: of people, 69, 105–8; of princes, 87, 92–4
enlightenment, 103ff.
equality, 85
Ernst of Hesse-Rheinfels, 179, 184; letters to, 185–8
Euripides, 58
evil, justification of, 6, 9–11

federalism, 117–18
Fénélon, 171n.
Filmer, 22, 45, 60, 61, 62, 191
Fontenelle, 39
French imperialism, 33ff., 121ff., 146ff., 194–5

George I, 39
Germany, political history of, 182–3
Gierke, O. von, 26n., 29n., 118n.
Great Design of Henry IV, 177n.
Grimarest, letter to, 183–4
Grotius, 1, 8, 29, 71n., 113–14, 118n., 127, 167, 172, 185, 186n., 187

Hanover, Leibniz' efforts on behalf of, 38–9
Hansch, letter to, 18
Harrington, 193–4
Hegel, 10, 12, 78n.
Herodotus, 92
history, writing of, 167–70
Hobbes, vii, 1, 2, 3, 5, 22, 23, 26, 27–28, 29, 30, 32, 33, 45, 47, 57, 60, 61, 62, 65, 70, 82n., 113, 118–20, 166, 187, 192, 196, 198
Holy Roman Empire, 1, 27, 31, 111ff., 121ff., 174, 180–3
Homer, 92
Horace, 67, 197–8

international law, 32–3, 175–6

205